APR 2 - 1996

Education in Germany

The German education and training system has been the subject of considerable attention from other nations, and has often been seen as a model for other systems. In the Federal Republic, responsibility for educational matters is devolved to the state parliaments, giving the system a degree of autonomy which does not exist in countries with centralised education systems. In order to fully examine the reasons behind the traditional success of the German system, and the implications this has for the UK debate, David Phillips brings together articles from some of the best known names in the field, including Mitter, Glowka, Hearnden, Führ, Robinsohn, and Prais and Wagner.

The book is organised into four parts. Part I examines the historical inheritance of the present education system, Part II covers standards and assessment and Part III discusses vocational education and training, an area of the German education system which has attracted much admiration. Finally and crucially, Part IV addresses questions about the future of the current education system in a unified Germany.

David Phillips is a Fellow of St Edmund Hall, Oxford and is a Lecturer in the Department of Educational Studies of Oxford University. His particular interests are in comparative education and policy studies and he is the author of several books and many articles in these areas. He is editor of the *Oxford Review of Education* and series editor of *Oxford Studies in Comparative Education*.

International developments in school reform
Series editor: Bob Moon

Other titles in this series include:

Educational Reform in Democratic Spain
Edited by Oliver Boyd-Barrett and Pamela O'Malley

Education and Reform in France: The Mitterand Years 1981–1995
Edited by Anne Corbett and Bob Moon

Education in Germany

Tradition and reform in historical context

Edited by David Phillips

London and New York

First published 1995
by Routledge
11 New Fetter Lane, London EC4P 4EE

Simultaneously published in the USA and Canada
by Routledge
29 West 35th Street, New York, NY 10001

Phototypeset in Times by Intype, London
Printed and bound in Great Britain by TJ Press (Padstow) Ltd, Padstow
Cornwall.

British Library Cataloguing in Publication Data
A catalogue record for this book is available from the British Library

Library of Congress Cataloguing in Publication Data
A catalogue record for this book has been requested

ISBN 0–415–11397–0

Contents

Part III Vocational education and training

Part IV Education in the New Germany

Illustrations

Preface

In nearly all parts of the world there is an interest and fascination with the way other national systems of education are organised and worked. Demographic change, economic transformation, technological innovation and the explosion of knowledge have created a veritable maelstrom of ideas within which schooling and education generally are centrally situated. The important shifts in political and ideological structures over the last decade has contributed a further dimension to this complex interplay of ideas. How others educate their children, young people and, increasingly, the population as a whole, is now the subject of intense intellectual curiosity amongst the media, politicians and the increasingly aware generation of parents.

On these issues there is also a vast array of expertise working in the fields of comparative, development and international education. Strong academic bases exist for these interrelated fields through institutions of higher education and within national and trans-global agencies. Journals and other publications, as well as the new technological means of accessing data and information, provide a forum for theoretical and methodological debate.

This present series of books seeks to provide a range of sources to inform both the policy making and political community as well, it is hoped, as contributing to debates among specialists in the field. The word source is important. The series, and the individual selections made by editors, does not seek to provide a comprehensive account of the structure of any particular education system. A number of educational encyclopaedias and guides, as well as international publications, now serve that purpose. Rather the series seeks to give readers an inside view of the issues and arguments that characterise contemporary debate. For that reason a strong emphasis has been placed on the translation of key texts, where the normal language of debate is other than English, or alternatively the selection of contributors who, whilst writing in English, either work within the system or have a detailed working understanding of the context. Translation, of course, poses problems in its own right, as indeed does a series framework based on nations or regions, but giving access to the ways of understanding, habits of thought and assumptions from within a specific cultural context is an important aim of the series. And in that respect it is hoped to remedy the imbalance in the exchange of ideas that global access to the English speaking medium can bring.

Editors who are specialists in the area have made their own choices about the organisation of the different volumes and the selection of contributors. Many of the authors go beyond specifically educational concerns to touch on the social, political and economic influences that are intertwined with the process of change and reform. In this sense the series provides a source to stimulate curiosity, examine wider social and cultural issues and provide a starting point for further study and exploration.

Bob Moon
The Open University
England

Acknowledgements

The articles in this book were previously printed by the following publishers; the editor and publishers are grateful for permission to reprint them in the present volume:

I THE FORCES OF TRADITION

1 †Robinsohn S. B. and Kuhlmann J. C. (1967) 'Twenty years of non-reform in West German Education', *Comparative Education Review* XI/3: University of Chicago Press.
2 Hearnden A. (1985) 'Problems in German secondary education', in G. Kloss (ed.) *Education Policy in the Federal Republic of Germany 1969–1984*, Department of Language and Linguistics, UMIST.
3 Mitter W. (1986) 'Continuity and change: a basic question for German education', *Education* 33: Longman Group UK Ltd.
4 Phillips D. (1987) 'Lessons from Germany? The case of German secondary schools', *BJES* XXXV/3: Blackwell.
5 Führ C. (1994) 'The German University: basically healthy or rotten? Reflections on an overdue reorientation of German higher education policy', *European Education*: M. E. Sharpe Inc.

II STANDARDS AND ASSESSMENT

6 Prais S. J. and Wagner K. (1986) 'Schooling standards in England and Germany: some summary comparisons bearing on economic performance', *Compare* 16/1: Carfax.
7 Phillips D. (1991) 'Assessment in German schools', *Journal of Curriculum Studies* 23/6: Taylor & Francis.
8 Glowka D. (1989) 'Anglo-German perceptions of education', *Comparative Education* 25/3: Carfax.

III VOCATIONAL EDUCATION AND TRAINING

9 †Kloss G. (1985) 'Vocational education – a success story?', in G. Kloss (ed.) *Education Policy in the Federal Republic of Germany 1969–1984*, Department of Language and Linguistics, UMIST. Acknowledgement is gratefully expressed to Diana Kloss for reprint permission. Günther Kloss was formerly Director of the University of Manchester/UMIST European Studies Centre.

10 Dougherty C. (1987) 'The German dual system: a heretical view', *European Journal of Education* 22/2: Carfax.

11 Raggatt P. (1988) 'Quality control in the dual system of West Germany', *Oxford Review of Education* 14/2: Carfax.

12 Marshall S. (1991) 'The genesis and evolution of pre-vocational education in West Germany', *Oxford Review of Education* 17/1: Carfax.

IV THE NEW GERMANY

13 Mitter W. (1992) 'Education in present-day Germany: some considerations as mirrored in *Comparative Education* (July 1991)', *Compare* 22/1: Carfax.

14 Phillips D. (1992) 'Transitions and traditions: educational developments in the new Germany in their historical context', *Oxford Studies in Comparative Education* 2/1: Triangle Books.

15 Führ C. (1992) *On the Education System of the Five New Länder of the Federal Republic of Germany*, Bonn: Inter Nationes.

Introduction

David Phillips

SOME HISTORICAL PERSPECTIVES

While Anglo-German political relations have enjoyed rather more than the usual run of ups and downs over the past century or so, British interest in educational provision – whether in Prussia, or in Weimar or Nazi or post-war Germany – has been demonstrably sustained. There is a certain historical inevitability in the fact that in recent years – that is, at a time of considerable economic difficulty – educationists and policy makers in the British Isles have devoted very serious attention to education in Germany.

The main imperative for such interest has indeed been the economic rivalry of two great European industrial nations. 'Germany is the land of schools,' wrote one commentator in 1910, 'and she is rapidly taking a leading place in the world.'[1] That 'leading place' economically was at first the object of outraged allegations of unfairness, followed later by unhappy resignation. Addressing the subject of Anglo-German relations in 1912, another author put the issue of trade competition in these terms:

> Twenty years ago the English people may have resented German competition because they actually did consider it unfair, and not without some plausible reasons. German trade originally ousted English trade from many markets because conditions were not equal, because the standard of living was lower in Germany, because wages and profits were smaller and hours longer, and because the goods 'made in Germany' were often a cheap and nasty imitation of British goods.[2]

The author in question goes on to talk of resentment about Germany's tariff restrictions, while her own trade was able to grow 'under the sunshine of British Free Trade'. In 1912, however, he continues, the Englishman

> admits that the average German works harder, that he is better trained, that he shows greater adaptability to the needs of his customers, that he possesses a better knowledge of foreign countries and foreign

languages. The praise of German qualities and German attainments is today the burden of every British Consular report.[3]

Some eighty and more years on the picture is much the same.

In the ten years or so leading up to these analyses education in Germany had been investigated in great depth by the British Board of Education and the Director of its Office of Special Inquiries and Reports, Michael Sadler, who wrote widely on most aspects of education. In January 1916, he was writing in *The Times* on the subject of 'imitating' German educational practice.[4] German education, he writes, 'makes good use of all second-grade ability, which in England is far too much of a waste product'. This key advantage is one which still occupies the attention of educational policy makers today, and I shall return to it later. Michael Sadler provides a check-list of achievements:

> Whatever we may feel about its capital defect – its idol-worship of the State and its subordination of conscience to system and success – German education has high merits. [. . .] [It] has made the nation alert to science. It has made systematic cooperation a habit. It has taught patriotic duty. It has kept a whole people industrious. Combined with military training, it has given them the strength of discipline. It has made profitable use of second rate intelligence. It has not neglected the mind.

Such a verdict, reached it must be remembered in the midst of war, summarises the outcome of years of attention to the merits of an education system which had been the envy of Europe and America for over 100 years.

In the nineteenth century it was the German universities that had attracted British and American students in large numbers. The German university represented for many progressive British academics the model of what a modern university should be. There was great enthusiasm for the scientific work of the great German universities and for the German idea of academic freedom encapsulated in the formula *Lehr- und Lernfreiheit* and in the concept of the unity of teaching and research. 'The French university has no liberty and the English universities have no science,' wrote Matthew Arnold, 'the German universities have both.'[5]

Several other Britons in public life could be quoted in this connection. One will suffice. Henry Fisher, later President of the Board of Education and Warden of New College, Oxford, was studying towards the end of the century in Göttingen. In his autobiography he sketches the attractions of the German university:

> During the last two decades of the nineteenth century the German universities enjoyed a wide reputation for freedom, courage and learning. To sit at the feet of some great German Professor, absorbing his publications, listening to his lectures, working in his seminary, was

regarded as a valuable, perhaps as a necessary passport to the highest form of academic career. Every year young graduates from our universities would repair to Berlin and Heidelberg, to Göttingen and Bonn, to Jena and Tübingen. The names of the German giants, of Ranke and Mommsen, of Wilamowitz and Lotze, were sounded again and again by their admiring disciples in British lecture-rooms.[6]

Fisher goes on to speak of 'two generations of . . . remarkable men, who had given new hope to every branch of human knowledge'. As one of Anthony Trollope's characters had expressed it in the 1850s, 'You'll have those universities of yours about your ears soon, if you don't consent to take a lesson from Germany.'[7] And there was indeed many a lesson to be learnt, both from university and from school provision.

German universities demonstrably led the world in many branches of the arts and sciences; Prussia, by Michael Sadler's time, had had compulsory schooling for a hundred years and more; teaching approaches were widely admired in some subjects, particularly foreign languages; great advances had been made in vocational training, which was to become compulsory in Germany after the First World War. And the crucial, though elusive, link between educational provision and economic success had been identified and its probability accepted.

Why, though, did Britain lag so far behind, given the impetus of the industrial revolution? One hypothesis that explains the phenomenon is that the British consistently failed to *teach* the skills that had built up their industrial success. Those skills were developed by individual engineers and inventors, outside of the educational system, working in an entrepreneurial spirit. The formal education system provided a *classical* education, shunning the practical. When other Europeans came to learn about these skills they returned home to pass them on via their formal education and training systems.

This is what Michael Sadler had in mind during the First World War when he wrote of Germany '[making] good use of all second-grade ability' or '[making] profitable use of second rate intelligence'. The Germans, alongside the other skills they have been concerned to nurture through their educational provision, have been at pains to train young people, both in formal schooling and outside of it, in precisely those middle-ranking vocations on which the economy so crucially depends, and it is the prolonged lack of such organised training in the United Kingdom that has caused our British political masters and their civil servants and advisers, as well as academic commentators, journalists and other writers, to turn their attention to Germany again as the end of the century approaches.

SOME ASPECTS OF EDUCATION AND TRAINING IN GERMANY

Germany, as a federal republic, devolves responsibility for educational and cultural matters to the *Land* (state) parliaments. Each *Land* (in the old Federal Republic there were ten *Länder* plus West Berlin; with the accession of the former German Democratic Republic (GDR) there are an additional five) therefore has a degree of autonomy which does not exist in countries with centralised education systems.

The autonomy the *Länder* enjoy, however, cannot allow them to deviate too far from 'natural' expectations of what the education system should deliver, and so there are also federal planning and policy bodies, the KMK (the standing conference of ministers of education) being the most obvious for the co-ordination of policy for the period of compulsory schooling.

A process of *juridification* results in educational provision being enshrined in law, and so it is clear to all involved with the system within an individual *Land* what types of school are provided, what the syllabus content is for particular years in particular types of school for the various subjects taught, how and at what stages children will be assessed, etc. This unequivocal clarity regarding provision must be seen as one of the strengths of the system, despite criticisms of bureaucratisation.

Since education is a matter for *Land* parliaments, it is also a subject for political decision-making. Whether or not to introduce the comprehensive school (*Gesamtschule*), for example, has been a political matter which has resulted in some *Länder* experimenting widely with such schools, while others have resisted them. Decisions reached in the five new *Länder* of the former GDR have been largely determined by CDU thinking on education, and so all of them quickly envisaged the rapid introduction of the grammar school (*Gymnasium*) and other 'selective' schools, to replace the 10-year common school which had provided a wholly undifferentiated education for all children between the ages of 6 and 16.

The eleven *Länder* of the old Federal Republic have retained a school system which is the most conservative in Europe. With various exceptions it consists of the *Gymnasium*, the academic secondary school preparing pupils for university entrance; the *Realschule*, an intermediate school with a long and distinguished history preparing pupils for a range of technical and middle-management careers; and the *Hauptschule*, the 'main' type of secondary school, actually for a minority of pupils in Germany's tripartite system and now having the unenviable label of 'sink school', since it is no longer clear for what its products are qualified. Alongside these schools there exist in some *Länder* comprehensive schools which cannot be considered truly comprehensive owing to the competitive presence of other types of school.

The five *Länder* of eastern Germany all proposed, following Unification, to introduce the grammar school and a *Realschule* of some kind; only one envisaged the *Hauptschule*; three did not foresee the introduction of comprehensive schools in any form. The conservative nature of German school provision will thus be confirmed and strengthened by the new *Länder*.

Defenders of the differentiated German system point to several features which mitigate its apparent rigidity:

- parents may *choose* which type of school their children attend;
- there is the possibility of lateral transfer from one type of school to another, syllabuses being devised with this in mind;
- leaving certificates of each type of school are not restrictive, but provide vertical access to other stages of education;
- some *Länder* in any case have an 'orientation stage' before a final decision is reached as to which type of school a child is best suited to attend.

But the greatest strength of the school system up to age 16 is probably the strong intermediate school (*Realschule*) which provides essential education and training for pupils not aiming specifically at a university education. They fulfil the task which the technical schools would have had in England and Wales, had they been developed in the way the 1944 Education Act envisaged. The new German *Länder*, while mostly rejecting the *Hauptschule* on the grounds that it has failed in the west, are putting their faith in the expanded *Realschule* for non-grammar school pupils.

Assessment in German schools is continuous and regularised. A 6-point scale is used, with grades 1–4 representing satisfactory attainment or above. Pupils may score only *one* average of 5 in their end-of-year report; a 6, or more than two 5s, will in most cases result in their not being able to proceed to the next class. A class can only be repeated once; thereafter a pupil who has failed to 'reach the goal of the class' will have to transfer down to another type of school.

Standards are high. A much-quoted British study of 1985 (see pp. 95–134 of this volume) purported to show that attainment in mathematics by those in the *lower* half of the ability range in England lags behind that of equivalent German pupils by about *two years*.

Vocational training, based on a 'Dual System' of co-operation between employers and the state, has long been regarded as exemplary in the Federal Republic. It is compulsory – on a part-time basis – for *all* pupils up to age 18 who are not in full-time education. At age 16, 72 per cent of school-leavers enter vocational training of some kind. There is a noticeable trend for 18-year olds to enter the Dual System, even though they have gained the right to a university place by passing the final school-leaving examination (*Abitur*). Some 16 per cent of new trainees are choosing this route to a vocational qualification.

A report by Her Majesty's Inspectorate published in May 1991 identified the strengths of the German approach thus:

* clear commitment to training by employers;
* accreditation and assurance of standards by Chambers of Commerce and Industry;
* the requirement that employers offer training contracts with a guarantee that appropriate training will be given;
* the significance of the fully trained master craftsman (*Meister*) in Germany.

In higher education the *Fachhochschulen* (roughly equivalent to our former polytechnics) are enjoying great favour, and they will be considerably expanded. They provide a shorter (3-year) course than the universities, with a strong bias towards practical subjects and their application. These institutions, building on the traditions of the *Realschule* concept and the highly developed vocational training system, provide a further indication of the seriousness of purpose of education in Germany when it comes to assessing and meeting the needs of a modern industrial society.

RECENT CROSS-NATIONAL ATTRACTION: ENGLAND AND GERMANY

The reasons why any one country is attracted to the education system of another country at a given time are normally quite complex. Such attraction has to do usually with perceived failings in the home system, and it does not always treat the target system with appropriate objectivity, often using particular aspects of its provision for the political purpose of stark, and selective, contrast.

It was not surprising that in the period leading up to the Education Reform Act of 1988, the most far-reaching educational legislation in England and Wales since the famous 1944 Act, there was much mention of education in Germany. Her Majesty's Inspectors of Schools chose the Federal Republic as the object of the first of their investigative studies to be published in series form since the days of Michael Sadler. Their report, published in 1986,[8] summarises the main attractions of the German system, before analysing those 'features and characteristics' which 'strike informed English observers as having important messages for us':

> The Federal Republic's system sets out to provide qualifications for all its pupils. It is not wholly successful in this, but its achievements are impressive. Within its differentiated system of education and training it appears more successful than we are in retaining a large proportion of pupils in general education or in education and training until 17 or 18 years of age; in providing attainable goals for them to work towards;

and in not hiving off different groups of pupils in ways that cut them off from the mainstream of general education.

These arrangements in general education, linked as they are with a training system in which industry plays a leading and responsible part, combine to give a broad range of pupils a range of qualifications to aim for; the possibility of threading their way through an interrelated system; and a sense of hope in that they are not dropped out of the system early on.

It is this framework that has an important and cumulative influence upon the expectations of teachers, pupils, parents, employers and the nation at large. Because there is understanding of and broad agreement about what education is seeking to achieve in respect of pupils' needs, parental aspirations, employers' general requirements and the nation's social and economic intentions, the standing of education, of its teachers and its institutions, is relatively high. At all levels these conditions have largely beneficial effects upon pupils' attitudes toward education and consequently upon the standards they achieve.

Later in the report we can isolate some of the features of educational provision that provide further evidence of its attractiveness to those working in the mid-1980s towards the new arrangements formalised in the 1988 Act:

- The most important fact to bear in mind about the Federal Republic's system of assessment generally and about the *Abitur* in particular is that for the Federal Republic it works. Many teachers and officials put much effort and money into developing curricula and subject- and assessment-guidelines and to overcoming local inconsistencies. Ultimately, however, the system works because virtually everybody involved seems determined that it should do so. [...] It is, as much as anything else, an article of faith. This wide agreement about education and its assessment is in itself an important message for English education where such agreement, undertaking and trust are lacking.
- The curriculum is in the lead and has public confidence and clarity; teacher training in all its practical aspects ... is well-tried and effective.
- The educational system in the Federal Republic is efficient at achieving quickly a broad consensus about which subjects to teach, in which years and for how many pupils.
- There can ... be a greater confidence that pupils' work in each year and ability group bears a clear relationship to subsequent work than is often the case in England.
- There is a degree of openness and general accountability about the assessment system in the Federal Republic which would be much appreciated by pupils, parents and employers in England.

I have expressed the main attraction of German educational provision in these terms, which would be unsurprising for a German audience:

> The Germans have decided what it is their school system offers; it is clearly stated and known to all who have a part in the system. For better or worse this incontestably clear approach does mean that parents know what precisely they can expect for their children from a particular school and they are able, through well established procedures, to make sure that it is provided.[9]

Writing in 1989 Detlef Glowka, a German educationist with expert knowledge of the British scene, summarised in five categories those aspects of the German education system which had been singled out for particular attention by Her Majesty's Inspectors and others. They were:

- the continuous assessment of pupil performance;
- the compulsory nature and breadth of the curriculum;
- the wide distribution of school-leaving qualifications and the systematic correlation between them;
- the developed and systematic paths towards accredited vocational education;
- the regulating force of central guiding and controlling authorities.

'It appears', Glowka says, 'that in these five areas something could be learnt from the Germans'; and he notes that they constituted central features of the 1988 Education Reform Act. (See pp. 140–58 of this volume.)

At the same time attention was being given to an important research report from the National Institute of Economic and Social Research in London. The study in question, by Prais and Wagner, examined schooling standards in England and Germany and made comparisons 'bearing on economic performance'. It has since been widely quoted in support of moves in the United Kingdom towards greater curricular control along German lines. Its authors were concerned principally with the attainment of pupils in the middle and lower half of the ability range, especially in mathematics. Among their findings we can quote three as being of most significance in the context of the UK policy debate:

- Over half of all German pupils, compared with only just over a quarter of the pupils in England, attain a standard above or equivalent to a broadly based set of O-level passes.
- The German system provides a broader curriculum combined with significantly higher levels of attainment in core subjects, for a greater proportion of pupils than does the English system.
- Attainments in mathematics by those in the lower half of the ability range in England appear to lag by the equivalent of about two years' schooling behind the corresponding section of pupils in Germany.

This latter finding in particular has been given great prominence by commentators at all levels. If it is legitimate, it reinforces the view of Michael Sadler some seventy years earlier that Germany was profiting from its attention to the education of those not aspiring to the highest level of academic attainment; it certainly reinforced the tendency of the then Department of Education and Science in London to support its arguments about policy with reference to developments in other leading industrialised countries.

There have also, of course, been some features of education in England that have proved attractive to German observers. Glowka mentions such aspects of educational provision as teachers' centres, the Open University, community education, curriculum development in all its variety, the established position of the comprehensive school, and the development of primary education. Many of these areas have attracted attention in the Federal Republic, even if they have not been consciously emulated. Glowka writes too of British patterns of liberality and democracy in education which could be perceived as being at risk during and after the 1988 reforms, and I imagine that it is the freedom to experiment, permitted through the traditional high degree of autonomy enjoyed by institutions and individual teachers, that made the British system enviable to outside observers.

To Glowka's list we might add the close relationship that exists at university level between teacher and student. Though some German critics might see the British university as a mere extension of school (a harsh and unfair judgement in my view) others would see great benefit in teaching arrangements that allow students close day-to-day contact with those who teach them. In the ancient Universities of Oxford and Cambridge such contact is even more pronounced, as a result of the highly developed tutorial system. The United Kingdom has nothing approaching the *Massenuniversität*, with all its attendant problems. On the negative side, however, there is no *right* of access to a university education, however good an individual's examination results might be.

THE PRESENT STUDY

Four themes have been identified to provide the structure for this edited collection of papers on education in Germany by German and British authors.

1 *The forces of tradition*. This covers the historical inheritance of the present system, its political control, the processes of juridification which have reinforced the 'conservative' nature of educational provision, and the difficulties of introducing and managing reform.
2 *Standards and assessment*. The assessment procedures in German

schools have received a lot of attention outside of Germany (most notably from HMI in 1986), despite their shortcomings and much criticism from German educationists. High measurable standards in education at all levels have also been noticed abroad. The important study by Prais and Wagner, included in this volume, sparked off a long debate and was often quoted by Ministers in the run-up to the 1988 Education Reform Act.

3 *Vocational education and training*. Again, this is a subject in German education which has received much attention as a model from which other countries might learn. Germany has had compulsory vocational education since 1918, and despite its current problems the 'Dual System' continues to be viewed with much envy in the UK and elsewhere. It formed the subject of a further HMI report in 1991.

4 *Education in the new Germany*. Against the background of the unification of the two Germanies there are important questions to be addressed about the future development of an essentially conservative system in a country which is playing a leading role in a new Europe but has faced economic problems of a kind to which it is unaccustomed.

The papers selected for inclusion were written over a long period, the earliest dating from 1967. It was decided not to attempt any editorial updating of the individual contributions, but to let them stand as indicators of the state of aspects of education in the Federal Republic of Germany at the time they were written. Thus, for example, Robinsohn and Kuhlmann's controversial paper of 1967 (included in the first section) reflects a particular critical stance on the slow pace of educational reform in Germany taken by two scholarly observers at a time of considerable educational change in other countries of Europe. Some overlap between the contents of the papers has also been tolerated, in order to preserve their inner cohesion. Editorial changes have been minimal, limited mainly to the omission of some superfluous material. Reference to 'West Germany' is of course inevitable in papers written before the Unification of the two Germanies in 1990.

It is hoped that the bringing-together of the fifteen papers which make up this volume will provide those interested in education in the Federal Republic with a commentary on some key aspects of educational development in that country since the war and some insights into current issues. It will be seen, I think, that the main perceived advantages of the German education system, as seen from the UK, are closely allied to the general thrust of reforms in England and Wales under successive British governments since Prime Minister James Callaghan's Ruskin College speech of 1976. Those advantages have to do largely with accountability at all levels, with greater centralised control coupled with responsible, regulated autonomy, with government-controlled authority over the curriculum and assessment, with the raising of standards, and with the encouragement of increased public respect for education generally.

Though it is clear that there is much in educational provision in the Federal Republic that would not lend itself to the uncritical adulation of educationists in the United Kingdom, its general coherence at home, its acceptability to most people involved with it, and its acknowledged high standards, continue to provide a challenge to British policy makers which has been on the agenda now for well over a century and to which reaction has been long overdue.

NOTES

1 Robert M. Berry: *Germany of the Germans*, London (Sir Isaac Pitman & Sons Ltd) 1910, p. 73.
2 Charles Sarolea: *The Anglo-German Problem*, London (Thomas Nelson and Sons) 1912, p. 54.
3 Ibid., p. 55.
4 Michael Sadler: 'Need we imitate German education?', *The Times*, 14 January 1916.
5 Matthew Arnold: *Schools and Universities on the Continent*, London (Macmillan and Co) 1868, p. 232.
6 H. A. L. Fisher: *An Unfinished Autobiography*, London (Oxford University Press) 1940, p. 79.
7 The novel in question is *Barchester Towers*.
8 DES: *Education in the Federal Republic of Germany: Aspects of Curriculum and Assessment* (An HMI Report), London (HMSO) 1986.
9 See 'Lessons from Germany? The case of German secondary schools' in this volume (pp. 60–79).

Part I
The forces of tradition

1 Two decades of non-reform in West German education [1967]

†Saul Robinsohn and J. Caspar Kuhlmann

This chapter will limit itself to problems of the function and structure of primary and secondary education, for it is at the junction of primary and secondary education that the principal issues in national educational policy have arisen. Here is to be found the major dysfunctionality of certain educational systems, including the German – in the lag in training qualified personnel and in 'democratizing' education.[1]

The title of this chapter demands some explanation. It is not meant to be polemic but to indicate that, in contrast to some other European countries, the adjustment of the educational system to the socio-economic and cultural developments of the mid-twentieth century has not yet really taken place in Germany. The authors do not consider certain changes in the organization of schooling and instruction which have occurred during the post-war years to have altered the system of West German education in any important degree. It is significant that a high official of the Bavarian Ministry of Education after enumerating a number of internal reforms, such as the participation of primary school teachers in deciding on selection for secondary schools, a concentration of subjects in the upper secondary schools, the introduction of social studies, the organization of study groups, and certain changes in the organization of the timetable, declared: 'The secondary school has completed its reform'; and concluded: 'peace must now return for a long period.'[2]

PATTERNS OF REFORM

The experience of total disruption after the Nazi period led many within the leading groups in Germany to look for security in old and trusted traditions. The conservatism which has prevailed in post-war Germany is a product of the overwhelming desire to recapture material well-being and social stability and a distrust of 'new beginnings' and experiments. Most of the leading university scholars rejected proposed reforms of the German secondary school and recommended retaining the traditional 9-year *Gymnasium*. Thus the Senate of the Hamburg University claimed in its memorandum of 1949 that 'training and education for the highest degree of effectiveness is such an important and urgent political task for a democratic state that all other political considerations ... are of no account, all the more so as any genuine education is in itself strong enough to avert the danger of unsocial isolation.'[3] Thus, in a nutshell are summed up 150 years of idealistic traditions in education – a belief in a pre-stabilized harmony between educational and social freedom.

The early post-war years were marked by conflict between desire to restore the status quo before Hitler and the proposals of German reform groups and the 're-education' policy of the occupying powers.[4] In 1947, the Allied Control Commission had defined its concept of 'democratizing' education in a directive to the German ministers containing the following criteria: equality of educational opportunity; free tuition and teaching materials; an additional ninth year of obligatory schooling; education for international understanding; educational guidance; health supervision; academic training for all teachers; democratic school administration. Other points concerned curriculum and structure: 'All schools should lay emphasis upon education for civic responsibility and a democratic way of life, by means of the content of the curriculum ... and by the organization of the school itself'; and 'schools for the period of compulsory education should form a comprehensive educational system. The terms "elementary education" and "secondary education" should mean two consecutive levels of instruction, not two types or qualities of instruction which overlap.' This implied the introduction of a 6-year primary school and 'organically integrated curricula of all schools to allow for later transfer.'[5] Not that all these criteria were met by the educational systems of the occupying powers themselves, but they were supposed to indicate the general current of progressive education from which Germany had been excluded for the previous twelve years.

In the initial phase of the post-war period these principles were transformed into blueprints for reform in all *Länder*. They were, however, abandoned within the shortest span of time. Many points of the directive have never been implemented. Because of the unexpectedly speedy resumption of German independence and the quick realization of the futility of re-education dictated from outside, the allies stopped insisting on their implementation. The result was to discourage genuine German reform impulses. Cultural advisers contented themselves with the support of 'internal reform,' which was quite acceptable to their German counterparts and of course open to any number of interpretations.

If, in contrast to conditions after the First World War, there was no widespread and optimistic readiness for reform and innovation, actual needs were sooner or later bound to enforce change. Against these economic and social dynamics the opposition of conservative forces was all the more fierce.[6] Within the strictly vertical school organization, reinforced by methods of strict selection and achievement control, the official representatives of the intermediate and secondary schools fought for the '*Eigenständigkeit*' (distinctive task) of their institutions. We must not assume, however, that professional conservatism would have prevailed had there not existed a large measure of social support for it. When the sociologist Helmut Schelsky criticized the school for appropriating to itself the privilege of allocating social chances in a *dirigiste* manner, this was not said in criticism of the selective character of school organization.[7] On the contrary, he intended to defend parents' rights and, as witnessed by his criticism of the *Rahmenplan* (see below), to isolate this factor from its social context and to maintain the school, especially the secondary school, as a cultural preserve.[8]

In view of later developments it seems fair to say that things might have been different had not the 'traditional remoteness of the state from a mode of thought which employs social categories,' the lag of the social sciences in Germany caused by the Nazi period, and the 'anti-sociological effect' (as Hellmut Becker put it) retarded the application of social scientific methods to these problems.[9] Eventually, surveys and interviews, the results of which have appeared recently,[10] were to show that certain groups, notably industrial and agricultural laborers, were grossly underrepresented in intermediate and secondary schools. If, on the surface, justification for this situation can be found in the low level of aspirations of the parents themselves, further analysis suggests that underneath this apparent acquiescence there is a distinctive recognition of the value of education and a corresponding feeling of frustration about the inability to attain it, which is widespread among educationally underprivileged groups. If we are to speak of a state of emergency in education, says W. Strzelewicz, 'it is to be found in this realm of our socio-cultural situation,' and he concludes that nearly every second adult in the Federal Republic lives with a feeling of not having had his chance.

To many it seemed the 1950s were the low tide of educational engagement and scholarship in post-war Germany. In 1956, a leading educationist wrote: 'A general fatigue has fallen upon educational thought in Germany, and sluggishly, without any new impulses, pedagogy is dragging itself along.'[11] This was probably exaggerated, since, from its inauguration in September 1953 down to 1959, the *Deutscher Ausschuß*, was preparing its plan for a reorganization of German education. It was perhaps the tragedy of this commission and of its members that their work had to be done mainly in the setting of an older reform pedagogy and on the basis of personal experience and observation rather than on the much needed foundations of statistical survey, precise evidence, and systematic social analysis.

For it was the gradual maturing of such methods which marked the turning-point in the public treatment of educational problems. Surveys of manpower-demand, started by the Bavarian *Kultusminister* Rucker, paid increasing attention to the questions of academically trained manpower, of a growing teacher shortage, and of the amazing variance in the degree of schooling in the various *Länder* of the Federal Republic. The results of such surveys were summed up and spotlighted by Georg Picht, a philosopher and leading *Kulturpolitiker*, who declared the teacher shortage to be the signal of educational disaster. At about the same time Ralf Dahrendorf initiated and publicized further investigations into the problem of educational inequality, and a number of politicians introduced these issues into parliamentary debate.[12] Economics of education proved to be a most powerful lever. Friedrich Edding, its first and most prominent advocate in Germany, stated its importance in the following way: 'A large part of public opinion in all countries is now convinced that educational attainment is not only an expression of material wealth, but that the future wealth of a country in any sense and its position in the world are strongly influenced by education.'[13]

It should be emphasized that this new approach was considerably influenced by the example of other western countries and by the activities of international organizations. This is especially true of the results of international economic surveys and analyses. The OECD Washington Conference of 1961 had demonstrated that West German schools lagged behind comparable countries in providing qualified manpower. Two years later the Conference of the Ministers of Culture initiated the first thorough survey of the demand for education. The Ministers of Education concluded that 'German cultural policy, following a period of reconstruction, has now entered a new chapter in which parallel needs in all countries within modern industrial society give new and strong impulses to the further development of school and higher education policy.'[14]

There is no denying the vitalizing effect on German discussion of educational reform of economic and sociological investigation and international comparisons. But this wholehearted embracing of economic reasoning has no doubt created its own problems. There is not only the obvious difficulty of equivalence and comparability, but behind the outcry against what is being disparagingly called '*Ökonomismus*' and '*Soziologismus*' lies the understandable fear that quantitative approaches may conceal and even distort vital questions of function and quality. For example, a new government in Baden-Württemberg, upon taking office, defined the aims of its educational policy in predominantly economic terms, and the Minister of Education simply formulated his goals as: (1) a rise in the number of secondary school graduates to 15 per cent of the age group; and (2) a rise in the number of 'intermediate' graduates to 40 per cent.[15] Detailed planning was initiated on this basis.[16] One can hardly be surprised if such crude methods, apparently neglecting social and cultural motivation and the needs for curricular and structural adjustment, presently lead to increasing individual failure and to institutional dysfunctionality.

A more recently published manpower survey shows a proper insight into the limitations of this approach, when, after proving that according to his calculations the need for academically qualified manpower will be met by the present organization, the author declares that his results should not weaken the demand for an expansion of higher education. On the contrary, he argues, the time has come to transform the institutions of higher learning from professional schools into colleges of general education.[17]

THE GERMAN SCHOOL SYSTEM AT MID-CENTURY

In the early 1950s the characteristic features of the German school system had changed only slightly since the beginning of the century.[18] There remained a vertical organization with its accompanying differentiated types of schools, pupils, and teachers and, in particular, a dual system of general education and vocational training; highly centralized administrations, within each *Land*; and strict methods of grading and selection.

At the age of 10 +, after four years of common elementary schooling (*Grundschule*), children are selected for different school tracks. In 1953, about four-fifths of all elementary school pupils – those who never attempted the examinations for one of the selective schools and those who had failed them – went on to the upper elementary school which was, and in the main still is, a straight continuation of the *Grundschule*.[19] After 4 (in some *Länder* 5) years of further 'basic general' education these students leave to begin vocational training, including obligatory theoretical instruction at a 'vocational school' (*Berufsschule*) which, however, occupies less than 7 hours a week on an average.[20] In 1953, the group leaving elementary school included 66.3 per cent of the 14- to 15-year olds.[21]

In the 10 to 14 age group one out of ten studied at an academic secondary school (*Gymnasium*).[22] Its graduates, who in 1953 numbered 3.3 per cent of the average age group,[23] had completed nine grades in one of three main types of program – classical, modern language, or mathematics-science.

There were, and in the main still are, few if any possibilities of transfer from one main tier to the other. Only a very limited number of continuation schools (*Aufbauschulen*), and these mainly in rural regions, offer a 6-year course for later secondary school graduation. However, a third type of school existed in some *Länder* after the war and has steadily grown in importance – the Middle School (*Mittelschule*), now generally called *Realschule*. In 1953, 5 per cent of the 10 to 14 age group were at *Mittel-* or *Realschulen*; 6.1 per cent of the 17-year olds reached 'intermediate graduation.'[24] This diploma is also offered – evidently as a substitute – by the academic secondary schools and by continuation classes at elementary schools.[25]

Even these mere quantitative data reveal a significant feature of the system – the extremely small apex of the educational pyramid. No less important is the indication that the obvious inadequacies of 'elementary' education did not result in the abolition of the vertical system but in the creation of a three-tier organization. It should be noted that a somewhat analogous development can be observed in vocational education, in which a limited number of students now get their education and training at more highly qualified full-time vocational schools (*Berufsaufbauschulen, Berufsfachschulen*). Once again, the establishment of auxiliary schools to take care of those for whom the existing system was clearly inadequate was preferred to outright reconstruction of the post-primary, including the vocational, phase of education.

To understand the school organization thus roughly sketched, one has to realize that it reflects an educational theory that assigns three different tasks to the three types of school. The elementary school is supposed to prepare its pupils for practical vocations; the middle school for positions of 'intermediate responsibility' (*mittlere Führung*) in the economy and administration of the country; the *Gymnasien* prepare for the leading posts, largely presupposing that further academic training will ensue. Indeed, in 1959, 97 per cent of the male graduates of the *Gymnasium* continued their studies at institutions of higher education.[26] The view that the potential populations of these three types can be distinguished by three corresponding kinds of ability has been basic to their establishment and is still discernible, not only in popular opinion, but even in school legislation. One still speaks of 'practical,' 'practical-theoretical,' and 'theoretical' aptitudes – a classification which was not uncommon in the school systems of other countries.

The theory and practice of vertical organization are reinforced by the hierarchy of school curricula and the rigid system of grade organization and promotion which make transfer from one type of school to the other extremely difficult. In one *Land*, in 1953, 7.5 per cent of the secondary school pupils were children of laborers, 25 per cent were children of academically trained parents, with corresponding shares of 42 per cent and 2.5 per cent respectively in the general population.[27] That there is no pretension to 'different but equal' or of 'parity of esteem' is made clear by the radically different training of teachers – *Volksschullehrer* being trained at Teacher Training Colleges (*Pädagogische Hochschulen*) and secondary school teachers at the university, with distinctly different programs of training. (Middle school teachers have alternative arrangements.) Salaries for teachers at elementary, middle, and secondary schools were, in 1956, in the ratio of 5 : 6 : 9.[28] In 1950 per-pupil expenditure at elementary schools was one-third that for secondary school pupils.[29]

A few words ought to be said about curricula, examinations, and achievements. Levels of achievements from instruction at all three types of school in Germany are high, and are recognized as such both within the country and abroad. In the absence of accurate comparative data on the results of alternative educational systems,[30] we have no reason to doubt these popular judgements. In spite of the customary, but probably not too serious, outbursts of dissatisfaction at one stage or the other, 'consumers' of the products of the schools are reasonably well satisfied. Elementary school graduates usually leave adequately prepared in reading, writing, and elementary mathematics; the students of *Realschulen* have more mathematics and science, one or two foreign languages, and certain office and other technical skills to prepare them for their tasks in '*mittlere Führungspositionen*'; secondary schools try to give their students knowledge drawn from a curriculum of some thirteen subjects, still with an emphasis on the humanities. However, close examination reveals that the offerings of the schools are dated, in particular in science and technology, and admittedly inadequate in social and political education.[31]

A quantitative look at the highly selective system of examinations and grade promotion reveals some startling facts. In each of the years 1955 to 1957, 3 to 4 per cent of elementary school pupils and middle school pupils had to repeat their grades. In the secondary grades the figure was 6 per cent and it is at present about 9 per cent.[32] According to a calculation of the *Wissenschaftsrat*, only one-third of those studying in grade 3 of the secondary school in 1950 eventually were graduated.[33] Analyses of selected age groups have shown that fewer than 20 per cent of secondary school graduates reach graduation without repeating one or more classes.[34]

In sum, then, the deficiencies in German education are not unlike those which reforms in other highly industrialized countries have tried to remedy: important decisions about a pupil's future career are usually made when he is 10 years old; not more than one out of every five pupils attempts a secondary education, and the majority of these eventually fail; only 5 to 6 per cent of secondary school graduates are children of laborers (who constitute about half of the entire population); about two-thirds of all boys and girls have practically completed general schooling at the age of 14 or 15; the curriculum does little to mend these deficiencies of social integration and orientation.

However, the instinct towards conformity of German society – a society which has only partially absorbed the social and cultural implications of high industrialization – has made for harmony and contentment with its traditional school system. Moreover, it should also be borne in mind that any change in the German educational system would have to be effected under a constitution which reserves 'cultural autonomy' to the individual *Länder*. This complex problem of cultural federalism, including the competence and limitations of the *Ständige Konferenz der Kultusminister* (Permanent Conference of the Ministers of Education and Culture, abbreviated to KMK), will be discussed more fully in the concluding section, but its implications appear throughout.

ATTEMPTS AT REFORM

In a recent survey of the educational system in Germany, the authors write: 'Even though . . . no thorough reorganization of the German school system has taken place, we have largely succeeded in realizing within its framework social and educational principles which are common today to all democratic countries.'[35] Such optimism seems hardly justified when the present system is measured against the educational program which the Ministers of Education of Western and Eastern Germany drafted as early as 1948 in their Stuttgart-Hohenheim resolution. This program reiterated in principle the recommendation of the *Pädagogisches Zentralinstitut* as far back as 1932 to modify the tripartite organization, but it also envisaged further advance towards a more comprehensive system.

Indeed, certain changes that have occurred within the tripartite school system require mention: free tuition and free teaching materials in most of the *Länder*; a ninth, and in some cases a voluntary tenth, year of elementary schooling in all *Länder* except Bavaria; the opening of certain complementary avenues to secondary school graduation for marginal groups; and in Berlin the introduction and consolidation of common 6-year primary schools for all children.[36] A more significant innovation, but one which hardly contributes to integration, is that of the apparently firm establishment of the middle school (*Realschule*). Possibilities of transfer from one type of school to another have been extended in some *Länder* through the introduction of foreign language instruction in elementary schools and through the addition of a number of continuation classes in elementary and middle schools. From 1950 to 1965, the number of secondary school graduates (*Abiturienten*) has risen from 4.2 per cent to 6.9 per cent of the age group, that of *Realschule* graduates from 8.7 per cent (1954) to 12.4 per cent (1963).[37] But are these developments educational reform, or are they rather examples of a process which comparative education often has demonstrated – that quantitative as well as qualitative deficiencies of an educational system are usually met by modifying the existing structure before undertaking more radical reform?

The best way to find out why no real structural, much less functional, reform has taken place is to consider the two general plans for educational reorganization published during the past decade – the '*Rahmenplan*' and the 'Bremer Plan.' Both were based on a national, though by no means empirical, survey of German schools. Since both plans have become known abroad and have been reviewed in the *Comparative Education Review*, their description can be brief.[38]

In 1953, a committee of experts, the *Deutscher Ausschuß für das Erziehungs und Bildungswesen*, was jointly established by the federal government and the *Länder* 'to survey the German system of education and to promote its development through advice and recommendation.' After offering a series of suggestions and recommendations on several issues and unsolved problems in German school and adult education, the members of this committee came to realize that nothing short of a proposal for the reconstruction (*Neuordnung*) of the whole system of education would be an adequate fulfilment of its assignment.[39] Only loosely, if at all, connected with the official institutions of science, scholarship, and political power, the authority of the *Ausschuß* rested exclusively on the competence of its members. A very modest budget did not allow for a substantial research program, and the *Ausschuß* concluded its work in 1965 after about twelve years of operation, having issued analyses and recommendations on a wide range of subjects but concentrating, in the second half of its existence, on questions of school curriculum, organization, and teacher training.[40]

Starting with the proposition that the whole system of schooling and education in Germany 'had not caught up with the changes which have altered the situation and consciousness of society and state during the last fifty years,'[41] the committee, early in its existence, presented to the German public a number of measures to promote a more democratic and more effective kind of schooling – intensified political education; a full academic, though not a common, education for all teachers; the introduction of a ninth and later a tenth year of obligatory schooling; and a better differentiated upper elementary school (*Hauptschule*).

The *pièce de résistance* of the committee's work was, however, the *Rahmenplan*, published in 1959, which attempted to modify the established tripartite structure, although it never really touched its foundations. Its most radical suggestion was to establish an intermediate, 2-year *Förderstufe* during which teachers of all three types of school should work together to identify and further the abilities and interests of their pupils with the help of differentiated methods of instruction. Only a minority of clearly gifted pupils would transfer, as before, to the more strictly academic type of *Gymnasium* (called '*Studienschule*') at the end of the fourth year. All others would be directed to the upper elementary, the middle, or the academic secondary school (*Gymnasium*) following completion of the orientation years in the *Förderstufe*. The tripartite system was thus retained while attempting to provide for easier transfer than heretofore possible. A not overly courageous plan, one might say, overtly trying merely to improve methods of selection and promotion and retaining, as a compromise measure, academic secondary education for the very few and not daring to touch the newly established differentiation between the elementary and the 'intermediate' type of school, although perhaps covertly envisaging later improvements for social and even organizational integration. However, even this modest proposal failed.

The 'Bremer Plan,' a blueprint for the reorganization of German schools, submitted in 1960 by the Teachers Union (*Arbeitsgemeinschaft Deutscher Lehrerverbände*) after 8 years of preparation, differed from the *Rahmenplan* only in proposing to make the common stage part of the regular continuation of the primary years for all, thus doing away with the residue of dual organization and the old-type *Gymnasium* represented by the *Studienschule* of the *Rahmenplan*. Why, one may ask, did the Union in the main reiterate the very moderate previous plan? There is little doubt that pressure from certain groups within the organization prevented a more radical solution.[42]

It was the Social Democratic Party which, in 1964, came out with bolder proposals based upon a horizontal organization. The *Förderstufe* in this plan would have been a transitional solution, and the long-range aim was an integrated comprehensive middle stage of grades 7 to 10.

These three blueprints have in common a realization of a fundamental problem – namely, tripartite division, a disposition to modify this through basic change of organization, and a lack of political power to secure implementation. What had been envisaged before 1933, ordered in 1947, and proposed in 1964 had not come much nearer implementation in 1966.

So far, only the *Land* of Hessen has systematically tried the *Förderstufe*, so that actually 6.7 per cent of the fifth and sixth grade pupils attend classes of this kind.[43] Another example of an attempt at better integration, the Multilateral Schools (*Additive Gesamtschulen*) dating from an earlier, partly American idea (*Schuldorf Bergstrasse*) are to be found in the same *Land*. Only Berlin plans a number of comprehensive schools proposed in the SPD blueprint.[44] Four schools of this type are under construction, in which common-core instruction up to the tenth grade will be combined with differentiated courses. Schleswig-Holstein has had a similar school but it was abolished by the *Land* Parliament.[45]

Another approach to reform might obviously come by way of a revision of curricula. So far, one such attempt dealing with only the secondary school has been made. The aim of the Saarbrücken agreement, reached by the Conference of the Ministers of Education in 1960, is 'concentration' of studies at the upper secondary school emphasizing the acquisition of study skills and habits and deepened insight rather than on broad information. (Nine subjects are still required for graduation, however.) More recently, one suggestion has gone as far as proposing a college stage leading from secondary school to the university.[46] The prospects for a more thorough revision of school curricula to bridge the gap between the different schools at the lower secondary level are dim, although there is a growing realization that improved social studies programs, extended foreign language instruction, and a modernized mathematics and science curriculum may gradually narrow the distance between the various types. Organized attempts at curriculum development are, however, still in their infancy.[47]

Similarly, signs of change can be found in the development of vocational education. The dual system is slowly being modified through the integration of the full-time schools where practical, theoretical, and general education are combined. Education and training are thus not only rationalized and intensified, but possibilities for opening additional avenues to higher education are at least indicated.[48] The *Deutscher Ausschuß* itself has deplored the fact that so far only 2 to 3 per cent of the recipients of higher education are reaching it via the *Zweiter Bildungsweg*, that is, through vocational and further education. With an eye on the significance of such parallel approaches in countries like England, an extension of appropriate provisions has been suggested for Germany.

The essential question, however, is not that of opening up parallel approaches, but rather that of overcoming 'the separation of technical and vocational training from general education,' which, according to a UNESCO declaration, 'contributes to social sterility.'[49] In this sense the *Deutscher Ausschuß* plan for reshaping vocational education is really closely connected to the *Rahmenplan*, since, at present, offerings of general education in vocational training are fragmentary. Since vocational training is still the path for some 80 per cent of all young people, there is no suggestion of 'secondary education for all' as yet.[50]

In short, thus far innovation is initiated and tolerated only in experimental institutions; the system in its entirety resists change.[51] The gap between planning for educational change and actual implementation is partly explained by the lack of institutions in which social planning competence and political power are closely linked. In the absence of such institutions, political authorities can afford to ignore existing plans or they prefer to neutralize them.

FORCES RESISTING REFORM

It should be noted that powerful groups of both 'producers' and 'consumers' of the 'output' of the educational system have rejected fundamental criticism directed against it and have opposed any major change. The producers include teachers of secondary, intermediate, and vocational schools and their professional organizations; the consumers are represented by parents' organizations, universities, and commercial and industrial groups. With notable exceptions, their universal argument has been that any radical reform would lead to an intolerable loss in quality. Taking their cue from the principle of productive efficiency, they have warned against 'experiments with the school.'[52]

Since the barbs of the critics and the tools of the reformers are directed mainly at the secondary stage, it is the spokesmen for the traditional secondary schools who react most vigorously. In the reforms projected they see elements antagonistic to their educational creed as well as to their social status. Emphasizing, here as elsewhere, the essentially scholarly character of their assignment – and, we may add, being relatively unimpressed by the methods and findings of the behavioral sciences – they hold that the different schools correspond to 'different kinds of life experience ... to the manifold conditions and forms of the spirit' and to different social tasks and individual interests. 'Every new attempt at reform,' it is declared, 'reinforces these grave-diggers of German education. We protest strongly against any kind of change in the structure of the *Höhere Schule*.'[53] They are joined by representatives of the *Realschulen*, who, fearing future reintegration of their thriving institutions in a common secondary stage, resist reforms, relying on the support of organized industry and trade. The universities, as institutions, have without exception rejected reforms which aimed at changing the existing 9-grade *Gymnasium* structure, and parents' organizations have joined them.

Although some leading groups in commerce and industry have become aware of the need for investigation and reform, their official bodies have so far combined in supporting the existing system. They have warned against *Etatismus* and *Dirigismus*; they have opposed any immediate extension of obligatory full-time schooling to include a tenth year; and they have supported the preservation and, indeed, extension of the *Realschule*. Not that these groups do not recognize the need for improved curricula, especially for better science programs and more technological experience in the various types of school, but they wish to achieve these aims by short-term and pragmatic measures.

A formally guaranteed 'equality of opportunity' and the conviction that 'those who are able will succeed' serve as rationalization and justification of the existing system. The established churches of both confessions have relied on an appeal to christian-humanist values in their pronouncements on educational reform. The Catholic Church especially has consistently urged the maintenance of the very small (usually mono-confessional) village schools with the avowed aim of preserving the united community-church-school influence and of counteracting the impact of modern secularism and 'materialism.' (About 50 per cent of all West German state schools were 1- and 2-grade schools and about 14 per cent of all elementary school pupils attended such schools, according to the federal statistics for 1962.) The churches have, in the main, rejected changes in *Gymnasium* education basing their opposition on its responsibility for the preparation of future clergymen.

In the absence of serious research, discussions on the 'pool of ability' were greatly influenced by the investigations of one of the remaining advocates of eugenics and Social Darwinism, K. V. Müller, who as late as 1959 declared that 'ability is a biological category' and 'unconditionally rooted in hereditary traits' and that any socio-political measures aimed at changing 'the natural correspondence of school selection and social selection' were futile.[54] For at least a decade the official attitude of the secondary schoolteachers' associations, of conservative parties, of organized industry and commerce, and of a number of ministries relied heavily on Müller's 'expertise.' They maintained that only about 3 to 5 per cent of the population are gifted enough to benefit from higher education.

Radical criticism of the procedures of selection and allocation and the public doubting of the validity of tripartism were regarded as endangering the existing high standard of scholastic and industrial achievement. Evidently a revision of the basic concepts of ability and talent was needed before the school system could be transformed.[55]

Discussions were further muddied by the injection of cold war ideology. The secondary schoolteachers' associations tried to discredit the *Rahmenplan* by pointing to its resemblance to the program of the Trade Unions. Modest reforms, like the extension of elementary education and the reform of rural schools, have been called 'Socialist,' 'levelling down,' 'Eastern,' 'communist.'

The positions of the leading political parties have also tended to inhibit reform. By 1949 the Christian Democrats (CDU) had formulated a common educational policy. In the immediate post-war years some of their leading politicians supported measures of far-reaching educational reform. Since that time and until recently, however, the party has identified itself with a policy of stability and of resistance to long-range planning, with official church policy, and with those groups who see in traditional, humanistic education a safeguard against radical change. Members of the Liberal party (FDP) have taken conflicting positions in matters of education, although some of its spokesmen have been among the most active promoters of reform.[56]

Although some shifts have occurred since the first period of public discussion, positions have, in the main, remained stable. To count the Social Democratic Party (SPD) among those resisting change would certainly be misleading, but it has not been consistent in urging it either. In the city states, to be sure, it did take the initiative in introducing the extended common elementary school, but in the case of Hamburg let itself be discouraged when it lost an election over this very issue. And in Hessen in 1947–50 the Social Democrats missed the chance to reorganize education in accordance with plans proposed by the Christian Democrat Minister of Education. On the whole, the SPD never tried to organize public pressure in educational matters as did pressure groups on the opposing side. Apart from the peculiar problems of a party striving hard to win wide public confidence, its uncertain position can be explained by the ambivalent attitude of the largely left-wing Teachers' Union itself.[57] We have seen that even the 1960 Bremer Plan shows signs of compromise between the advocates within the Union of horizontal and of vertical organization. Although some of their sub-organizations had taken the initiative in reform action, it is characteristic of the attitude of the Union that in a number of instances it withdrew support from measures proposing innovations when questions of salary and status, for instance, were at stake. Indeed, the discussions of the second phase of reform (from 1959 on) show that it was not only the resistance of the opposing groups which weakened the chances of reform but also the lack of conviction of its advocates who had not succeeded in defining a clear program.

If, more recently, changes can be seen at all, they are to be found more in the modified positions on the educational 'right' than on the 'left,' if such terms may be permitted. Thus the Farmers' Association, previously committed to the rural community with its one- and two-class schools, now welcome the introduction of central schools and orientation classes, in order to improve standards of production and organization. Representatives of the *Philologenverband* have also modified their positions a little. Still they have not admitted that secondary schools have a social class bias or agreed that enrolments could be greatly increased. However, even the very discussion of these questions using objective evidence is in itself new and promising. Evidently, their leaders could not help but be impressed by the accumulating evidence of research showing the range of untapped talent reserves,[58] for example that two-thirds of the 'gifted' children of lower income groups never even attempt a secondary school education,[59] and that this low level of aspiration must be explained by the inability to overcome language and other cultural barriers.[60] The educational goals of the *Gymnasium* itself are now open to discussion, and the original *Rahmenplan* proposals have been somewhat refined.

To summarize, the strong tendency towards conformity of co-operating groups within West German society has, in the absence of equally strong counterforces and of any real challenge by social research, succeeded in either mobilizing public opinion against structural reforms or in neutralizing it. Rational discussions of educational problems have often been thwarted by the intrusion of ideology. Cultural federalism has tended to act more as a brake on innovation and experimentation than as an inspiration to pioneering competition. Finally, public pressure 'from below' has not been present because of the low level of educational aspiration in some social groups.

THE CHANCES FOR CHANGE

Some encouraging prospects for change are now appearing as factors which have so far inhibited reform have weakened and as factors leading to reform have gained strength. There is a growing demand for more qualified and mobile workers at all levels, the realization that improved curricula at all stages are urgently needed, and the recognition of manifest dysfunctions in the present system.

During the first phase of reform discussion, at a time of scarcity and economic reconstruction, a latent fear of academic unemployment convinced bourgeois as well as socialist groups that rigorous selection was justified. Since economic recovery, the material basis for this policy has changed. As a result, there has been a growing consciousness that a revision of selection procedures together with a necessary expansion of education and training are required. We have here an illustration of the generally observable ambivalence of economic arguments concerning educational organization. In times of stress, representative groups of commerce and industry will press for highly selective, vertically differentiated systems to secure efficient industrial production and to yield immediate results. Economic theory, on the other hand, taking a long-range view, will emphasize the need for a general rise in the quality of education for all groups in order to meet the demands of science and technology.

The figures on prospective requirements in the fields of 'education and culture' contained in the KMK forecast for the period 1961–70 were impressive enough to encourage the extension of education and training, if not sufficient to prompt educational reconstruction. A growing realization of the need for further planning and research brought about two parallel, but not necessarily complementary, developments. Planning and research units were attached to some ministries and a number of independent research institutes were founded. The ministerial units largely follow explicit political directives, while the independent institutes still have to identify their criteria for research priorities and to refine their instruments. Nevertheless, there are some signs of improved communication between the various representatives of research, planning, and policy making as well as a growing body of information.

The feeling of dissatisfaction with the present methods of selection has led to the use of statistical means to question the reliability of such instruments. So far this work has not brought about a general use of objective instruments. However, straight selection procedures are gradually being replaced by the introduction of initiatory stages (*Anfangsstufen*) at secondary schools complemented by observation classes (*Beobachtungsstufen*) in grades 5 and 6 of elementary school. But such measures only postpone the inevitable decision between the present vertical and a comprehensive school organization. As soon as a larger number of aspirants begins to knock at the doors of secondary schools, processes of observation will have to be introduced. These are certain to lead to a modification of the present system of vertical differentiation. It is the same alternative in all comparable counties.

The first limited results of experiments with genuine *Förderstufen* show that at this intermediate stage the number of children transferring to secondary schools is significantly greater than in the ordinary system (60 per cent at the six experimental schools compared with 43 per cent at the same schools before, and an average of 36.5 per cent in the *Land* concerned).[61] Furthermore, it is mainly the percentage of children from lower income groups that has increased.[62] It has further been shown, although not yet conclusively, that the predictive value of evaluation at the end of an integrated 'intermediate stage' (*differenzierender Mittelbau*) is much higher than that of earlier methods of transfer and evaluation (at the end of the fourth grade).[63] Furthermore it has become clear that in Germany as elsewhere one of the reasons that some groups do not achieve secondary and higher education can be traced to initial handicaps of their socio-cultural milieu, such as language barriers or lack of parental support. These cannot be overcome by making formal statements about equality of opportunity. There have been several attempts to meet this deficiency at both the motivational and the organizational level. For example, students and young scientists have started campaigns of recruitment and individual assistance among the children of farmers and industrial laborers. The start which has been made on replacing the one- and two-class country schools (*Zwergschulen*) with consolidated central schools will certainly gain momentum, possibly opening a further avenue towards more comprehensive forms of educational organization (another example of the frequently observed phenomenon that reform of an educational system starts from points of manifest dysfunction before it extends further).

In addition to the *Gesamtschulen* projected for Berlin and in a few instances practised in Hessen, a number of other experiments may prove important, such as the all-day schools in a number of larger cities and the introduction of foreign language instruction in elementary classes.[64]

One of the most serious problems is the absence of genuine methods and instruments for curriculum revision and development. Only slowly is the 'manpower demand' approach being complemented by a 'social' and 'cultural demand' approach. The commitment of reformers to questions of structure and organization can only be broadened through the recognition that inquiries ought to be undertaken about the information and skills of mobility and communication which all children need for a free and effective life. Whether the structural approach will soon be joined to a functional-curricular approach is impossible to predict; but whenever it happens, curriculum reform too will lead to new forms of common schooling and to new modes of differentiation.

Whatever the inspiration coming from social science and from educational thought and whatever the achievements of planning operations, the educational system of the Federal Republic will still face the intricate problem of 'educational federalism,' the 'cultural sovereignty' of the various *Länder*. No 'concurrent' federal legislation in educational matters is provided for in the basic law of the country. The assessment of the effects of 'cultural autonomy' is a matter of controversy. To the authors it seems evident that, in the main, it has proved detrimental to educational progress, especially since, within the federal system, in the individual *Länder*, educational administration is decidedly centralized. This centralized and bureaucratic tendency is reinforced by the agreement between the various *Länder* to preserve a single system through the KMK machinery. This is the only possibility since the principle of unanimity gives the right of veto to any single *Land* and in practice limits agreements to those negotiated between the ministerial officials. The München resolution, passed in February 1954 by the Heads of the *Länder* Governments, firmly established the principle of the unified system and, as Walter Schultze has recently said, thus sanctioned the slogan of 'peace to the schools' and paralyzed systematic and controlled experimentation and reform. The Düsseldorf agreement of the following year was, to be sure, amended a decade later in 1965 by the Hamburg meeting of the same body;[65] and a new policy was formulated by the 100th plenary session of the KMK in March 1964, envisaging long-range planning and educational experimentation. These proclamations have yet to be acted upon.

It is to be hoped that the Council of Education (*Bildungsrat*), established in July 1965 and in operation since last year [1966], will pave the way for a real breakthrough.

A retrospective glance at the work of the *Deutscher Ausschuß*, in a way the Council's predecessor, may indicate the prospects for the new body. That committee of experts did not hesitate to tackle many of the vital problems of German education, but it stopped short of issuing bold and unequivocal measures of reform. It generated a surge of intensive discussion, sometimes going to the very roots of German educational thought, but it was never able to secure political decision and action. A comparative analysis of the activities of consultant bodies and public commissions suggests that their effectiveness depends on the existence of an institutional link with political power and on permanent contact with public opinion. By these criteria the committee's chances were always slim. No such links existed, nor was the majority of its members equipped to trigger a popular movement. Finally, their financial resources were consistently small.

These limitations do not apply to the *Bildungsrat*. It lacks neither funds (if not to commission research, at least to secure expert knowledge) nor the opportunity to draw upon the resources of statistical services, science, and scholarship. Many sub-committees and expert groups have been organized and links between the experts and their government counterparts have also been established. Whether even this machinery will be able to overcome the deadlock remains to be seen. The answer will depend largely on effective mobilization of public interest and political forces.

NOTES

1 R. Poignant, *L'enseignement dans les pays du Marché Commun* (Paris: Institut Pédagogique National, 1965). German translation, Frankfurt am Main: Diesterweg, 1966, p. 275.

2 E. Hohne, 'Gedanken zur Neuordnung des Höheren Schulwesens in Bayern,' *Anregung. Zeitschrift für Höhere Schulen*, 10 (1964), pp. 73–9.

3 Denkschrift der Universität Hamburg, *Die Schule in unserer Zeit*. 'Zur Frage der Neuordnung des Hamburger Schulwesens' paras 6 und 7 (Hamburg: Universitätsverlag, 1949).

4 'The programs of German educators after the war show strong support for school reform, in many cases consistent with the Occupation plans for education' (R. F. Lawson. *Reform of the West German School System, 1945–1962.* University of Michigan Comparative Education Dissertation Series, No. 4, p. 97). This conclusion can be easily substantiated by a detailed analysis of the programs and actions of the Social Democratic, Communist, and Liberal parties, of circles of progressive teachers – among them veterans of the Weimar school reform movement – of some Christian Democratic Ministers of Culture, of several *Evangelische Landeskirchen*, and others.

5 A note on Directive No. 54 in H. Merkt, *Dokumente zur Schulreform in Bayern* (München: Richard Pflaum, 1952), p. 163, and Omgus, ed. Title 8, *Education and Religious Affairs.* 8. 301 (1947).

6 A. Flitner, 'Die gesellschaftliche Krise unseres Bildungswesens,' *Universitas*, 20 (November 1965), pp. 1155–70.

7 H. Schelsky, *Schule und Erziehung in der industriellen Gesellschaft* (Würzburg: Werkbund, 1957).

8 H. Schelsky, *Anpassung oder Widerstand? Soziologische Bedenken zur Schulreform* (Heidelberg: Quelle und Meyer, 1963).

9 H. Becker, 'Sozialforschung und Bildungspolitik' in *Quantität und Qualität* (Freiburg i. Br.: Rombach, 1962), pp. 331–46. (A reprint from a lecture given at the 14th Deutscher Soziologentag, Berlin 1959.) Becker was one of the first and most consistent advocates of a multi-disciplinary approach in educational research.

10 Cf. W. Strzelewicz, H. Raapke, W. Schulenberg, *Bildung und gesellschaftliches Bewußtsein. Göttinger Abhandlungen zur Soziologie.* (Stuttgart: Ferdinand Enke, 1966), Vol. 10, especially pp. 29–37 and 577–90.

11 F. Bollnow, 'Das veränderte Bild vom Menschen und sein Einfluß auf das pädagogische Denken,' *Erziehung wozu? Pädagogische Probleme der Gegenwart* (Hamburg: Kröners Taschenbuchausgaben, 1956), vol. 241, p. 35.

12 'Erhebung über den Bestand an Ingenieuren und den Bedarf an technischem Nachwuchs in der Bundesrepublik, erstellt vom Bayerischen Staatsministerium für Unterricht und Kultus im Auftrag der Ständigen Konferenz der Kultusminister der Länder in der Bundesrepublik Deutschland,' München, 1957. Georg Picht, 'Die deutsche Bildungskatastrophe,' *Christ und Welt*, Stuttgart, February 1964. Ralf Dahrendorf, *Bildung ist Bürgerrecht* (Hamburg: Nannen, 1965).

13 F. Edding, *Ökonomie des Bildungswesens* (Freiburg i. Br.: Rombach, 1963), p. 73.

14 Ständige Konferenz der Kultusminister, *Kulturpolitik der Länder 1963–1964* (Bonn: Bundesdruckerei, 1965), p. 34.

15 *Kultus und Unterricht.* Amtsblatt des Kultusministeriums Baden-Württemberg, 10th July 1965, Schulentwicklungsplan, pp. 594–5.

16 Cf. H. P. Widmaier, *Bildung und Wirtschaftswachstum.* Schriftenreihe des Kultusministeriums Baden-Württemberg, series A, No. 3. Stuttgart, 1966.

17 H. Riese, *Entwicklung des Bedarfs an Hochschulabsolventen in der Bundesrepublik* (Wiesbaden: Franz Steiner, 1967). G. Bombach of the University of Basel reiterates the author's view in his preface to the book.

18 Cf. J. B. Conant's letter to Professor Becker, published in *Frankfurter Allgemeine Zeitung*, September 27, 1966.

19 In 1953, 79.5 per cent of the 10 to 14 age group remained in the *Volksschule*. F. Edding und R. von Carnap, *Der relative Schulbesuch in den Ländern der Bundesrepublik* (Frankfurt am Main: Hochschule für Internationale Pädagogische Forschung, 1962), Table 3.

20. W. Lempert, *Lehrzeitdauer, Ausbildungssystem und Ausbildungserfolg* (Freiburg i. Br.: Rombach, 1965), p. 338.

21 Edding und von Carnap, op. cit.

22 11 per cent. Ibid.

23 Wissenschaftsrat, *Abiturienten und Studenten* (Tübingen: Mohr, 1964), p. 53. The quota had dropped from 4.2 per cent in 1950.

24 Edding und von Carnap, op. cit. The figure was 5.1 per cent in 1957. See F. J. Weiss, *Entwicklungstendenzen des Besuchs Allgemeinbildender Schulen in den Ländern der Bundesrepublik Deutschland* (Frankfurt am Main: Deutsches Institut für Internationale Pädagogische Forschung, 1964), p. 26.

25 Of all students leaving school after the tenth grade, 28.5 per cent came from the *Gymnasium* in 1962. Weiss, op. cit., p. 27.

26 Wissenschaftsrat, op. cit., p. 74.

27 K. W. Leyerzapf in an unpublished manuscript at the Institut für Bildungsforschung, Berlin. See also: R. Geipel, *Sozialräumliche Strukturen des Bildungswesens* (Frankfurt am Main: Diesterweg, 1965), pp. 95–7.

28 F. Hilker, *Die Schulen in Deutschland* (Bad Nauheim: Christian, 1963), p. 75.

29 G. Palm, *Die Kaufkraft der Bildungsausgaben* (Freiburg i. Br.: Walther, 1966), p. 61.

30 An important attempt is being made by the International Project for the Evaluation of Educational Achievement, *International Study of Achievement in Mathematics: A Comparison of Twelve Countries* (New York: John Wiley & Sons, 1967). More caution, however, should have been exercised in the interpretation of the results than had been shown in some of the widely publicized previews.

31 Cf. Report of the Institut für Sozialforschung an der Johann Wolfgang Goethe-Universität, *Zur Wirksamkeit politischer Bildung*, in Forschungsberichte der Max-Traeger-Stiftung, Frankfurt am Main, 1966.

32 G. Pröbsting in *Material- und Nachrichtendienst der Arbeitsgemeinschaft Deutscher Lehrerverbände*, No. 92. 1959, p. 22; calculated from: Statistisches Bundesamt, Wiesbaden, *1956–61*, Series 10. I. *Allgemeinbildende Schulen*, pp. 122, 127.

33 Wissenschaftsrat, op. cit., p. 47.

34 Widmaier, op. cit., p. 168.

35 W. Schultze, Chr. Führ, *Das Schulwesen in der Bundesrepublik Deutschland* (Weinheim: Beltz, 1966), p. 125.

36 In Schleswig-Holstein, Hamburg, and Bremen the common 6-year primary school had been introduced in 1948–9, but abolished a few years later.

37 Wissenschaftsrat, op. cit., p. 53; *Development in Secondary Education*, OECD, September 1966, p. 7; F. J. Weiss, unpublished manuscript, Institut für Bildungsforschung, Berlin; *Arbeitsmaterial der Kultusministerkonferenz*, Dokumentation No. 15, Bonn, 1965, p. 49.

38 U. K. Springer, 'West Germany's Turn to *Bildungspolitik* in Educational Planning,' *Comparative Education Review*, 9 (February 1965), pp. 11–17; J. H. Van de Graaff, 'West Germany's *Abitur* Quota and School Reform,' *Comparative Education Review*, 11 (February 1967), pp. 75–86.

39 Deutscher Ausschuß für das Erziehungs- und Bildungswesen, *Empfehlungen und Gutachten*, Series 1. 1955, p. 3.

40 The budget of the *Deutscher Ausschuß* in the first year of its existence amounted to 57,000 DM and that of the *Bildungsrat* in 1967 to 1,046,000 DM. Schorb-Fritzsche, *Schulerneuerung in der Demokratie* (Stuttgart: Klett, 1966), p. 48; 'Haushalt der Geschäftsstelle des Deutschen Bildungsrates,' letter of February 2, 1967.

41 *Deutscher Ausschuß*, op. cit., p. 27.

42 Cf. *Minutes of the Annual Congress of Teachers and Educators*, Berlin, 1952; see also: *Um Schule und Stand*, No. 3, 1954, pp. 38–40.

43 *Kulturpolitik in Hessen*, edited by the Minister of Culture in Hessen (Frankfurt am Main: Diesterweg, 1966), p. 8.

44 Hamburg has also proposed a plan for a 'highly differentiated comprehensive school.'

45 Cf. the debate in the Schleswig-Holstein Parliament on September 26, 1960.

46 H. v. Hentig, 'Gedanken zur Neugestaltung der Oberstufe,' *Analysen und Modelle zur Schulreform*, *Neue Sammlung*, 3rd. Sonderheft, 1966, pp. 31–58.

47 Cf. S. B. Robinsohn, 'Bildungsreform als Revision des Curriculum.' (Berlin: Institut für Bildungsforschung, 1967). Mimeo.

48 Cf. the recommendations of the KMK for an intensified system of *'Berufsaufbauschulen'* in 1959 and 1965.

49 H. Abel, 'Der berufliche Bildungsweg nach den Vorschlägen des Deutschen Ausschusses für das Erziehungs und Bildungswesen im internationalen Vergleich' in *Studien zum europäischen Schul- und Bildungswesen* (Weinheim: Beltz, 1966), Vol. 1, p. 41.

50 Ibid., p. 45.

51 R. Lawson explains this absence of an overall reform by stating that 'an isolated practice cannot function in an antagonistic context' (Lawson, op. cit., p. 208). See also, S. Mueller Shafer, *Post-war American Influence on the West German* Volksschule, University of Michigan Comparative Education Dissertation Series, No. 3, especially pp. 244–9.

52 Cf. *Deutscher Philologenverband zur bildungspolitischen Diskussion, Bildung und Schule.* Düsseldorf, 1965; Verband Deutscher Realschullehrer, *8. Realschullehrertag in Hannover*, May 30, 1966; *Der deutsche Verband der Gewerbelehrer.* Wolfenbüttel, 1960; *Die Direktorenvereinigungen aller Bundesländer und West Berlins*, Annual Meeting, September 24, 1965; *Westdeutsche Rektorenkonferenz*, June 9, 1965; and the common statement issued in October 1965 by Deutscher Industrie- und Handelstag, Deutscher Handwerkskammertag, Bundesvereinigung der Deutschen Arbeitgeberverbände, and Bundesverband der Deutschen Industrie.

53 Philologenverband Nordrhein-Westfalen, *Leitsätze für eine organische Ausgestaltung des gegenwärtigen Schulwesens* (Düsseldorf: Schwann, 1964); and Philologenverband, Landesverband Nordrhein-Westfalen (January 30, 1947). Quoted in J. Schnippenkötter, *Zum Nordwestdeutschen Plan für höhere Schulen* (Bonn, 1947), p. 29.

54 K. V. Müller, *Umfang, Standort und Nutzung unseres Begabungsnachwuchses* (Celle: Schweiger und Pick, 1939), p. 1.

55 Cf. A Huth, 'Was fordert die Wirtschaft von der Schule?' *Die Bayerische Schule*, No. 9, 1952. Stifterverband für die deutsche Wissenschaft, *Aufstieg der Bergabten* (Essen, 1958), p. 11. For a critical approach see Ch. Caselmann, 'Die mögliche Lenkung der Begabungen,' *Probleme einer Schulreform* (Stuttgart: Kröner, 1959); J. B. Conant, 'Development of Talent in Europe and in the United States,' *The North Central Association Quarterly* (April 1960), pp. 265–72; H. Roth, 'Wandlung des Begabungsbegriffes,' *Jugend und Schule zwischen Reform und Restauration* (Hannover: Schroedel, 1961); W. Schultze, W. Knoche, E. Thomas, *Über den Auslesewert der Auslesekriterien für den Schulerfolg an Gymnasien* (Frankfurt am Main: Hochschule für Internationale Pädagogische Forschung, 1963).

56 The FDP voted for the Education Act in Berlin in 1947, voted against it in 1951; supported the introduction of a common 6-year primary school in Bremen in 1949, insisted on its abolition in Schleswig-Holstein in 1951.

57 A good example is the fate of the *'Differenzierter Mittelbau'* (a kind of 4-year *Förderstufe*) in Niedersachsen, cf. note 36.
58 W. Arnold, otherwise known for his conservative concept of education, estimated that the number of students could easily be doubled, as far as intelligence was concerned. *Rechtfertigt die Leistungsfähigkeit der heutigen Jugend den Ausbau differenzierter Bildungseinrichtungen?* Würzburger Rektoratsrede; Würzburg, 1964.
59 K. V. Müller, op. cit., p. 21. See also H. Walter, *Die soziale Welt* (1959), p. 22.
60 It is R. Dahrendorf who by constant emphasis has driven home the fact that low-income classes are underrepresented in secondary education, in *Offene Welt*, 71 (1961), pp. 535–46. Somewhat earlier Ch. Lütkens had characterized the school as a 'middle-class institution', in *Kölner Zeitschrift für Soziologie und Sozialpsychologie*, Sonderheft 4, 1959. Moreover, the incidence of failure among working-class children in *Gymnasien* was greater than of middle-class children of similar intelligence. See H. Adam. 'Soziale Unterschiede in der Schulbildung begabter Kinder,' (Frankfurt am Main, 1960) Mimeo.; and H. K. Schwarzweller, 'Educational Aspirations and Life Chances,' a paper read at the World Congress of Sociology, Evian, 1966. Others, among them Kob, Loehrke and Gebauers, Hitpass, Grimm, Petrat have shown how poorly motivated German workers are towards secondary education. See also R. F. Hamilton, 'Affluence and the Worker,' *American Journal of Sociology*, 71 (September 1965), pp. 144–52. Geipel, Peisert, Aurin, C. L. Geissler, and others have emphasized the regional aspect as a determinant of different levels of schooling.
61 E. Geissler, R. Krenzer, A. Rang, *Fördern und Auslesen* (Frankfurt am Main: Diesterweg, 1967), p. 14.
62 Ibid., p. 36.
63 Cf. *Der Differenzierte Mittelbau*, edited by the Minister of Culture of Niedersachsen (Hannover, 1963), especially pp. 9–28.
64 A more extensive, though still incomplete list is to be found in Chr. Führ, 'Die Schulversuche in der Bundesrepublik,' in 'Sicherung von Schulversuchen durch pädagogische Forschung' (Dortmund Schuldezernat, 1965) Mimeo.
65 Cf. H. Heckel, 'Das Hamburger Abkommen der Ministerpräsidenten,' *Studien zum europäischen Schul- und Bildungswesen*, Vol. 1 (Weinheim: Beltz, 1966).

2 Problems in German secondary education [1985]

Arthur Hearnden

In recent years there is probably no country in Western Europe which has appeared more resistant to the idea of comprehensive education than the Federal Republic. It was largely this that prompted the OECD inspectors to be so critical in their report[1] which was published in a German version under the suggestive title *Bildungswesen mangelhaft (Education system: Poor)*. The fact that there were so few comprehensive schools – whether of the 'additive' or the 'integrated' kind – seemed to suggest that the selective system was largely impervious to the social pressures which transformed most of the education systems of West European countries in the 1960s and early 1970s. But it was not so much that Germany was isolated from the social pressures, rather, that the method of coping with them was different.

There was a rather English flavour to this. Most commonly it did not consist in abolishing selection in accordance with pronouncements about fundamental principles – in the way that, for example, would be typical of France – but rather in the pragmatic style of letting the *Gymnasium* (grammar school) sector expand to meet the demand for the kind of education it had to offer. Though one could not go so far as to describe the result as comprehensive what it did mean was that many *Gymnasien* were responsible for a much wider range of ability than tradition decreed.

This was particularly so in the less populous areas, some of which were discovered to be a kind of 'educational Siberia'. It is true that empirical research was rather later in getting going in Germany than elsewhere in Western Europe, but when it did get going it reached what became ritual statistically disadvantaged groups – girls, Catholics, working class, rural children – which often overlapped with one another. Very often the difficulty was that there was simply no *Gymnasium* within range. And one of the things that happened as a result of social pressures was simply that a great many new *Gymnasien* were created in places that had not had them before.

Though this strategy largely drew the sting of the comprehensive movement there has, nevertheless, been a moderate growth in the number of *Gesamtschulen* (comprehensive schools) in the last few years, and this seems to be the logical result of the earlier expansion of the grammar schools. For as this develops and largely engulfs the *Realschule* (intermediate school), so the underprivileged character of the *Hauptschule* (upper primary school) becomes even more apparent. It is largely on this *Hauptschule* – or secondary modern – base that the *Gesamtschulen* are being built, with the aim of ensuring that in theory at any rate, every educational opportunity remains open to those who do not attend *Gymnasien*.

This is something of a convenient generalisation – the picture is rather more complicated in fact – but when the appropriate reservations have been made there seems to be enough evidence on which to predict the emergence of a bipartite system, with politics determining whether an individual *Land* comes down on the side of a heavily *Gymnasium*-based system or a heavily *Gesamtschule*-based one. Indeed there is already an established convention whereby the *Länder* are thought of as in two groups for educational purposes, the so-called A-*Länder* and the B-*Länder*.

This is a perfectly understandable and constitutional situation, but in the past decade it has seemed increasingly important to reconcile it with some kind of national co-ordination. The national planning bodies – first the *Bildungsrat* (Education Council) and then the *Bund-Länder-Kommission* (Federation-*Länder* Commission for Educational Planning) have spent years constructing a framework which could accommodate political diversity of this kind while at the same time giving some kind of coherence to the educational system as a whole.

The way in which it was chosen to do this was not through the structure of the school system so much as through the structure of the qualifications system. The principle was that it need not matter whether you attended a *Gymnasium*, a *Realschule*, a *Hauptschule* or a *Gesamtschule* – what was important was that the leaving certificates of these various types of school should all be equally valid as passports to the next stage of education. Thus anyone who had satisfactorily completed an *Abschluß* (leaving certificate) at what we would call the 16 + stage would have an entitlement to enter an *Oberstufe* (secondary level II) and work for the *Abitur* (grammar school leaving certificate), or its vocational counterpart in the *Fachoberschule* (upper secondary technical school). This was to be equally acceptable for higher education whether it was obtained in a *Gymnasium* or a *Gesamtschule*.

This was a skilful way of getting round the awkward problems of selection and of federalism in that it was fastening on to a secure and established feature of German culture – the *Berechtigungswesen* (system of qualifying examinations). Anyone who is at all familiar with the ladders of advancement in German professional life will know how much more clear-cut this has been in comparison with England. From the *mittlere Reife* (*Realschule* leaving certificate) onwards each stage has its own particular orthodoxy in relation to employment levels and status.

So it was quite astute to make use of tradition to help to solve the problems. The *Berechtigungswesen* provided a ready-made and recognisable ticket system. But in the event there was more difficulty about adapting it to a mass system of education than was ever anticipated, or at least acknowledged. What the planning strategy did was to sanction the issue of tickets on a very large scale – and it was inevitable that there should soon be more tickets than there were seats on the train. When that happens it is not usually very long before other selective mechanisms come into play, and discredit and disillusionment follow.

This is not a problem that is confined to Germany. The emphasis on paper qualifications is becoming steadily stronger in the UK. It can be seen in the remarkable rise in the numbers taking examinations in schools. It is why so much heat has been generated over the various plans to create a single system of examining at 16 +. It accounts for the suspicion of internal assessment and the rallying round external examinations which put a premium on objectivity, fairness, national standards and so on. And in the UK we have, I think, been fortunate to have a long established examining tradition of this kind, and a system which is accepted as reasonably fair in its distribution of academic advantages. But even with this depth of experience there are still serious problems of comparability arising.

Comparability has naturally become a matter of major concern in Germany, too, and to an extent and in a way that the German approach to school examining was not really designed to cope with. It is an even more difficult problem there than it is here. The basis of assessment in German schools has traditionally been internal and if it worked reasonably well it was because there were collective norms of achievement which had been assimilated by teachers who were all trained in a similar way. But it was not designed for the kind of competition for university places which has developed in recent years whereby the various marks achieved are averaged out to one place of decimals in order to achieve a rank order on the basis of which places can be distributed. This kind of *Notenarithmetik* cannot really be said to have enhanced the quality of education in the *Oberstufe*.

This problem has been aggravated by another change which has taken place – in the construction of the *Oberstufe*, i.e. sixth form, curriculum. Here is an area where the contrast with the position in England is interesting. Our sixth-form curriculum is constantly being criticised for being too narrowly specialised and we have been through an extensive and abortive exercise designed to broaden it. In Germany, on the other hand, it was too broad and so a great deal of energy has gone into trying to reduce the demands of the so-called *13-Fächer-Schule* (13-subject school) – and, in contrast to here, a quite fundamental change has, in fact, been introduced.

In place of the standard range of subjects which used to be all taken up to the age of 19 there is now a bewilderingly complicated points system for the calculation of the final average mark or *Gesamtqualifikation*. It is in academic terms a very sophisticated system and, given the large number of pupils who have to be assessed, probably as accurate as one is likely to get. What is of particular interest is the division into *Grundkurse* and *Leistungskurse*, i.e. basic courses and intensified courses. Basic courses provide a 'common core', others more advanced or unusual subjects.

What were the arguments for the change? They can be expressed platitudinously as being to provide greater scope for the individual abilities and interests of pupils and for the exercise of individual responsibility in making choices – a responsibility which is in keeping with the increased independence of young people aged between 16 and 19. Or they can be expressed cynically as bowing to pressure to make life easier for young people aged between 16 and 19 because they are not as prepared to work conscientiously as they used to be. Another justification would be that it was supposed to improve the preparation for university study, give young people an incentive to decide rather earlier on their academic and vocational aspirations. In this sense it fell into a general pattern of streamlining education, of which the university counterpart was the limitation on the period of study – the notorious *Regelstudienzeiten*.

This streamlining involved a special sacrifice, the significance of which was seriously underrated at the time. Schools are not just places to study academic subjects and take examinations; if they are to educate successfully they need also to have a securely anchored corporate life. Now it is natural for us in the UK to be inclined to lay great emphasis on this, in view of our particular traditions of seeing the school as a community with a wealth of extracurricular activities. The German tradition was quite different but in its own way just as strong. The community was not the school but the class. A class, by virtue of being together for virtually all subjects throughout school life, had a certain social cohesion about it which was supportive, reassuring and at its best could also be positive and constructive.

The greatest disservice which the new system did was to break up this cohesion. Some observers feel that the resulting loss of corporate identity has been bewildering for the young people concerned, but there are others who consider the alarm to be exaggerated. It is too early to come to any very definite conclusion about this – it is something that will greatly vary from school to school, just as the quality of corporate life varies from school to school in England. In theory it is perfectly possible for the pastoral role of the *Klassenlehrer* (class teacher) to be taken over by a *Beratungslehrer* (personal tutor/counsellor) but it is a task that will not be filled automatically and will require a certain imaginative adjustment.

What then of the academic advantages which were hoped for? If it was supposed to make life easier for the universities there is not much evidence of success. The alarm signals in the universities are considerably more strident than they were before the changes were introduced. Perhaps it is not yet possible to diagnose fully the significance of this but it echoes the kind of controversy with which we are familiar in this country.

We have been concerned about the variety of pre-university preparation. There has been such a proliferation of syllabuses in basic subjects that the students coming up to the universities do often seem to have very little knowledge in common. As a consequence, a great deal of valuable time is lost making up the leeway. The problem has arisen largely because of the diffuseness of British education and the lack of any one authoritative source to determine what the content of the curriculum should be. It has the advantage of allowing teachers a great deal of initiative to innovate, but we have been more aware in recent years of the disadvantage of the confusion that this can cause.

Germany, on the other hand, is a country of *Richtlinien* (regulations) enshrined in the *Schulrecht* (law relating to schools), and by comparison with the teachers in English secondary schools German *Studienräte* (grammar school teachers) sometimes appear to be in the position of the young man in the poem:

> There was a young man who said Damn
> It appears to me now that I am
> Just a being that moves
> In predestinate grooves
> Not a taxi nor a bus but a tram.

Of course the *Richtlinien* are different from *Land* to *Land* but they were never all that different. Yet now one hears university teachers complain that there is nothing predictable any more about what the first year students have done at school.

The *Gesamtschulen* generally feature in discussions of this kind and the impression is often given that there is a much wider range of interpretation of *Richtlinien* than before – even though their actual quantity has increased. This is considered bad enough in subjects where there is a direct progression from *Leistungskurs* to university subject. But at a time when there still has to be a *Numerus clausus* in some subjects and some universities and students cannot necessarily bank on their first choice of course, the loss of flexibility which has resulted from the espousal of specialisation is even more damaging.

It is difficult to assess how justified these complaints are. It may be partly that Professor George Turner, when he was President of the

Westdeutsche Rektorenkonferenz (West German Committee of Vice-Chancellors) and hence a spokesman for the universities, was rather more outspoken than his predecessors. But it is also true that there has been a tendency among young people in the *Oberstufe* to avoid the more difficult courses – just as in this country there is a tendency (though not too marked) to steer clear of the very difficult A-levels. The German term for this is *taktisches Lernen*. The tactic involved is clear enough, namely to choose those subjects in which there is the best chance of a high mark in order to get the average mark up and hence improve the prospects of entry.

There have, of course, been attempts to judge the situation more objectively. Like, for example, the survey in which a Physics professor at the University of Bonn assessed the knowledge of 75 per cent of entrants to university physics courses and found that a third of them were well below the minimum standard considered appropriate.[2] Physics is, of course, one of the most demanding subjects in the school curriculum and there seemed to be an element of *taktisches Lernen* even inside the *Leistungskurse*, whereby the emphasis was much more on mathematics than on physics.

It is difficult to say whether surveys of this kind are a help or a hindrance. The question of standards is so delicate that any survey provides rich material for political exploitation. Thus, for example, it is usually the case that the results are broken down by *Land* and a crude comparison between the CDU- and SPD-governed *Länder* emerges – generally along the lines that the CDU-*Länder* produce better students and that the SDP-*Länder* produce more students.

This kind of controversy is then further fuelled when comparative research is done on the standards achieved in *Gymnasien* and *Gesamtschulen*. North-Rhine Westphalia published in 1979 the result of investigations which show that by the 16 + stage the comprehensive pupils have fallen markedly behind their counterparts in the selective system in German, Mathematics, English and Physics, i.e. in the four subjects that form the basic core of our culture.[3] Those who are familiar with the comprehensive school controversies in this country will know how much more complex the issue really is than is conveyed by generalised arguments about achievement in, say, Mathematics being '10 per cent better in the selective system than in the comprehensive one'.

Indeed this suggests that there is a great deal for the Federal Republic to learn from the way in which comprehensive schools have developed in England. For there is not only the theory on which to draw, but a good many years of solid practical experience of building up schools which have to compete academically with one another and indeed with the private sector – and will have to compete still more as the numbers begin to fall and rationalisation dictates school closures. The main lesson may well be the need for caution about the *integrierte Gesamtschule* in its most thoroughgoing interpretation which denies any justification for grouping ability.

Less insistence on this more extreme interpretation of the *integrierte Gesamtschule* could well be beneficial to the cause of comprehensive education in the Federal Republic. Because it will only survive in a way that is consistent with German cultural unity if it can compete on reasonably comparable terms with the selective system. And the danger of this not happening is very apparent.

The controversy that for several years posed a threat to cultural unity is the question of the acceptability of leaving certificates. The alignment of the various *Land* systems has been built up with painstaking care in the post-war years and central to it is the idea that whatever the *Land* in which a leaving certificate is obtained, that certificate is accepted currency throughout the Federal Republic. For over ten years the comprehensive school certificates at various levels had a provisional recognition only because the *Gesamtschule* was, and in most *Länder* still is, technically in an experimental phase. The political exchanges between the CDU- and SPD-*Länder* (with the CDU-governed Lower Saxony siding with the SPD-*Länder*) became so charged over the issue that a split into two blocs which would not recognise each other's qualifications was by no means out of the question. Only in the summer of 1982 did the *Länder* ministers of education finally manage to sign an agreement.

A further possible interpretation of this political sensitivity is that the school system as a whole – whether *Gymnasium*- or *Gesamtschule*-based is suffering from demoralisation. This recalls another phenomenon of secondary education in Germany in recent years, namely the spectacular rise in the popularity of private schools. Certainly there is a great deal of talk about the crisis of motivation in the state schools and it may be that this has been aggravated by the difficulty of providing appropriate pastoral care. One senses that the authorities have tried to overcome the problems by issuing more and more guidelines for teachers who in turn feel that the changes being introduced have a depersonalising effect upon the life of the schools.

Hence it is tempting to see the private system as an independent alternative in which sound educational principles can thrive despite bureaucracy. If this were so it would be refreshing, but there is, of course, the possibility that the private sector simply illustrates another aspect of the demoralisation of modern society and caters largely for problem children whose parents cannot handle them. A systematic study of the private schools would present a very mixed picture; some are probably outstanding, like the famous *Odenwaldschule*, others probably abysmal.

Whatever the reasons for their success, however, the phenomenon of the private schools together with the problems of the state schools, and the worries in the universities do appear to form part of a general picture which conveys some sort of mismatch between what is happening in the school system and what is being asked of it by society. Grave doubts are more and more frequently being voiced about the close coupling of the education system and the qualifications system. The pressure which this is putting on the schools is diverting them from some of the more fundamental tasks of education and contributing to the abdication of responsibility for inculcating enduring values and norms of behaviour.

'Was kann Schule leisten?' is therefore the question that needs to be asked – not 'was soll?' but 'was kann?', i.e. is it possible for schools to meet all the various demands placed upon them? And if they opt to meet primarily the utilitarian ones are they making the right contribution. Are they contributing to the crisis of motivation among young people or merely victims of it?

NOTES

1 Organisation for Economic Co-operation and Development (OECD), *Reviews of National Policies of Education: Germany*, Paris, 1972.
2 Inter Nationes, *Bildung und Wissenschaft*, 10/11–79 (e), pp. 136–7. Many other surveys with similar results have been reported; see, for example, *Die Welt*, 25.7.1981, or *Die Zeit*, 2.10.1981. See also Heldmann, Werner, *Studierfähigkeit. Ergebnisse einer Umfrage* (= Schriften das Hochschulverbandes, 29), Göttingen, 1984.
3 Der Kultusminister des Landes NordrheinWestfalen (ed.), *Gesamtschule in NordrheinWestfalen* (= Strukturförderung im Bildungswesen des Landes Nordrhein-Westfalen, H. 38), Köln, 1979. See also Fend, H., *Gesamtschule im Vergleich. Bilanz der Ergebnisse des Gesamtschulversuchs*, Weinheim, Basel, 1982; Bund-Länder-Kommission für Bildungsplanung und Forschungsförderung, *Modellversuche mit Gesamtschulen. Auswertungsbericht der Projektgruppe Gesamtschulen*, Bühl/Baden, 1982; Haenisch, H., Lukesch, H., *Ist die Gesamtschule besser? Gesamtschulen und Schulen des gegliederten Schulsystems im Leistungsvergleich*, München, 1980.

3 Continuity and change: a basic question for German education

Present-day questions in education in the Federal Republic of Germany against a historical background [1986]

Wolfgang Mitter

INTRODUCTORY COMMENTS

In this century education in West Germany has passed through three innovatory movements of basic significance. Although they were only partially successful they have made a marked impression on formal education within the country's schools and other institutions. As a result of comprehensive changes in the socio-economic, political and cultural structures these innovatory movements have, furthermore, had a strong influence on informal education. Reciprocal effects between developments in formal and informal education can be established by finding examples in the behaviour patterns of people at school, in family life, in business and in the street.

The first of these innovatory waves affected the whole of Germany after the First World War. It was a part of the world-wide movement for educational reform among the protagonists of which can be reckoned important educationists with varied aims, such as John Dewey, Celestin Freinet, Pavel Blonsky and, in Germany, Georg Kerschensteiner, Eduard Spranger and Paul Oestreich. If the effects of this reform wave are considered in their entirety, we can speak of the first attack on traditional schooling which, in general terms, was characterised by rote learning and the encyclopaedic assimilation of facts. Open methods of teaching and learning, such as group teaching and other methods of teaching which aimed to arouse children's desire to know and their imaginative powers, found their way into the elementary schools. Even grammar schools were affected by the movements of reforming education. Such movements could be seen particularly in the preference for interpreting individual works of literature and historical events as opposed to the traditional transmission of encyclopaedic knowledge.

The second innovatory wave can be regarded as one of the direct consequences of the Second World War. It is identifiable because of the joint efforts of education officers in the various military governments, particularly in the American and British occupation zones, and of German educationists and politicians who used their powers and energies to rebuild education from the chaos which the collapse of the National Socialist regime had left behind. Among the German educationists special mention should be made of the Minister for Education in Hesse, Erwin Stein, who played a decisive part in establishing the German Institute for International Educational Research in Frankfurt-on-Main. In spite of the manifold differences of opinion between Allied officers and German educationists on the one hand and between the political parties on the other, there was a widespread consensus as far as the basic aims of the new policy for education were concerned: these aims were the resuscitation of respect for the dignity of people and the promotion of equality of opportunity and fairness in education.

Increasing numbers of the public felt that the achievement of the second aim was making inadequate progress and hence came the criticisms which laid the foundation of the large-scale reforms which characterised educational development in the Federal Republic of Germany in the late 1960s and early 1970s. As this third wave has run on direct into the present era, allow me a few comments to describe its most important features. First of all the student movement must be mentioned. Its spectacular expressions were, indeed, short-lived but they had far-reaching effects because they were the start of changes in the social situation and in things hitherto taken for granted in the universities. Secondly, reference must be made to the extensive work of the German Council for Education, an advisory body, which, during its existence (1965–75), published a large number of remarkable reports and recommendations. Finally, the change in the Federal government in 1969, which led the 'social–liberal coalition' to power, brought to maturity the first visible results of an educational policy that was clearly expressed in the publication of the *Education Report '70*. As well as equality of educational opportunity the following aims were listed in the programme of educational reforms:

- the modernisation of the education system with reference to planning, school building and organisation;
- the democratisation of education and culture in which it must be emphasised that the West German interpretation involves, not merely the opening of school and society to strata of the population hitherto under-privileged, but also co-operation and joint decisions by teachers, parents, members of the community, and finally even by pupils in the way schools are set up and organised;
- the introduction of curricula which aim to replace or, at any rate, restrict the function of traditional timetables. Underlying this desired change was the provision in Saul Robinsohn's 'School Reform from the point of view of Curriculum Revision' for, on the one hand, the formulation of overlapping and detailed aims and, on the other,

instructions on teaching methods and guidelines on evaluation in order to complement the previously established lists of curriculum contents.

To sum up, it may be emphasized that all three innovatory waves resulted in a condition which can be variously described as consolidation, stagnation or even destruction. Such an appraisal depends for its acceptance not only on what, in fact, has happened, but also on the point of view of the individual critic. The Weimar Republic's reforms were given up or perverted into purposes which the National Socialist officials declared to be 'true' German education. The radical initiatives of the post-war period after 1945 were slowed down in the early 1950s by an educational policy which critics have called 'restoration' and indeed this may be the characteristic of the whole period from the end of the 1940s to the mid-1960s. Although, in my view, such a harsh criticism must be seen as biased and even exaggerated, it does show that the education system in the Federal Republic of Germany is linked directly with those of the Weimar Republic past in both their reformative and their conservative components.

The third innovatory movement which was embodied in the 'large-scale reforms' became separated off from the turning point of the spirit of the age as soon as the conservative politicians and intellectuals designated (and welcomed) the present period as one of 'consolidation'. At this point it should certainly be added that this last change in the system of education was making itself known as early as the mid-1970s – long before the change of government in October 1982 which brought the 'Christian–Liberal' coalition to power.

The 'consolidating' forces scaled down or even suppressed the reformative achievements of the previous innovatory waves. In general, however, it can be justifiably stated that in given circumstances these reformative achievements have been absorbed into the general development of the formal and informal educational system of the Federal Republic of Germany. The lasting effects of the most recent period of reform will be dealt with later in more detail. In itself the period of reconstruction after the Second World War laid the foundations for an educational philosophy and its translation into practical terms which are rooted in the values of democracy, tolerance and international co-operation and it is to be hoped that this is so to a more profound and more reliable extent than was the case in the Weimar period. Finally, it has become evident, especially in recent years, that the initiatives of the educational reforms of the 1920s are being renewed. This can be seen in that the predominant interest of the educationists and even of the general public has shifted from the 'large-scale' reforms to 'internal school reform', that is, to the problems which motivate teachers, pupils and parents in the very place where learning and teaching take place.

This brief review may indicate that the German system of education, as evidenced in the changes described, harks back to a long tradition which reveals too its international connections. In particular this review shows up features relating to the general political and social history of the eighteenth and nineteenth centuries, not to mention the relationships which reach back into the more distant past.

THREE ESSENTIAL FEATURES OF CONTINUITY

The dominant role of the state

In Germany the staté plays the leading role in the organisation, administration and control of schools and other educational institutions. This feature goes right back to the period of early absolutism, when German princes began to regard policy affecting schools as an important task. The 'state' means, as the Germans understand the term, just as do the French for example, the centralised structure for legislation and government which can make use of a hierarchically constructed administration. The general nature of this fundamental stipulation was laid down in article 144 of the 1919 constitution and confirmed by article 7 of the Basic Law of 1949: 'The entire school system is subject to the supervision of the State.'

State organisation applies particularly to the horizontal stages of primary and secondary education. But at university level the influence of the state is restricted to 'supervision' in the real sense of the word, for, within this framework, the universities are allowed considerable autonomy in the responsibility for their own concerns.

The state monopoly is limited in the field of pre-school education. It is thus in favour of the small local authority units and the churches, as well as of private individuals and institutions. Another limitation occurs in the field of vocational education within industry. Here the state is content with outline legislation and allows the non-state chambers of trade and commerce extensive rights to regulate their forms of training.

The tension between uniformity and variety

State monopoly in the education system and political and administrative federalism do not present us with a paradox because the constituent *Länder* of the Federal Republic each possess a centralised administrative structure. German federalism can be traced back to the Middle Ages and came to a climax after the Thirty Years' War. At that time it was underpinned by the religious division, the effects of which on the education system have indeed lost their importance since the 1960s. Certainly the history of German education bears witness, also, to remarkable efforts to achieve a 'national education'. These efforts achieved their expression with varying degrees of intensity from the beginning of the nineteenth century and have two roots. One of these comes from the spiritual impetus which educational theory experienced in Germany in the eighteenth and nineteenth centuries. Calling for particular mention are Wilhelm von Humboldt's influence on the Prussian and German universities and grammar schools, the influence of the educational theories of Pestalozzi and Herbart on the elementary school and on the training of elementary schoolteachers, as well as Georg Kerschensteiner's importance in preparing the way for modern vocational training. The other root comes from the political movement at the beginning of this century, which produced converging tendencies which combined at the beginning of the Weimar Republic and were clearly expressed in the Reich law on elementary education of 28 April 1920.

The very fact, however, that things came to a halt with this one Reich law and that the possibilities of Reich legislation provided in the Weimar constitution could not be used indicates that federalism was a dominating force in the education system. The important status of the constituent states in matters of education, which was reflected in the independent responsibility they obtained for all state institutions – including the legal supervision of universities – has consequently a historical basis; even under the totalitarian dictatorship of National Socialism unifactory efforts came to naught, but only because of internal conflicts in the political leadership.

The Federal Republic, building on the developments in the western occupation zones from 1945 onwards, linked up with the traditional federative structure and further strengthened it. Admittedly, a change in the constitution in 1969 gave the Federal Authority outline legislative powers for the development of the university system and for collaboration in educational planning. Even in these fields the constituent states remain responsible for legislation affecting any changes in normal standards and practices.

Accordingly, the state-supervised nature of the education system is, in essence, to be seen in the jurisdiction of the constituent states, which collaborate in various specialist bodies, such as the Standing Conference of Ministers of Education and, in conjunction with the Federal government, in the Federal and State Commission for Educational Planning and Promotion of Research but which remain formally autonomous in the development of school buildings, the educational content of syllabuses and the certification of teachers. The above-mentioned examples of co-operation – and especially the awareness of an educational public which disregards state boundaries – certainly ensure that, even allowing for the important status of the states in matters of education, the traditional links of an education system which is unified, at any rate in fundamental questions, continue to be effective. This endeavour finds expression also in the decisions of the Standing Conference of Ministers of Education. So far as the most recent part of the history of education is concerned, mention must be made, in particular, of agreements on the reorganisation of the last two years in grammar schools (1972 and 1977) and on the reciprocal recognition of the end-of-course standards in comprehensive schools (1982). On the other hand it must not be forgotten that the pressure for unanimity in this body frequently slows down the initiation of decisions and may sometimes even defer them.

The dual system in vocational education

Whereas, in the course of recent decades, schooling for general education has been subjected to more or less serious changes, the idea of continuity can be applied with particular justification to the dual system of vocational education, particularly as, up to the present, this statement applies to both East and West Germany. In the educational systems of both these countries the large majority of adolescents (i.e. in age groups 15–16 to 18–19) pass through the dual system. Its history can be traced back to the apprenticeship system for artisans, which is an inheritance from the medieval form of training. In contrast to what happened in other West European countries, the German apprenticeship system, which was subdivided into numerous trade training courses, underwent a revival at the end of the nineteenth century, and this was sufficiently evident to encourage industrial firms to develop their own 'modern' forms of apprentice training. In this connection it must also be emphasised that this modernised method of the traditional way of preparing young persons for vocations in trade and industry was justified by its representatives' assertions that it was not only a highly appropriate system of training but also an excellent means of combining the acquisition of knowledge and skill with moral education. This concept has persisted until the present day.

The revival of the apprenticeship system was further developed (and was to some extent consolidated) when continuation schools were set up in Germany with the object of supplementing apprentice training on the job by part-time attendance at school. In this way the continuation schools were among the predecessors of the later Vocational Schools, which were gradually developed in the first decades of the present century. Between 1919 and 1938 part-time attendance at them until the age of 18 became compulsory for all boys and girls not in full-time attendance at the upper level of a secondary school (whether for general or vocational education). Both the German Democratic Republic and the Federal Republic of Germany have accepted and developed still further this inheritance with its 'dual system' of vocational education. Consequently, it is today possible for boys and girls to have to attend a vocational school for two or three days a week even if they are unemployed or are working at an unskilled job and do not therefore have the recognised status of apprentice.

Two further essential characteristics are significant so far as the dual system is concerned. On the one hand we have to note the division of powers between the school authorities of the constituent states, who bear the whole responsibility for the educational elements of the course, and the employment agencies, which consist of the Chambers of Trade and Commerce and the Chambers of Agriculture. These latter non-state institutions are responsible for the practical (vocational) training within the legal parameters which have been laid down by the Federal Legislature. The division of powers does not guarantee, however, that all young people not in full-time attendance at the upper level of a secondary school are absorbed into the dual system as such.

On the other hand, this system has certainly been shown to offer a strong impetus to the employing firms; they are involved in apprentice training, not just because it ensures and develops continuity in the workforce, but also because they intend to keep the state clear of any involvement in vocational training (apart from the legislation on parameters). I shall turn to the present-day problems of the dual system in more detail when I examine school organisation.

PRESENT-DAY PROBLEMS ARISING FROM THE TENSION BETWEEN CONTINUITY AND CHANGE

Organisation

Like other European countries, Germany can look back on a history of education which is centuries old and in this history the dominant principle in the organisation of education was the vertical one. This organisation was determined by the parallelism between the grammar schools – with, in Prussia, their junior schools preparatory to the main school – and the elementary schools. A boy's school career was usually predetermined from his sixth year onwards; either from a preparatory school to the grammar school, and thence to the university or alternatively, from the elementary school to vocational training at a trade and later in industry (education for girls was not systematically developed until the end of the nineteenth century). The vertical principle was, however, clearly affected by the existence of a manifold 'intermediate area' which, from the 1920s, has coalesced into the secondary technical schools of today. Also the cultural difference between town and country schools was opposed to the vertical principle without, in fact, calling its existence into question.

The vertical principle was broken by two educational reforms; both were far-reaching and were joined in a historical compromise between ideal conceptions and political reality. I am referring to:

- the demarcation of grammar school and university, the dividing point being the school-leaving examination qualifying for university entrance;
- the already-mentioned Reich school law of 1920 as a result of which

the compulsory 4-year primary school was created as a part of the continuing 8-year elementary school. The abolition of the preparatory school, devised (in Prussia) to ensure entry into the grammar school, was confirmed in 1949 by the Basic Law of the Federal Republic of Germany.

In contrast to this primary school reform, the organisation of the secondary stage with the grammar school at one extreme and the upper stage of the elementary school (classes for age groups 11 to 14) at the other, with the secondary technical school in the middle, remained unchanged until 1945. The way from the upper stage of the elementary school led to practical vocational training (from the 1920s usually in the form of the above-mentioned dual system); from the secondary technical school the way led to the extended and specialised technical college system; from the top form of the grammar school the way led of course to the university.

After 1945 the American and British Military Governments made various attempts to lengthen the primary school course by two years and to introduce comprehensive schools at the secondary stage. I have already mentioned the basic moves to change curricula which the Military Governments instigated; in contrast to these, their efforts to make organisational changes came to naught. Let me now leave this historical review and begin to analyse how things developed at the various horizontal stages.

1 Whereas primary education (except for the 6-year course in West Berlin and Bremen) has remained fixed at 4 years, there has been a remarkable expansion of pre-school education. It was one of the essential features of the period of reform in the 1960s and early 1970s. The discussion which paved the way for and went along with this development revolved mainly around the fundamental position of pre-schools within the education system. But from the end of the 1970s this discussion had almost entirely ceased to appear in policy considerations affecting education. One reason for this apparently surprising change may be found in the fact that nowadays, in contrast to the situation ten years ago, most parents no longer have any difficulty in finding vacancies for their children in nursery school. This change can be attributed to the rapidly falling birth-rate.

2 Although the organisation of the primary school with what is predominantly a 4-year course has remained unchanged, the classes for 11- and 12-year-old pupils have been given the job of acting as an assessment stage for all pupils so as to ease for them the transition to the secondary stage. The most important function of this assessment stage is to postpone the decision about what the pupil wants to do (and should do)

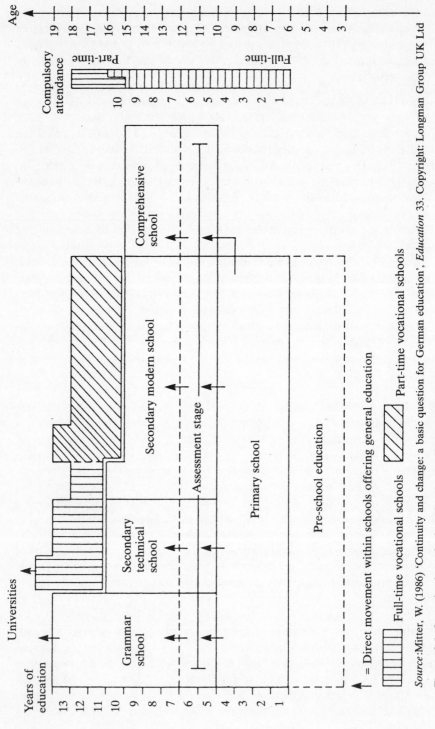

Age

19
18
17
16
15
14
13
12
11
10
9
8
7
6
5
4
3

Compulsory attendance

Part-time

10
9
8
7
6
5
4
3
2
1

Full-time

Universities

Years of education

13
12
11
10
9
8
7
6
5
4
3
2
1

Grammar school

Secondary technical school

Secondary modern school

Comprehensive school

Assessment stage

Primary school

Pre-school education

↑ = Direct movement within schools offering general education

⊞ Full-time vocational schools

⊟ Part-time vocational schools

Source: Mitter, W. (1986) 'Continuity and change: a basic question for German education', *Education* 33. Copyright: Longman Group UK Ltd

Figure 3.1 Organisation of education in the Federal Republic

at the age of 10 + and thus to ensure a more reliable decision. To this end, various models of external and internal differentiation have been developed, especially in mathematics and foreign languages (usually English). Original proposals which aimed at allowing teachers to direct their pupils to the different forms of the tripartite system of secondary education came to grief. The choice of secondary school course for the children continues to be the responsibility of the parents, even if (analogous with the former regulation about completing the primary school course) they are required to ensure that the assessment stage is formally completed.

3 In the Federal Republic of Germany the earlier part of the secondary stage continues to be dominated by the tripartite system, the basis of which, as I have already indicated, was laid down during the nineteenth-century. Even in the constituent states (chiefly Hesse and West Berlin) which in the last two decades have established also comprehensive school systems, the existence of the traditional tripartite system has not been seriously called into question. This statement applies of course, much more explicitly to the majority of constituent states which have never given their (few) comprehensive schools anything more than experimental status, as is particularly the case in the South German states of Bavaria and Baden-Württemberg. The tripartite system comprises the secondary modern school, which has developed from the former upper stage of the elementary school, the secondary technical school and the lower and middle stages of the grammar school. The secondary modern school, which is in the rural areas today chiefly organised as a 'central school', prepares its pupils for

1 vocational training in the dual system;
2 work in the lower or intermediate range of the public service (combined with training which includes attendance at a part-time vocational school);
3 attendance at a full-time vocational school (technical college).

In spite of various attempts made by the constituent states, the secondary modern school has got into a critical position so far as its achievement levels and social status are concerned. This applies particularly to towns; in them the secondary modern school finds it increasingly difficult to compete with the expanding secondary technical schools and grammar schools. The secondary modern school is in constant danger of declining into a school for 'left-overs', i.e. one which is attended by boys and girls of low achievements and, also, by the majority of the children of immigrant workers.

4 Between the selective grammar school and the non-selective secondary modern school, the secondary technical school has not only established

itself but also, during the last twenty years, has expanded as an alternative selective institution. It is different from the traditional secondary modern school in offering an additional year (age 15–16) and a wider range of subjects (e.g. English as a compulsory and French as an optional foreign language). Therefore, at the end of its course the way is open to full-time vocational training (in technical colleges) and also to the dual system as well as to the top classes of the grammar school.

5 The grammar school has probably undergone the greatest changes during recent decades. From a basically 'elitist' school with relatively strict selectivity it has become a school for pupils from all strata of the population. These pupils are young people who are aiming to go to university or, at least, to complete the intermediate course (to age 16 +). In earlier times the grammar school was criticised because of its selectivity, which was geared to social factors. This is not the case today, or, at least, not to the same extent. What continues to be a matter for dispute is the concentration of the school work and the choice of subjects so as to achieve university entrance. In the late 1960s and 1970s, i.e. at the crest of the third innovatory wave of the present century, the grammar school was often regarded as out-of-date and its position in the field of secondary education was attacked (particularly in connection with efforts to introduce comprehensive schools as the overall compulsory secondary schools). In recent years, by contrast, the repute of the grammar school has risen again in many sections of the population, admittedly nowadays as an institution through which many may rise and not, as in earlier days, through which only a few could do so.

The changed position of the grammar school can be seen also in that an increasing number of pupils leave at 16 + to begin vocational training in the dual system, or what is more frequently the case, to begin a full-time course of vocational training. For such pupils the grammar school fulfils the same educational function as the secondary technical school.

The 3-year course geared to university entrance begins at age 16 +. From 1976 this course has been reorganised to become the so-called Reformed Upper Level course, in accordance with the decision of the Conference of the Ministers of Education of 1972. Instead of the traditional system of teaching, in which the subjects were taught in self-contained class groups (as continues to happen in the main school course of the grammar school), there was established a course system, to which detailed reference will be made later. Like the grammar school as a whole, the Reformed Upper Level course reflects a basic dissension in so far as it has not expressly adjusted to its changed function in respect of the expectations and requirements of the system of employment. In this connection we may comment that, as well as its traditional function of preparing its pupils for the university, the grammar school has become for increasing numbers of pupils a course which leads to vocational training (of the intermediate level) or even direct to a job in the system of employment. In spite of these far-reaching internal changes the Reformed Upper Level course has also retained the traditional concept of the grammar school, according to which its function is defined solely as being preparatory to the university.

6 Full-time vocational education presents a highly differential system which consists of technical colleges of various types and offers a multiplicity of specialist courses. Attendance at an advanced technical college can also lead to a general leaving certificate or a specialist one or to a qualification which confers the right of admission to a technical University. In the early 1970s some reformers demanded that 'integrated forms' should be developed, aiming to achieve co-operation between, or even amalgamation of the top form of the grammar school and full-time vocational education. But such moves did not get beyond the experimental stage.

7 Like full-time vocational education, the dual system can be considered a part of the advanced secondary field. In the same way it presents a highly differentiated system, the story of which goes back a long way in the history of German education, as has already been indicated in some detail. In West Germany today, it is indisputably true that the dual system has, in many respects, been maintained, albeit in its modernised form. Admittedly, three problems remain unsolved:

1 in spite of great efforts, the free economy has constantly been unable (as has the public service) to take on apprentices for training;
2 there is difficulty in preparing or establishing training courses which meet the changing requirements of the employment market and which have regard to the increasingly important principles of mobility and ready adjustment to changing circumstances;
3 the courses and the curricula offered to young people in the (part-time) vocational schools bear no relationship to actual work on the job.

8 The efforts to modernise vocational training as a whole have included in recent years the following innovations:

1 the organisation of a basic vocational training in which apprentices are given in their first year fundamental knowledge and skills over a wide range;
2 special training courses for pupils with leaving certificates, i.e. for those leaving the grammar schools who do not want to (or cannot) aim at university courses;
3 projects for young people which are pre-vocational and preparatory for a vocation which bear no relationship to work on the job (see para. 7 above).

9 In the period of 'large-scale reforms' the universities underwent considerable changes, particularly in the right to attend university and in their organisation (participation in certain decision-making processes by assistants, students and members of the non-academic personnel; closing down traditional faculties in favour of areas of special subjects; introduction of the presidential system in place of the traditional rectoral one, etc.). In this respect the past ten years have achieved a degree of 'stabilisation'. On the other hand the universities continue to be burdened with the ever-growing number of students and it seems unlikely that the crisis which this has caused will diminish during the next decade when financial restrictions will bring about additional aggravating factors. This critical position is caused particularly by the legal position according to which, in the Federal Republic of Germany, admission to university education is regarded as a fundamental right. Admittedly, in a number of disciplines, in particular medicine, restrictions on admissions have been introduced (in the shape of regulations imposing fixed numbers). Quite apart from the fact that, in the disciplines concerned, conditions of study are not even improved by these regulations, these fixed numbers merely force the students to apply for admission to other fields of study, which thereby become overcrowded. Among the fields of study to which in recent years financial grants and establishment of chairs have drawn particular attention, we must mention especially communication and information studies. This re-orientation has certainly happened in many places at the expense of the humanities and the social sciences.

10 In the 1960s and 1970s teacher training was fully integrated into the university system, mostly into the universities themselves. The most important problem facing teacher training today is that students are being qualified as teachers without there being for most of them any prospects of obtaining jobs as teachers. Some universities (e.g. Hildesheim) have established, as alternative courses, arrangements for in-service training of teachers. Admittedly, this innovation encounters traditional objections, which can be attributed to the tradition that in-service training is seen to be a matter which is organised by school authorities and carried out in their own in-service training institutions.

The content of educational courses

I should like to restrict myself here to consideration of the teaching and educational plans of German secondary schools. They have always emphasised the idea of a broad general education. Here too let us first look for a brief measure of agreement with the past. In all schools offering a general education, this expression has a fundamental meaning. The standards, namely 'higher scientific education' in the grammar school or 'popular education' in the elementary school, were indeed strictly distinct, one from the other, in the vertical system; the claim, such as it was, that the system transmitted to the pupils a core of educational content which society and the state regarded as, and stated to be, compulsory, applied nevertheless to all children and young persons. In determining all this in practical terms a good deal of arbitrariness made itself felt and this is common knowledge to the theoretician and historian of education. He encounters this set of problems particularly when he sees obsolete syllabus content and school subjects persisting on the one hand, and the struggle to put into practice new and legitimate claims on the other. An example of the complexity of this problem is evidenced by the discussion about the value, or otherwise, of teaching Latin in present-day grammar schools in West Germany.

Let us return to the historical review. The general education core of subjects always included German, arithmetic or mathematics, natural and social sciences (or nature study and local history and geography) as well as religious knowledge, which was a necessary ingredient in traditional German schooling; in contrast to this core of subjects any forms of specialisation were definitely in a lower category; they were regarded as essentially a matter for vocational education. In secondary education, in addition, at least, one foreign language was a part of 'general education'; as a rule there were two, even possibly three and, indeed, classical and modern languages in various combinations. This fundamental situation has remained essentially unchanged to this day so far as the primary school and the lower stage of the secondary school are concerned. We must just add that, in recent decades, there has been added to the core of subjects, on the one hand, political education (i.e. education in social and community matters) and, on the other (admittedly only in secondary modern schools) the educational field covering the facts about, and conditions in, the working world. In a contrary sense, as has already been indicated, the introduction of the reformed upper level course in the grammar school has involved restrictions in the general obligation to study many subjects and has extended the pupils' opportunities for choice. In comparison with the British and American system, the adherence to a compulsory core of subjects even in the reformed upper level course is rather surprising. These subjects comprise German, at least one foreign language (two in many constituent states), mathematics, one of the natural sciences and one of the social sciences. Whether history should be one of the core subjects is a matter of dispute. In grammar schools in Hesse this subject is once more compulsory, following a ruling to that end by the Supreme Court of Hesse in December 1981. This court ruling is having an influence beyond the boundaries of Hesse, at any rate in its influence on opinions.

PARTICULAR PROBLEM AREAS

1 As in other countries, those persons concerned with policy affecting education and teachers in the Federal Republic of Germany must come to terms with the new technologies, which are finding their way into the schools. This task is brought about on the one hand by the wishes and demands of the labour market, but also is paying some heed to the growing interest of many young people in the new field of learning itself. The main focus of attention in this field has been directed so far towards secondary education, where there has been much controversial discussion about the place and status of the new technologies in teaching. Should the innovation be concentrated on establishing and developing the communication studies and information techniques as if they were a new subject to be taught, or, on the other hand, should the innovation be accepted as a teaching principle which pervades all subjects and fields of study as suits their particular needs? Whereas at present the first alternative is predominant in what is happening in schools, the long-term view might well gain more and more ground in the years to come.

2 As a consequence of economies in government budgets, research has to struggle against restrictions. This shortfall is compensated by the co-operative agreements made between university institutes and industrial firms, which are nowadays very much encouraged by the government. In contrast, in this field also the humanities and social sciences suffer from this development because for them it is hardly possible to obtain financial support from industrial firms. Admittedly, there are special arrangements for promoting research, such as, in particular, the German Research Community and the Volkswagen Foundation, which give support to the 'disadvantaged' disciplines. But this is not regarded as adequate and it has caused the Conference of Rectors (Vice-Chancellors) to complain about the imbalance in the promotion of research.

3 From the early 1970s, the education of children of foreign workers has presented a specific problem. It has in no ways been satisfactorily solved, and improved conditions of teaching are needed. It would, however, amount to a biased way of looking at this problem if we were to ignore the efforts already made in this field, particularly to introduce teaching to help and encourage these pupils, and to develop teaching in the relevant native language as well as in German. In addition, agreements by treaty have been made with some countries (e.g. Italy and Greece) to send appropriate native teachers to Germany for a specified period. In principle, all these efforts are made more difficult because the non-German children (and their parents) do not have German citizenship; consequently, tension persists between the

demands of integration and those of re-integration (by which is meant return to the countries of origin).

POLICIES AFFECTING EDUCATION IN THE CONTEXT OF THE EXTERNAL CHALLENGES OF THE PRESENT

As in other countries, policies affecting education and teaching in the Federal Republic of Germany have to come to terms with external challenges which, it seems, can be concentrated into three problem areas. In the first place there is the question of financial restriction, already mentioned more than once. In general it must be stated that the budgets have imposed no essential cuts on the education sector, if we are talking of absolute figures. But because of the great increase in the age groups which have now come through to the upper secondary stage and the third stage (universities), there have certainly been actual reductions in per capita expenditure (i.e. in relation to the individual pupil).

Secondly, the education system must respond to the wave-like movements in the demographic sense. These movements affect organisation (e.g. size of classes) and the supply of teachers and other educational personnel in the schools. Whereas the upper secondary stage and the third stage are still confronted by large age groups to an increasing extent, the primary stage and, also to an increasing extent, the lower secondary stage have to face, in the main, reduced age groups. The education authorities have, on the one hand tried to provide the schools of the upper secondary stage with teachers, partly on a limited contract basis. On the other hand, efforts have been made to keep primary schools open, even if the official guidelines provide for closing them because of insufficient numbers of pupils.

Thirdly, the education system has to come to terms with the changed and still changing expectations and demands of the labour market. In particular, schoolteaching and educational work in all its aspects must pay heed, as has already been mentioned, to the consequences of the new technologies (microcomputers etc.). There is, in our day, a particular need to make the rising generation closely acquainted with patterns of behaviour which are strongly characterised by flexibility and creativity. It is not easy to cope with this task because, on the one hand, it has to be done as part of an extremely dynamic process and, on the other, it has to compete against the basic question – just as important, if not more so – which is posed at all levels of education by the education of children and young persons in basic human values, such as human rights, peace, democracy and protection of the environment.

4 Lessons from Germany? The case of German secondary schools [1987]

David Phillips

INTRODUCTION

> It is not hard to discern the ideas which mould education in France and Germany, because these ideas are deliberately accepted by the educational authorities, and to be traced in their regulations. It is far less easy to discern the governing ideas in English [. . .] education, because in [that country] there is more variety, more clashing of systems, a struggle for existence rather than a victorious creed and purpose. Yet unless we can track the underlying ideas, we move in the dark.[1]

Kenneth Baker's enthusiastic citing during his tenure as Secretary of State for Education and Science, of the advantages of selected European models, and especially that of the Federal Republic of Germany, was nothing new. The above was written in 1903, at a time when there was great interest, as we shall see, in the system of education then in existence in the German Empire, a time when Michael Sadler was critically receptive to the German model.

In his 1987 North of England Conference speech in Rotherham the Secretary of State spoke of 'our maverick education system' which 'has been a source of pride and much self-congratulation'; the system was 'one of those institutionalised muddles that the English have made peculiarly their own'. He highlighted the contrast with practice elsewhere in Europe:

> For at least a century our education system has been quite different from that adopted by most of our European neighbours. They have tended to centralise and to standardise. We have gone for diffusion and variety.[2]

Diffusion and variety can, however, be seen as the great strengths of our system: its 'most admir'd disorder' is something which should be abandoned in favour of greater order, control, standardisation, centralisation, prescription or whatever, on the lines of other European systems, *only* if we can be convinced of their superiority. Closer analysis of the West

German secondary system can help to identify some of the problems which, though they may not be seen as of critical importance within the German system, where the continuance of tradition is highly valued, can serve as warnings to our policy makers if and when they assume that the simple importation of certain organisational procedures or principles of other systems will help solve the perceived problems at home.

This chapter looks at aspects of control as it exists in the education system of West Germany today and an assessment will be made of its consequences. Mention will be made of the question of standards of pupil achievement as between the Federal Republic and England. The various types of secondary school will be described and an attempt will be made to explain why the post-war development of Germany did not encourage that progressiveness in education which has been a feature of the British system. Some conclusions will be reached which take into account the caveats of Michael Sadler and of the inspectors who produced the 1986 report.

Around the turn of the century the office of special inquiries and reports of the Board of Education was producing, under Michael Sadler's direction, an important series of 'special reports on educational subjects' which spanned a wide range of interest in foreign systems. Volume 1 of these reports had contained two papers by Sadler, and several by others, on aspects of education in Germany. Subsequent volumes continued the interest in what was happening in Germany, Volume 3 including, for example, a paper by Sadler on 'problems in Prussian Secondary Education for Boys with special reference to similar questions in England'. And Volume 9, published in 1902, devoted some 612 pages solely to Germany.[3]

Education in Germany in the nineteenth century had been in many respects the envy of Europe. The German universities in particular had achieved an unsurpassed greatness and some of the best British and American students and scholars had beaten a path to their doors.[4] The schools too were widely admired. Sadler, as had Matthew Arnold before him, felt great enthusiasm for their progress: 'The construction of the modern school system of Germany', he wrote in another context in 1912, 'will stand out in history as a classic example of the power of organised knowledge in furthering the material prosperity of a nation'[5] – a theme to which I shall return. But even Sadler was careful to conclude his remarks on a cautionary note: 'German and British education have much to gain from a closer understanding. But both are deeply rooted in history, and some of the finest qualities of the one cannot be superadded to the finest qualities of the other.'[6]

It is important to note that this salutary warning is repeated, some three-quarters of a century later, in the preface of the 1986 HMI report on education in the Federal Republic:

it is easy to forget that a country's education system at any one time is as influenced, in its structure and nature, by its history, politics and the characteristics of the country and people as it is by those situations and imperatives that are common to many countries in the difficult business of educating the young. A consequent risk is that we pick and choose those features that are attractive to us in relation to our problems in the belief that we can unravel them from the seamless robe of the system of which they are an integral part and weave them into the very different warp and woof of our own.[7]

Throughout this present paper the forces of tradition in the German system will provide a *Leitmotiv*, and throughout it will be *principles* of German education rather than *practice*, which will be seen as providing models of interest to the British system: many examples of practice will often serve better as warnings against than as incentives for imitation.

I

For every Pfennig that the German pays in taxes, he expects and receives a Pfennig's worth of government. He enjoys being looked after, and if he fails to hear the whirring of the wheels of public administration, he feels that something has gone wrong.[8]

This view, expressed by an American observer over ninety years ago, provides the familiar caricature of the German, specifically the Prussian, bureaucratic and legislative machine. Caricatures, however, are only effective precisely because they contain a germ at least of truth. *Ordnung muß sein* – 'There *must* be order' – is a catchphrase which encapsulates a basic truth about the *durchorganisierte Gesellschaft* that makes up the German state and which it is important to bear in mind when discussing the education system of the Federal Republic at any level. Within the *Rechtsstaat* (constitutional state founded on the rule of law) education has been subject to a process of *Verrechtlichung* (juridification), of embodiment into the codified legal system of the country.

Thus, when a head teacher communicates with his staff on a matter like the setting of classroom tests he might well as a matter of course quote the appropriate legislation by particular paragraph, together with any amendment. Thus, as we are reminded in the HMI Report on Germany of 1986, the trainee teacher will be taught and examined in educational law.

Thus, when a teacher in a German school puts a grade at the bottom of a pupil's work he is engaging in an administrative act within the country's legislative framework. It is not too great an exaggeration to say that the grade is not awarded on a personal basis ('this is what I, your teacher Herr Mittermeyer, think of your work') nor is it awarded on behalf of the subject department, or the school, or the head teacher – it is awarded on behalf of the State, and the teacher, as a servant of the

State, is fully answerable for his action in awarding it and may be challenged in the courts to defend such action. The hand that writes the grades is controlled by an administrative arm attached, as it were, to the body politic.

The teacher's hand is tied, then, as far as the administration of the State's will is concerned, where that will is expressed through regulations and guidelines. Change is not possible to anything approaching the extent to which it is regarded as both possible and desirable within the British context:

> Schools being considered as subordinate elements of the hierarchical system of public administration, any substantial change within a school is not an educational matter that can be left to the professional freedom and competence of teachers, but a political one.[9]

Education in the Federal Republic is a matter for the individual *Länder*, which retain *Kulturhoheit* (cultural autonomy): the individual *Land* controls educational provision on a local basis. It is thus a mistake ever to talk of a *national* curriculum in the German context. Guidelines (*Richtlinien*) are published by the *Land* ministry on the teaching of all subjects, and teachers are expected to keep within them. The guidelines in modern languages, for example, might well state explicitly that the medium of instruction shall be the foreign language in question, and this precept will be accepted.

There are of course advantages and disadvantages in such prescription. In Germany it is particularly marked: not only is there high comparability of provision from school to school, but there is a rigid common system of assessment and reporting. The sound legal framework has been developed to protect the rights of all involved in the various processes: teachers, pupils and parents. Inevitably all three groups come under considerable stress from time to time, and we should not underestimate the harmful effects that high stress levels have on the proper functioning of education systems. But one main advantage should be borne in mind: the Germans have decided what it is their school system offers; it is clearly stated and known to all who have a part in the system. For better or worse this incontestably clear approach does mean that parents know what precisely they can expect for their children from a particular school and they are able, through well established procedures, to make sure that it is provided. This must be counted as one of the great strengths of the German system, and it is the aspect which clearly appeals most to the present Secretary of State.

II

The 1986 HMI report on Germany passes over the question of school stress with a brief reference to 'frequent articles in the press and complaints by parents that some pupils experience undue stress as a result of the system of staying-down' (para. 12.2, p. 32). But the subject is of much greater concern in Germany than that would suggest. New coinages such as *Schulstreß, Schulangst, Notenterror* (terror of marks), *Leistungsdruck* (the pressure to perform well) and talk of the *humane Schule* indicate the seriousness and widespread nature of the perceived problems.[10] In a survey of 1977 by the *Aktion Humane Schule* it was found that only 8 per cent of children liked the working atmosphere in the tenth class of the Gymnasium;[11] in a 1978 study of school stress commissioned by the Education Ministry of the Saarland two-thirds of pupils claimed high levels of anxiety about their school work;[12] a Frankfurt project begun in 1977 on the conditions of school success found that the less successful pupils became caught in a vicious circle: forced to do extra work at home, their motivation is affected and the extra pressure leads to poorer test results – and so the circle begins again.[13] Even the 1902 British Board of Education Report had a section headed: 'On the measurement of Mental Fatigue in Germany . . .'.

Fear of failure is often heightened by very high parental expectations. Parents know for example that university entrance in a *Numerus clausus* subject can depend on a mark difference of as little as 0.1 and are therefore anxious to make their children fully aware of the vital need to perform well. *Leistung* (achievement) is a virtue highly prized in Germany often at the expense of the processes which ideally facilitate it. *Achievement* of standards of which each individual is capable measured by criterion – referenced assessment might be regarded as an ideal arrangement, but the *Leistungsprinzip* tends rather to presuppose achievement of a norm in one particular type of school, a norm which allows for very little consideration of an individual's performance measured against his or her ability.

In the light of these problems it is difficult to be enthusiastic about the uncompromising rigidity of assessment procedures in German schools. When a *TES* sub-editor heads a piece on assessment in Germany 'Joseph's dream realised in West German Schools'[14] the temptation is to see advantages in the fact that in the UK there is sufficient autonomy and flexibility in the system to allow teachers to assess children in ways more appropriate to their circumstances. The basic approaches in the two countries lead to conflicting conclusions among educationists. On the one hand, for example, and to consider only the primary sector, an experienced observer of the German scene can say that 'in general it is just not possible to think of German . . . primary schools as relaxed, friendly, "happy" places geared to the learning needs of the individual child';[15] on the other a British commentator can declare enthusiastically that

> it is more than likely that [the German] primary schools have contributed to the atmosphere of hard work, discipline and respect for

excellence that is one of the main strengths of German society and German industry. It is hard to doubt that the competitiveness and the ambition which the primary schools systematically reward, have helped industry to be successful, whatever one may think of the intrinsic desirability of these characteristics.[16]

This leads us to consider the question of national prosperity and educational provision. Armytage relates German economic prosperity to 'a sound manpower base, rising from an organised educational system'[17] and other commentators expect to draw lessons for the British system and our own national output from, for example, the *Land*-controlled curriculum and rigid assessment procedures, or the highly developed system of vocational training in Germany.

Comparative studies of performance between nations are frequently undertaken these days and their results are treated seriously. There have been the large-scale IEA studies, for example, and more recently the interesting and much quoted investigation by Professor Prais and Karin Wagner reported in the *National Institute Economic Review* and in *Compare*.[18] In previous studies Prais and Wagner had calculated that the number of those in the German labour force gaining apprenticeships or other intermediate qualifications is double that in Britain. They had concluded that

German vocational training appeared particularly ahead in those occupations where mathematics, or even basic arithmetic, was involved – complex circuitry for electricians, book-keeping for office workers;

and their later study, focusing on the attainments of pupils in the middle and lower half of the ability range, looks especially at the apparent effectiveness of German secondary schools in mathematics teaching. The greatest differences between Germany and England [*sic*], they argue, are to be found when those particular sectors of the school population are investigated. Among their conclusions are that

over half of all German pupils, compared with only just over a quarter of all pupils in England, attain a standard above or equivalent to a broadly-based set of O-level passes;

that

the German system provides a broader curriculum, combined with significantly higher levels of attainment in core subjects, for a greater proportion of pupils than does the English system;

and that

attainments in mathematics by those in the lower half of the ability-range in England appear to lag by the equivalent of about two years' schooling behind the corresponding section of pupils in Germany.

Prais and Wagner rightly pay particular attention to the kind of education provided in the German *Realschule*, the type of secondary school roughly equivalent to the former technical, 'technical grammar' or 'central' schools where they existed in our tripartite system. These schools have always been a special strength of the German system and it is appropriate to emphasise their importance in providing realistic, valid and widely accepted goals for an intermediate range of the school population. We shall look at these schools in more detail later.

The main difficulty I have with such comparative studies as that of Prais and Wagner is that they concentrate on outcomes at the expense of processes. If we leave aside all quibbling about methodology and accept the general findings of such investigations we are still faced with the nagging problem that good results can always be achieved if conditions are such that good results *have* to be achieved. A system which has a highly bureaucratic method of continuous assessment, that requires common syllabuses and agreed teaching styles to be followed, that threatens repetition of classes and thereafter removal to another type of school, and that institutionalises a national idolisation of the concept of *Leistung*, is almost bound to succeed in producing higher measurable results than one which is more liberal, or flexible, or relaxed, or autonomous, or anarchic in style – critics will choose their preferred adjective.

German teachers still in general teach their lessons in a markedly formal style: the emphasis is on didactic teaching, on *Frontalunterricht*; and children are expected to 'learn the lesson' and will be asked to demonstrate, orally, that they have done so. There is little scope for more informal styles, let alone for the variety and experimentation that characterise British classrooms. Teachers too take a restricted view of their educative role: most *Gymnasiallehrer*, for example, would find the British notion of 'active tutorial work', or even of more general pastoral care, curious within the context of their interpretation and expectations of their professional role.

It would be quite wrong to create the impression that German schools are authoritarian and uncaring institutions: this they patently are not. But they do not operate within the framework of autonomous decision-making which makes for a learning environment which can adapt to local needs, as in the British comprehensive school.

We must also bear in mind when making comparisons with our own system the fact that the GCSE examination in particular ensures, through the national criteria, that there is greater standardisation of practice in the curriculum and that such matters as continuous assessment and profiling will inevitably assume greater importance in our schools. We shall not, however, reach a stage where repetition of a year will ever make sense, since there is as yet no concept of what constitutes a year's work in terms of content, teaching materials and methods.

The principles of German practice, which assumes commonality of purpose within the particular types of school, would clash in the British context with the practice of a de-segregated system of schooling and with approaches to teaching which allow individual interpretation of curricular needs. We should be wary of a process which leads from the definition of national guidelines and principles, to the drawing-up of curricula which ensure common content (to the extent, for example, that all 13-year olds studying history, say, will cover the same period or topics), through to the prescription of teaching styles and methods. Once the individual's responsible autonomy is interfered with at an early point in this process the development towards full state control will inevitably begin.

III

The West German school system preserves the traditional differentiation between three separate types of secondary school, a diversification in school provision much admired by Michael Sadler and one which of course found its rationale too in the Norwood Committee's belief that all pupils fall into one of three psychological or mental categories: the academic, the technical and the practical, each category being best served by a distinctive curriculum in an appropriate type of school.[19] The three types of the German system, the *Gymnasium* (grammar school), the *Realschule* (intermediate school) and the *Hauptschule* (main secondary school), similarly may be seen to cater for these psychological types; indeed the *Rahmenplan* (Outline Plan) of 1959 makes a parallel division which can be reduced as in Table 4.1.

Table 4.1 Division of types based on *Rahmenplan* (Outline Plan) of 1959

Psychological type	School type	Occupational type
Theoretical	*Gymnasium*	Intellectually leading
Theoretical–practical	*Realschule*	Practical with increased responsibility
Practical	*Hauptschule*	Instruction-following

I shall look at the three types of secondary school in turn and then consider the development of the *Gesamtschule*, the comprehensive school.

The *Gymnasium* is the most prestigious type of secondary school and one with a long and distinguished history.

> The humanistic grammar school, for long treated with hostility and under threat as far as its continued existence is concerned, has held its own by virtue of its inner strength.[20]

Those words were written in 1919 and the humanistic grammar school still survives, its 'inner strength' undiminished by the vicissitudes of successive reform efforts. It is remarkable how consistent the curriculum of this most traditional of all German school types has been. There was virtually no change in the balance of the timetable from the days of Humboldt, the progenitor of the *humanistisches Gymnasium* through the final decades of the last century to the Weimar years. And, indeed, the timetable of such a school in 1986 preserves the emphasis on language despite inroads made by the sciences. Language predominates. The proportion of time devoted to ancient and modern languages in the classical grammar school, leaving aside German lessons, stood at 55.88 per cent in Humboldt's day and still stands in the schools of Nordrhein-Westfalen, for example, as high as 40.62 per cent.

Traditionally the *Gymnasium* has been the school which prepares pupils for entry to the university, the final school-leaving examination (the *Abitur*) granting the right to university study in all subjects where the *Numerus clausus* does not operate.[21] Until the upper secondary level was reformed most subjects in the *Gymnasium* would have been studied right through to *Abitur* level. But in 1972 agreement was reached to initiate the so-called *reformierte Oberstufe* ('reformed upper-secondary level' – its detractors called it the *deformierte Oberstufe*, arguing that it was a deformation of the traditional broad-based curriculum). From the eleventh class onwards, i.e. following the period of compulsory secondary schooling and the successful completion of the intermediate leaving certificate, distinctions between the various forms of *Gymnasium* (humanistic, mathematical–scientific, etc.) disappear and pupils follow a combination of basic and specialist courses (*Grund- und Leistungskurse* – note here the institutionalising of the concept of *Leistung* in the nomenclature). Pupils must choose two specialist courses, one of which has to be a modern language or mathematics or a science. These courses take up five or six hours a week, and the pupils choose basic courses which occupy a further two to four hours, the ratio usually being roughly 2 : 1 between the two types. Parallels with the unsuccessful British N and F proposals, and now with possible combinations of A and AS level courses may be noted.

A significant problem with the reformed upper secondary level, apart from objections to it on the grounds that it has narrowed the traditional curriculum significantly, is that pupils engage in what is known as *taktisches Lernen*, i.e. they choose those subjects in which they are likely to score higher marks, rather than those which might be more appropriate for later university study, or indeed subjects in which they have more interest or even ability. With the *Numerus clausus* so severe in subjects like medicine and dentistry such 'tactical learning' becomes understandable. It is a good example, however, of 'playing the system': this is evident too in the existence of university students known as *Gerichtsmediziner* (literally 'courtroom medics') who have obtained a place to study medicine by proving that the teaching capacity in a given university has not

in fact been filled. There are lawyers in the Federal Republic who specialise in such matters.

Numbers of children attending *Gymnasien* can be seen in Table 4.2.
Proper comparison between the school populations in the three main
types of secondary school are only possible if the numbers in the lower
secondary level are compared. The proportions are interesting. There are
far more pupils in the *Gymnasien* and *Realschulen* combined than there
are in the *Hauptschulen*, and there are more pupils in the *Gymnasien*
than in the *Realschulen*. Far from dismantling their tripartite system the
Germans have actually reinforced it over the years by building in particular more grammar schools. With falling rolls the *Gymnasien* have been
making conscious efforts to attract pupils: there was a time when glossy
prospectuses were being produced to do just that.

Entry to the *Gymnasium*, as to the *Realschule*, depends on parental
preference. The principle used is guided choice based on reports and
opinions of both primary and secondary school teachers. Parents retain
the right of choice even if all advice is directed against them. Selectivity
is thus that of the parent. This is of course the reverse of the system
which operated in our tripartite arrangements, and it is a principle which
strengthens the German system considerably.

Another important principle, largely missing in the former British system,
is what the Germans call *Durchlässigkeit* (permeability): this allows pupils
to move from one type of school to another and to gain access to the
several types of vocational school and to higher education via various routes.
Curricula and school-leaving qualifications have been carefully aligned to
permit this to happen. *Durchlässigkeit* allows the Germans to counter criticisms that their system is too neatly discriminatory.

> Take a school pupil, guarantee him a modest living, send him to the
> university and let him study his favourite subject from school, if pos-
> sible an arts subject. The chance of producing someone disillusioned
> by his experience, full of pathetic irony, insecure cynicism and highly
> developed self-pity, is not slight.[22]

Such judgements of the current prospects for those embarking on a
university education are alas not rare. A further example of such low-
key cynicism, of a resigned coming-to-terms with the cul-de-sac into which
many thousands of aspiring academics are led each year, is to be found
for example in the novel *Von der Nutzlosigkeit, erwachsen zu werden*
('On the Uselessness of Being Grown-Up').[23] There the protagonist, an
unemployable Germanist, uses a striking metaphor to describe the position he and his fellow students found themselves in:

> We were sitting in a through coach without a destination and which
> had been uncoupled for some time, and the examination office and
> the professors were rattling on the carriage from outside, so that we
> inside might believe that it was still going somewhere.[24]

Table 4.2 West Germany: children in attendance at primary and secondary schools (1,000s)

	1970	1975	1979	1980	1981	1982	1983	1984	1985*
Grundschulen	3,978.2	3,914.7	2,991.0	2,770.7	2,588.2	2,439.5	2,352.7	2,291.2	2,190.1
Hauptschulen	2,369.2	2,510.4	2,363.0	2,273.7	2,187.0	2,061.5	1,894.0	1,714.3	1,638.7
Realschulen	863.0	1,147.2	1,365.2	1,351.1	1,323.5	1,278.1	1,214.4	1,132.2	1,049.0
Gymnasien	1,379.0	1,863.5	2,088.8	2,119.0	2,106.4	2,050.5	1,960.7	1,852.7	1,748.9
Gesamtschulen	—	165.8	214.4	220.3	225.6	226.3	224.7	220.9	216.6

Source: Statistisches Bundesamt Wiesbaden: *Bildung im Zahlenspiegel 1986* (Stuttgart and Maine, Kohlhammer, July 1986)
Note: (* = provisional figures)

Wozu noch studieren?[25] ('Why bother any more to study?') is the title of another recent book in which the experiences of young people of varying backgrounds and in several disciplines are related. The disappointments of a university career which has failed to produce the rewards expected are tragically evident.

The tragedy here is twofold: to be faced with the prospect of unemployment after a university education which has traditionally been held to be the key to success is sad enough; but even sadder is the assumption that *if* that education has not resulted in the anticipated success it has not of itself been worthwhile. The very formula *Wozu noch studieren?* presupposes that university study for its own sake, that a *higher* education, should no longer be a viable option.

In German universities there is a somewhat closer relationship between the course of study chosen and the student's intended career than is the case in Britain: hence the dilemma faced by Heinzen and Koch's hero. The conclusion, now being reached by *Gymnasiasten* in increasing numbers, is that it is better to seek employment after the *Abitur* than to face the uncertainty of a minimum of 5 years' university study. If this trend increases the traditional role of the *Gymnasium* in preparing students for university will have to undergo further reappraisal. The increased specialism of the *reformierte Oberstufe* may not prove as useful in such circumstances as the previous broader-based curriculum.

Already between 20 and 30 per cent of *Gymnasiasten* leave school at the end of the tenth class with the intermediate leaving certificate. And 30 per cent of those who gain the *Abitur*, designed it must be remembered as the *Hochschulreife*, the indication of preparation and fitness for university study, choose not to start a university career.

A research team from the Max Planck Institute for Human Development and Education in Berlin sees three serious challenges for the *Gymnasium*: (1) the continuing development of the other types of school, particularly the *Realschule* – the *Gymnasium* has lost its monopoly on preparation for higher education; (2) the consequences of its own expansion: more flexible teaching and a varied curriculum must be developed to legitimate pupils' completion of schooling at the end of the tenth class; and (3) there must be a redefinition of the relationship between the *Gymnasium* and the university and society as a whole.[26]

The *Realschule* has a long and distinguished history in Germany, its main period of growth beginning in the nineteenth century with the increasing awareness of the need to develop a more modern and realistic approach to the education and training of young people than that offered in the traditional grammar schools. They have been described as 'semi-academic intermediate schools' and I have already drawn the parallel with the British technical and central schools. They have expanded in number considerably since 1949, largely because many parents have regarded them as providing a more appropriate education for the needs of their children than the exclusively academic grammar schools. As the Max Planck researchers put it, 'the *Realschule*'s curriculum, more than that of the other types of school, [has taken] into account the most likely employment prospects of a certain group of secondary school pupils'.[27] So enthusiastic are the Max Planck authors in fact that they declare that the *Realschule* 'appears to be a model ... for a type of school that should be made universal'.[28]

Pupils of the *Realschule* would expect to become technicians, to move on to middle management in industry, commerce and administration as well as to train for careers in catering, nursing, etc. Possibilities have increased for *Realschule* pupils to transfer to the upper secondary level of the *Gymnasium* but most move on to vocational training after gaining the *Realschule* leaving certificate. The growth and considerable standing of these prestigious schools have provided an obstacle in the way of those wishing to press for a comprehensive system of education in the Federal Republic.

In contrast to the increased numbers of children attending both *Gymnasium* and *Realschule* numbers attending the *Hauptschule*, the 'main' secondary school, have been on the decline. In 1980 only one of the eleven *Länder* of the Federal Republic (Rheinland-Pfalz) had more pupils in the *Hauptschule* than in the other two types of secondary school combined.[29] In Nordrhein-Westfalen, the largest of the *Länder*, the *Hauptschulen* have lost 35 per cent of their pupils since 1978, and in 1985 they had for the first time fewer pupils on intake than the *Gymnasien*.[30] In this context a teachers' union leader is reported to have accused the *Gymnasien* of 'thrusting themselves forward as a sort of high-class comprehensive for all primary school leavers'.[31]

The *Hauptschule* has undergone a certain identity crisis. As its name implies it is designed to be the 'main' secondary school – yet, as the Max Planck researchers put it, 'it no longer serves the broad mass of the population for which it was established';[32] that 'broad mass' of average pupils prefers to go to alternative types of school, including the comprehensives.

The leaving certificate of the *Hauptschule* is recognised as being equivalent to that of the *Realschule*; for this to be realistic there is a certain alignment of curricula. The subjects which are given particular attention are those which will be essential, in accordance with the principle of *Durchlässigkeit*, if a pupil transfers to another type of school or continues in full-time education beyond the *Hauptschule*: mathematics and German and, very important in the German context, a foreign language, usually English. The alignment of curricula and the notional equivalence of school-leaving certificates have, however, worked paradoxically to the disadvantage of the *Hauptschule*. Its leaving certificate has dropped in value considerably: the Institute of German Industries has reported that, where 80 per cent of trainees had the *Hauptschule* leaving certificate in 1970, the equivalent figure for 1983 was only 42 per cent.[33] The Max Planck team conclude that there seems to be no reason to imagine that the *Hauptschule* will 'overcome its disadvantages *vis-à-vis* the other types of secondary school.'[34] It looks set to be regarded as the poor relation, in academic terms, of its competitors, while having to cope with the difficulties of catering for the needs of its large intake of children from Germany's immigrant population.

It is worth noting at this stage a development which has placated the supporters of comprehensive schools while preserving the tripartite system. This is the 2-year *Orientierungsstufe* (orientation stage), post-primary and pre-selection, which allows a diagnostic and prognostic phase during which a pupil's particular capabilities can be assessed. Grouping in the orientation stage usually operates only in mathematics and modern languages. Sometimes the orientation stage is directly related to school type, sometimes not; practice varies between the *Länder*.

The first point to make about comprehensive schools (*Gesamtschulen*) in Germany is that they have been regarded for most of their existence as experimental, even in those *Länder* which have been most in favour of their introduction. Secondly, they represent only a small proportion of secondary schools even today: there were in fact only some 297 *Gesamtschulen* in the Federal Republic in 1983 (in 1975 there were 216).[35]

Experiments with comprehensive schools were started in the 1950s and centred initially on Hessen, Niedersachsen and West Berlin. There are basically two types: the integrated type, which incorporates the traditional school types, and the co-operative (sometimes called 'additive' or 'school-type orientated') where the school types are retained but the schools co-operate in school centres. The former have been favoured by the SPD, the latter by the CDU *Länder*. Whatever the type, however, they exist alongside the other types of secondary school.

As might be expected, parental attitudes to the *Gesamtschulen* have been mixed. In October 1978 the main teachers' union found by means of a questionnaire survey of all existing comprehensive schools that about one in four of all pupils applying for admission to them were being turned away: it was revealed that all the *Länder* except Bremen were operating a *Numerus clausus* on admissions. This measure of the popularity of comprehensive schools contrasted starkly with a people's petition presented in the same year in Nordrhein-Westfalen against plans for co-operative *Gesamtschulen* (i.e. in this case school centres with three separate types of secondary school and an orientation stage) and signed by some 3.6 million voters. Parents saw this development as compromising their right of parental choice, since their children would be *selected* for the appropriate school type after the orientation stage.

The main reasons why comprehensive schools have not developed as quickly in Germany as their proponents would have hoped may be summarised thus:

1 The strong intermediate school has meant that realistic goals can be

achieved by the middle ability range whose parents might otherwise have been calling for alternatives to the academic *Gymnasien*.

2 The cultural autonomy of the *Länder* has enabled political decisions to determine the extent to which such a radical new approach to secondary schooling should be espoused.

3 The concept of *Leistung* militates against any type of school which does not rate achievement as highly as the *Gymnasium*.

4 Places in grammar schools have steadily increased while *Gesamtschulen* have been trying to get established.

5 The principle of *Durchlässigkeit*, it is argued, makes comprehensive schools unnecessary, since transfer between the various types of school is facilitated.

6 Parental choice of secondary school type operates.

7 The *Orientierungsstufe*, where it exists, delays choice until diagnosis and prognosis of ability have taken place.

8 Because the comprehensives exist alongside the other types of school they have to compete on an unequal footing: this curtails their potential for innovation.

It remains to mention that part-time vocational training is compulsory in the Federal Republic for all pupils not in full-time education up to the age of 18, a principle first introduced in 1920. The range of possibilities is very wide. Pupils not continuing to the upper secondary level may leave school to find unskilled work, attending a vocational school (*Berufsschule*) part-time, or they may enter the so-called 'dual system' of apprenticeship plus vocational school attendance, or they may start various other courses, including full-time training stretching over long periods.

As with secondary schools, the principle of *Durchlässigkeit* operates, and trainees may transfer, with appropriate qualifications, from one type of *Berufsschule* to another, and into various types of higher education, including the *Fachhochschulen* (roughly equivalent to polytechnics) and the universities.

The German approach to vocational training, though not of immediate concern in a paper on the secondary school system, is important in the context of the relationship between education and training and national prosperity. We have seen that German pupils do rather better than their English counterparts in mathematics; they are also trained to a high level in the trades and occupations they follow. It is a simple matter to gain subjective evidence of the advantages of such training. Anyone who has visited or lived in Germany will be aware of the knowledge and interest of most employees in the service industries, for example.

A brief look at some basic statistics reveals the difference in degree between provision in the UK and the Federal Republic: in 1981 in West Germany 92 per cent of 16 year olds, 89 per cent of 17 year olds, and 72 per cent of 18 year olds were participating in some kind of education and training; in the UK the corresponding figures were 84 per cent, 60 per cent and 42 per cent.[36] The Secretary of State, in his 1987 North of England Conference speech, made specific reference to the Federal Republic in the context of his concern about our relative lack of success in keeping young people in full-time education and training.

IV

In the immediate post-war period the Germans were preoccupied with reconstruction in the literal sense: their main concern was with providing the schools and the teachers to do the job at all and with eradicating the residual effects of twelve years of National Socialist influence. Rather than look forward to wide-ranging reform of the school system (which the Americans in particular would have liked) the German authorities preferred to look back to the reforming years of the Weimar Republic and to readopt a system which had been seen to work: the principle was 'On from Weimar'.

Stabilisation was the main concern of the young Republic: this stabilisation led to the comfort of stability over its first ten years, and that in turn led to a complacent distrust of reform. The catchphrase *keine Experimente!* (frequently quoted to characterise the atmosphere in education before the mid-1960s) reveals an unwillingness to interfere with the *status quo*: such an attitude is, however, understandable in a country which had seen so much upheaval during the previous fifty years, but it was an attitude stubbornly adopted in the face of very different policies in other countries of Europe.

The answer to the question 'Why did the Germans not seize the opportunity to make a completely new start?' may be summarised in five points:

1 The force of tradition was, despite the intervening years of Nazi hegemony, too strong to allow of any drastic departure from a system which had once been the envy of the world.
2 There was an understandable fear of any centralised control (Allied or German) – the only time there had been a Federal Minister of Education had been under the Nazis.
3 The teaching body – at all levels – was not the most progressive: in Nordrhein-Westfalen only 6.2 per cent of secondary school teachers were under 30 and 55 per cent were 50 and over; in Berlin the average age of fully trained teachers was 57 in 1948.
4 There was a feeling that the Allies did not necessarily have the answers to many of the important educational issues of the time, despite, for example, the British enthusiasm for the 1944 Education Act.
5 Counteracting the enormous physical and material hardships of the time naturally took precedence over projected reform plans.

During the twenty-year period that followed the establishment of the

Federal Republic in 1949 the CDU was in power and committed firmly to preserving the traditional tripartite system of secondary education: generally speaking it was opposed to any radical reform measures designed to achieve greater equality in education. There was too during this period a lack of educational research: among educationists in the universities 'a strong philosophical-historical tradition'[37] prevailed. Nor were there any marked developments in curricular matters: in fact, the word 'curriculum' is relatively new in its usage in educational contexts in Germany.

By 1972, in the aftermath of what had been dubbed 'two decades of non-reform'[38] it could be said of German secondary schools that

> despite all the efforts there still prevails the traditional picture of a highly selective school system based on the idea of grading down all the pupils who can't cope with the standards set by historically evolved curricula and inflexible teaching methods.[39]

That harsh judgement was reflected too in the critical OECD report on education in Germany which appeared in the same year:

> In an age when mass secondary and higher education are being rapidly developed in the other advanced states, Germany has made do with a system that until now has effectively shut off some 90% of the children from the possibility of entering university-level education; that experiences great difficulty in remodelling curricula to suit modern conditions; in which teachers appear to follow authoritarian models in their classroom behaviour; and that is bureacratically administered, lacking essential minimum elements of public, parental, teacher and student participation in decision-making.[40]

Despite or because of such gloomy judgements education has remained a subject of major political concern in the Federal Republic: the period of 'non-reform' was followed by a flurry of activity in planning and policy making at all levels, and the education debate is as crucial in the run-up to German elections as it was in 1987 in Britain. The neo-conservatism of the 1980s has not dampened the debate about comprehensive schools, and the SPD *Länder* continue to plan their expansion.

The German system appears to work well when judged by certain criteria: parental choice operates; there is comparability of parental expectation of and actual provision in the various types of school; teachers have attained a high degree of professional status; vocational training is excellent and measurable standards generally are high. Judged by other criteria, however, there are some obvious problems: competition between the various types of secondary school is now rife, to the considerable disadvantage of the *Hauptschulen*; curriculum development tends to lag behind other countries and to be restricted by ministerial guidelines; the propaedeutic function of the *Gymnasium* limits scope at the upper secondary level; the rigid assessment procedures create considerable unhappiness and stress; comprehensive schools develop at a snail's pace because they are always in competition with what the *Gymnasien* and *Realschulen* can offer.

How we in Britain might benefit from studying the German experience is difficult to determine, but I suspect that it is from the successful *Realschulen* and from the highly developed vocational training arrangements that the best lessons are to be learnt. The German approach to control of the curriculum and to assessment procedures might all too often serve as warnings of potential problems to those wishing to propose similar styles for our own system. They are embedded in the nation's culture and history to an extent that makes them appear wholly natural in the German context. Neville Postlethwaite recounts the story of a French Minister of Education who, when told that grade repetition led to a larger spread of achievement and was expensive, replied: 'Messieurs, je vous le crois, mais qu'est-ce que vous voulez que je fasse? Le redoublement, c'est une tradition de la France!'[41]

In reaching a conclusion about the nature of secondary school provision in Germany we are left with the paradox of, on the one hand, admiration for a system which appears properly co-ordinated and well defined – and one which produces impressive measurable outcomes – and, on the other hand, apprehension that these positive features are achieved through means which are not so easily sanctioned. Consider this assessment:

> Over-organisation, excessive supervision from above, State control over entrance to the professions . . ., the too linguistic character of the instruction, and a lack of variety of individual initiative are the evils from which German education is felt by many to be suffering at the present time.[42]

That harsh judgement, familiar to those who know the German system, leaves us with a checklist of concerns. The author is Michael Sadler. It was written, like the excerpt which opens this chapter, in 1903.[43]

NOTES

1 Percy Gardner: *Oxford at the Cross Roads* (London, Adam & Charles Black, 1903) pp. 3–4.
2 Kenneth Baker: Speech to the North of England Conference, Rotherham, 9 January 1987 (Text with *DES News* 11/87).
3 Sadler produced eleven such volumes between 1895 and 1903, 'the like of which had not been seen before in any country' (Lynda Grier, *DNB*).
4 See David Phillips: 'The German Universities – Citadels of Freedom or Bastions of Reaction?' *Comparative Education* (Vol. 17, No. 3, 1981).
5 M. E. Sadler: 'The History of Education', in: *Germany in the Nineteenth Century* (Manchester 1912) p. 111. Sadler singles out the following 'great achievements' since 1870: 'the strengthening of the Universities by the prudent munificence of the State; the diversification of secondary schools; the quickening of a new spirit among the teachers and pupils in elementary education;

the furtherance of technical education in all grades, but always upon a basis of liberal preparatory training; the extension of the period of compulsory education in many parts of Germany so as to cover the critical years of adolescence; and . . . the reform of higher education for girls' (ibid., pp. 111–12).

6 Ibid., p. 127.
7 *Education in the Federal Republic of Germany: Aspects of Curriculum and Assessment* (London, HMSO, 1986) p. v.
8 Ray Stannard Baker: *Seen in Germany* (London, Harper & Brothers, 1902) p. 3.
9 Karl Heinz Gruber: 'Ignoring Plowden. On the limited impact of the Plowden Report in Germany and Austria', *Oxford Review of Education* (Vol. 13, No. 1, 1987).
10 A research report by Willi Ferdinand (Essen, Neue Deutsche Schule Verlagsgesellschaft, 1973) is entitled *Über Hausaufgabenkummer, Zensurenärger und Hilfsschulmisere*, emotional coinages which add to the vocabulary of such terms.
11 From a survey of a total of 1,120 pupils in various types of school, reported by Bettina Schwake, *Die Welt* (12.10.77).
12 Reported by Dieter Bossmann, *Deutsches Allegemeines Sonntagsblatt* (18.6.78).
13 See report by Paul Korb, *Der Tagesspiegel* (7.8.79).
14 *TES* (13.1.84).
15 Gruber, loc. cit.
16 Max Wilkinson: *Lessons from Europe. A Comparison of British and West European Schooling* (London, Centre for Policy Studies, 1977) p. 33.
17 W. H. G. Armytage: *The German Influence on English Education* (London, Routledge & Kegan Paul, 1969) p. 94.
18 S. J. Prais and Karin Wagner: 'Schooling Standards in England and Germany: some summary comparisons bearing on economic performance', *National Institute Economic Review* (May 1985) No. 112; *Compare* (Vol. 16, No. 1, 1986).
19 Board of Education: *Curriculum and Examinations in Secondary Schools* (The Norwood Report) (London, HMSO, 1943) p. 2.
20 *Das Gymnasium und die neue Zeit: Fürsprachen und Forderungen für seine Erhaltung und seine Zukunft* (Leipzig and Berlin, 1919). (Present author's translation.)
21 Jowett had proposed such an examination and its associated rights as early as 1893 in a letter to Professor Jebb. (*Letters of Benjamin Jowett*, ed. Evelyn Abbott and Lewis Campbell (London, John Murray, 1899) p. 237.)
22 Teresa Vince: 'Leben aus der Ferne', *Die Zeit* (28.2.86) (Present author's translation.)
23 Georg Heinzen and Uwe Koch: *Von der Nutzlosigkeit, erwachsen zu werden* (Reinbek bei Hamburg, Rowohlt, 1985) (Present author's translation.)
24 Ibid., p. 87.
25 Werner Harenberg (ed.): *Wozu noch studieren?* (Spiegel-Buch No. 64), (Reinbek bei Hamburg, Rowohlt, 1985).
26 Max Planck Institute for Human Development and Education: *Between Elite and Mass Education* (Albany, State University of New York Press, 1983) pp. 215–16.
27 Ibid., p. 186.
28 Ibid., p. 194.
29 Ibid., pp. 174–5.
30 Paul Bendelow: 'Secondary moderns lose out in the numbers battle', *TES* (21.3.86).
31 Ibid.

32 *Between Elite and Mass Education*, p. 174.
33 Paul Bendelow, loc. cit.
34 *Between Elite and Mass Education*, p. 181.
35 *Grund- und Strukturdaten*, p. 22.
36 DES: Statistical Bulletin 10/85 *International Statistical Comparisons of the Education and Training of 16 to 18 year olds* (September 1985): Table 3.
37 Peter Seidl: 'Comprehensive Education in West Germany and Austria', *Forum* (Vol. 15, No. 1, Autumn 1972).
38 Saul B. Robinsohn and J. Caspar Kuhlmann: 'Two Decades of Non-Reform in West German Education', *Comparative Education Review* (XI/3, October 1967).
39 Seidl, loc. cit.
40 OECD: *Reviews of National Policies for Education: Germany* (Paris 1972) p. 55.
41 T. Neville Postlethwaite: 'Research and Policy-Making in Education: Some Possible Links', in: *Educational Research and Policy. How Do They Relate?*, ed. Torsten Husén and Maurice Kogan (Oxford, Pergamon Press, 1984) p. 196.
42 Michael Sadler: *The Ferment in Education on the Continent and in America*, Proceedings of the British Academy (1903) p. 7.
43 In parts of this chapter I have drawn directly on information in Arthur Hearnden: *Education, Culture and Politics in West Germany* (Oxford, Pergamon Press, 1976).

5 The German university: basically healthy or rotten?

Reflections on an overdue reorientation of German higher education policy [1993]

Christoph Führ

Karl-Heinrich Becker, 1919: At core our universities are healthy.[1]

Carl Jaspers, 1945: At core the university has preserved itself in its protected circumstances. . . . Because the spirit of science has not yet been destroyed, the university can now begin again without delay . . .[2]

(Blue Paper) Expert evaluation on the higher education reform of 1948: We can say against the widespread dissatisfaction with higher education that colleges and universities are the guardians of an old and basically healthy tradition.[3]

Hermann Heimpel, 1955: The proposition that higher education is basically healthy means that the idea of education derived from German idealism, and specifically Fichte, which lies at the basis of the German university, has perhaps been shaken but it has not been disputed: the application of science, the education of man through science; through a science which is not a propagated dogma but consists of a unity of research and theory.[4]

Dieter Simon, 1991: The German university is . . . rotten to its core. It requires a reorientation. What is needed is a policy which replaces growth-bound thinking first in higher education, and then in all the other provinces of science.[5]

Enough of these 'core' words! In the following, we shall forego any attempt to interpret these propositions in their historic context and in all their various nuances. And, we also shall forego offering a 'genealogy' of these theses. Hermann Heimpel was in any event aware of the connection between the statements in the 1948 blue paper (*Blaues Gutachten*) expert evaluation and C. H. Becker's words of 1919.[6] So, let us take these statements as reflecting how the German university understood itself. To that extent, these 'core sayings' are at the same time signposts of an historical development.

I

No one now would dare to declare the German university to be 'healthy at core' given the conditions of the mass university and its crisis in profiling and orientation. The question of what indeed the 'core' of the university is is difficult to answer. Until the structural reforms of the 1960s, some relatively plausible answers to this question could be found, e.g. the faculties. Since then, the faculties have been supplanted by extensively compartmentalized specialized domains, following the Anglo-Saxon model. It is hence debatable whether there exists a 'core' to the university at all in the former sense. If it in fact does no longer exist – and many would agree on this – it would, of course, be a matter of indifference whether it is 'healthy' or 'rotten.' Dieter Simon's statement signals 'core-less' times. In 1981, Niklas Luhmann noted: 'Whether the core is still healthy, whether it even exists at all, is something which no one can any longer determine. The structure is self-sustaining . . . The bureacracy deals with itself in bureaucratic forms.'[7]

This is surely correct. Yet, is the thesis of 'rottenness' fitting? Are there no areas of the university that are basically 'more healthy,' or at least less 'rotten' than others? Perhaps there are good reasons to claim that disciplines such as legal science, the historical sciences, medicine, the natural sciences, and engineering are less affected by the developments of the last decades than, for example, educational science, social sciences, and theology. But here too the situation varies from one university to another.

The chairman of the Science Council, Professor Dieter Simon, called for a 'reorientation' in 1991, and appealed for a higher education policy that 'supplants a growth-bound thinking in growth first in higher education, and then in all the other provinces of science.'[8] Simon is challenging the *Zeitgeist*. Yet, German higher education policy is still utterly captive to this belief in growth. The most recent demonstration of this is the 'Plan for the development of higher education in Germany,' approved unanimously on July 6, 1992, by the Conference of University Rectors (HRK):[9] 30,000 additional positions for academics in universities and specialized colleges are called for, and state expenditure of 9 billion DM annually to go along with it. This is justified in the first instance by the accumulated need that has been neglected since the 'decision to open' the universities of 1977. Prognoses for university beginner figures over the next two decades and the assumed demand of the labor market for an academically pre-trained labor force are crucial for planning: 'The individual desire to study will not diminish over the long term but indeed will more likely increase. This tendency will be further promoted by the labor market's rising demand for a workforce with higher qualifications. . . . In view of the continuing high demand for a university education, it is irresponsible to reserve university education for a small segment of the population. Universities must therefore respond to the continuing challenge to train one-third of a yearly cohort by altering the structure of university courses.'[10] The HRK is here referring to a 'distribution and coordination between basic courses and courses which develop and deepen a subject as well as vocationally oriented further education.'[11] In addition, specialized colleges should be expanded: 'Therefore an expansion of the traditional spectrum of disciplines is necessary if we wish to broaden specialized colleges . . . with a view to relieving some of the burden on the universities.'[12] Which specialized areas are meant here remains an open question. At present, specialized colleges are training two-thirds of engineers and almost half of those persons in information sciences and company management.

The HRK even has a critical word for the *Gymnasien*: 'The prospects of success of such changes in internal structure also depend upon the prior education of the applicants. We must have a minimum of unity.' The federal states must ensure that the final *Gymnasium*-leaving examination (*Abitur*) procedures produce a maximum fairness in the distribution of educational opportunities. That would defuse the question of the value of the *Abitur* not only as a necessary but also a sufficient proof of qualification for university studies and soften the call for 'specialized higher education entry examinations.'[13] Golden words! They have been part of the liturgy of the higher education reform debate for decades.

Does the 'reorientation' called for by Dieter Simon fit this picture? Probably not.

II

If we venture a retrospective glance over the last 200 years of the history of the German university, we will see that such 'reorientations' have never begun from within the institution of the university itself or been implemented within its own autonomous domain.[14] It was always the state that intervened and changed things. Thus, after being prepared by Wilhelm von Humboldt (together with Schleiermacher, Fichte, and Friedrich August Wolf *et al.*), the Berlin University was founded in 1810 by a cabinet order of the Prussian King Friedrich Wilhelm III (i.e., it was inaugurated by the Prussian state). The late Thomas Nipperdey stated: 'The Prussian University is one of Prussia's few world historical achievements, and its status remains uncontested down to this very day. Since the founding of Berlin University it has become the prototype of the modern university, from Baltimore, to Tokyo, to Jerusalem, even though for some time now only vestiges of it are still to be found in Germany.'[15] It is the 'reorientation' of these 'vestiges' with which we shall be concerned here.

This solitary more or less 'classical university reform' was overshadowed by the defeat at Jena and Auerstädt, a profound crisis of the state. Prussia's response to this challenge, as we know, was to institute reforms in the state, army, and education.

In our century, the university has shown itself to be an institution of considerable adaptability and continuity. It has withstood all the political and social upheavals associated with the years 1918, 1933, and 1945, at least in the west. 'At core,' it remains largely unchanged. We cannot dwell further on the transformations of the universities and higher education establishments in the east between 1945 and 1990 in the 'socialist cadre foundry': the Soviet occupation forces, the SED, and the state apparatus dominated by it set the tone in that respect.

Although the interventions between 1933 and 1945 had mostly to do with personnel (many Jewish and democratic scholars and students were expelled, often by terrorist methods), there was a 'university miracle' in the west in the reconstruction phase alongside of the 'economic miracle.' Well-known emigrants returned (e.g. the historian Hans Rothfels, the philosophers Plessner, Löwith, Horkheimer, and Adorno). Famous scholars, respected far beyond Germany, such as Edward Spranger, Martin Heidegger, Hans Georg Gadamer, Wolfgang Schadewaldt, Helmut Thielicke, Romano Guardini, Rudolf Boltmann, Bruno Snell, Friedrich Meinecke, Gerhard Ritter, Franz Schnabel, Percy Ernst Schramm, Hermann Heimpel, Ernst Robert Curtius, Alfred Weber, Werner Heisenberg, Otto Hahn, Walter Hulstein, and Ludwig Reisner, to mention just a few, helped in the intellectual reconstruction of the Federal Republic. Of course, the events of the 1960s showed that this was only a belated, deceptive show – one is almost tempted to say a pale reflection of the Wilhelmine and Weimar era.

As the number of university students doubled in the 1950s, the Science Council was charged in 1957 with working out a general plan for the promotion of the sciences. The recommendations of the Science Council for expanding higher education establishments specializing in science in 1960 were met with a lively response. This expansion was financed mainly by the federal states, which between 1946 and 1969 were solely responsible for higher education as part of their cultural autonomy. The establishment of new universities in, for example, Bochum, Bremen, Konstanz, and Bielefeld was surrounded by a broad public debate. This all took place in the aftermath of the great educational reform debate, in which the Conference of Ministers of Education, the West German Rectors Conference, teacher associations, and trade unions all made critical contributions. The planning and reform of education were the great themes of the 1960s worldwide.

In Germany as well, the reforms and simultaneous generous expansions of secondary and higher education created special burdens and problems from the early 1960s. In that period of 'educational euphoria,' our educational policies took an 'unrealistic turn,'[16] the consequences of which are still being felt. Three months before Georg Picht proclaimed 'disaster in German education' with profound repercussions, Ludwig Erhard, the Federal Chancellor, pointed out in his government declaration in October 1963: 'Unless Germany steps up its intellectual investments, it will necessarily fall behind other cultural and industrial countries. And this means that not only economic progress and prosperity, but also social security, are at stake. The federal government and the states must work together to resolutely confront this great common task. The German people must be aware that the tasks of education and research rank as high for our generation as did the social question in the nineteenth century.'[17] Six years later, the Federal Chancellor Willy Brandt wanted to give priority to education and training, science, and research, on the list of reforms. But since the oil crisis of 1973 other political questions have had priority. At the time, Picht advocated 'disengaging' the education system from the employment system. The first signs of such 'disengagement' became evident in the early 1980s, when tens of thousands of young academics, especially teachers, could not find suitable jobs.

The discussion on higher education reform acquired new urgency with the student unrest in the late 1960s. Hermann Lübbe, however, declared a 'myth' the claim that the higher education reforms were induced by the student movement. They had been under way for a long time already when academic youth came forward with their own agenda. Lübbe observes: 'The student protest movement did not develop as a result of pressure from a deadened state of affairs, but rather occurred in the midst of a very dynamic higher education reform policy whose effective beginnings dated to at least ten years prior to this protest movement.'[18] The high point of the student movement was during the 'Grand Coalition' (1966–9). At that time, a broad 'extra-parliamentary opposition' established itself as part of the discussion over the emergency laws and the Vietnam War. Although the majority of students rejected radical political groups, they granted them broad latitudes for their activities in colleges and universities because they did not participate in student elections. At that time, two political groundswells overlapped in a dangerous manner: the 'democratization' of the structures and the expansion of higher education establishments. A radical, socially critical discussion in secondary schools and in colleges and universities pushed for a reform of society through street demonstrations, sit-ins, and boycotting of classes, with education reform serving as a lever. The universities and politicians at that time for the most part reacted helplessly. Debates on higher education policy in the state parliaments (e.g. in Hessen) showed, as the *Rektor* of Frankfurt University, Professor Dr Walter Rüegg, put it: 'How terrifyingly distant the university has become from the public at large.'[19] This is the only explanation of the political readiness to effect extensive changes in the traditional structures of the German university in all the major parties. The German professorial university, in which academics, especially full professors, had priority rights of independent decision making on questions of research and teaching, as well as on personnel, within the bounds set down in state legislation, was restructured into a group university in an overly hasty manner by dint of political decisions taken by the state parliaments and often bearing little relevance to the actual situation. All groups active in the university – professors, assistants, students, and other personnel – participated in the decision-making process in different ways that varied from state to state. The traditional faculties were also largely disbanded. The normal four faculties were broken down into often more than twenty specialized areas. The expansion of higher education resulted in the introduction of a new form, the specialized college, at the end of the 1960s. The interstate treaty signed on October 31, 1968 on standardization in specialized higher education promoted the schools of engineering, with their long and proven traditions, as well as other specialized higher education establishments, to a rank approaching that of a university. In 1969, the Basic Law was changed under the Grand Coalition. Henceforth, the federal government would have policy-making powers in higher education. These changes were intended to place a greater share of the financial burden incurred by the expansion on the federal government and ensure anew the unity of higher education, which the reforms had called into question. The expansion and new construction of higher education establishments, including teaching hospitals, were made a joint task of the federal government and the states. On the basis of this new judicial situation, the federal parliament then passed over the following years a law promoting the building of higher education establishments, a law on higher education, and the federal apprenticeship promotion law. The federal government allotted 26.5 million DM between 1970 and 1992 just for promoting higher education; the federal states contributed equivalent amounts. This is in itself a considerable joint achievement! Even so, the colleges and universities were simply inundated by students.

Let us interrupt our brief historic sketch for the moment and merely state that the '1970 Report on Education' issued by the Social–Liberal federal government in 1970 envisaged that by 1980 half of an annual cohort of secondary-school pupils would complete their *Abitur* (the *Gymnasium* leaving certificate) and one-fourth of every cohort would be entering higher education. Instead of this 50 per cent, in 1980 19.2 per cent of pupils in one cohort obtained a university-entry diploma, and this relatively modest increase in the proportion of pupils receiving their *Abitur*, measured in terms of the objectives of 1970, had the effect that, since 1977, the surge of students into higher education could only be absorbed by an 'overload program,' and the number of disciplines with a *Numerus clausus* increased.

III

To commemorate Niklas Luhmann's 65th birthday, Andrei Kieserling compiled a paperback of some of Luhmann's essays on higher education reform from 1968 to 1992 with the title 'The University as a Milieu.'[20] Luhmann has been teaching since 1968 at Bielefeld University, founded in that year, and is a witness of his times. We select some of his comments relative to the question of how it was possible that the 'core' of the university was 'becoming rotten' in that period.

Luhmann complains, in particular, about the 'immense increase of regulations and formally mandatory decision-making processes' (p. 74). Democratization, according to him, means a 'multiplication of the burden of decision-making. One decision begets many others. Someone who participates on boards, commissions, committees, conferences, senates, and councils, must decide how he is going to vote. Often he must sit in on further sessions to ensure a balanced vote count' (p. 75). 'Even the efforts made to reform the reform on the organizational level, and to dismantle the gigantic demo-bureaucracies, which sprang up as a consequence of the "group university," are not sufficient, however urgently they were desired. The "group university" is fascinated with itself' (p. 52). 'Thus the participatory movement of the '68 generation . . . led to massive participatory bureaucracies and hence to an immense increment in organized excuses for why nothing happens' (p. 152). Luhmann calls the university an 'organized social *topos*' (p. 94).

As regards further expansion, Luhmann asked: 'In view of the sharp increase in the number of students, the first problem is the question whether perhaps a too large proportion of the population is studying – too large measured in terms of the possibilities of applying their education. . . . There are many more students today than formerly, and if the number of diplomas has not increased correspondingly, it follows that a process of selection is occurring, whether it is that many more students drop out than before, or that many students study without any aim at all beyond getting through their courses. Such selection would be a self-selection' (p. 80 f.). 'The problem is how rigorous should the selection be in the university to ensure that certain recipients, specific professions can be offered qualified personnel, or how easy should the selection process in the university be to promote individuality and developmental potential?' (p. 114).

Luhmann goes on to say that the question has been justifiably asked 'whether one can still speak at all of a unitary institution called the "university" ' (p. 85). 'In actual operation, the fact that the university is itself an organization has produced an impenetrable confusion as regards examinations, the approval of new chairs, injection of funds, etc. Organizationally what we have is an unwieldy intermingling of politically defined premises for decision-making and of desiderata deriving from teaching and research. The fact is, simply, that the organization has . . . caused a hypertrophy of decision-making possibilities, and hence attracts parasites. Politics parasites on the university' (p. 110). On the topic of professorial universities and group universities, Luhmann says: 'Something that was not very good has been replaced by something that was worse, i.e., the chance of a reform was missed. The structures could have been made more transparent with few and clear legal regulations, and thereby the despotism of certain professorial power plays could have been broken' (p. 111). 'But I am sure that the structure we now have will be unable to reach again the position which German universities had in science in the nineteenth century and, moreover, quite independently of funds' (p. 112). 'What is needed is . . . an overall idea for the social function of higher education, for its mission of educating and training. The Humboldt University was based on an idea of education that can no longer be resuscitated' (p. 82). Is that really true? It is true that Humboldt was thinking of small, flexible universities. The 'mass university' should, however, be rethought on the basis of Humboldt's ideas. They might also provide some pointers today.

IV

In the nineteenth century, the prime objective of educational policy was to ensure primary education for all; but the twentieth century has been characterized by a demand for 'secondary education for all.' Since the 1960s, higher education has been demanded for roughly half of an annual cohort. Indeed, the above-mentioned 1970 educational report of the Social–Liberal coalition government posits this goal for 1980 already! The historic consequence of the accelerated expansion of the *Gymnasien* since the 1960s, reinforced by Picht's 'apocalyptic catastrophe,' was a 'flood of students.' The hopes of higher education policy makers for a demographically induced decline in the number of new enrollments, for a tunneling process, was based on false forecasts. The only auxiliary was the 'overload program,' the openness resolution of 1977. The HRK declared on November 4, 1991, that it could no longer support this openness resolution, and on July 6, 1992, it specified what it needed to recuperate (this was discussed in a previous section).

One of the main arguments of the HRK for a further expansion of higher education is the thesis that there is a 'growing demand on the labor market for a workforce with higher qualifications.'[21] One may ask in rejoinder: Has this demand ever been studied comprehensively and critically in the recent period? The HRK rests its assertion on no empirical data at all. Did not the Conference of Education Ministers have about 16,000 unemployed young teachers in the west until recently? Are there not many young graduates in mathematics, biology, chemistry, physics, sociology, etc. who were unable to find a suitable job, and in some instances therefore begin a second course of study? Do not many young academics in the west have jobs for which neither university studies nor a *Gymnasium* diploma is necessary? In short, do we not have a considerable number of young academics who, while not being unemployed, nonetheless do not have jobs that conform to their training? It is high time that these questions are cleared up, before the argument of a 'rising demand on the labor market' is used further. Can we continue to afford the fact that almost one-third of new enrollments fail in their studies, and drop out? This is a clear sign of an overcrowded university whose educational function is being strained, and also of a lack of preparation for higher-education studies in the upper-level course system of the *Gymnasien*.

We may recall that in the early 1930s, when there were only about 120,000 students in the whole of what was then the German Reich (an idyllic number from the present perspective!), a public debate was going on about university reform against the background of a world economic crisis. In 1931–2, two illustrious Frankfurt professors, the constitutional lawyer Hermann Heller (who died as an emigrant in 1933) and the economist Adolf Löwe (who is still living at the age of 99 in Wolfenbüttel after returning from emigration), proposed a 'rigorous change in the conditions for admission.'[22] Heller pleaded for a thoroughgoing reform of educational objectives in the university and for reducing the number of students by about one-third. Heller wrote: 'Today's university is ailing first and foremost from the fact that it must be everything's and every-one's lassie. It has to be an educational commune, a place of research, and a professional training school all in one, and on top of that it is intolerably overcrowded by students, some more usable, some less . . . Thus the university is suffering from not only an acute but also from a chronic overcrowding.'[23] How much more valid is this criticism today?! Heller's proposal was then: 'An effective limitation of academic study, fairer in regard to the overarching problem of the examination system, could be achieved through a much more stringent screening-out of those who are unsuitable in the upper level of secondary school and even in higher education itself. In the upper secondary school, the prerequisites for a college-entrance diploma must be tested much more rigorously, and higher education must fundamentally only accept secondary school leavers with especially good grades.'[24]

In 1932, already Adolf Löwe considered that the number of youth who received their college-entrance diplomas (*Abitur*) was the key to all pres-ent problems in German higher education.[25] Therefore, today as well it is here that educational policy making should apply the 'lever' because the consequences of throwing open the doors of the fortress too wide resulted in the overflooding of higher education since the 1960s. It is not the place here to examine in detail possible paths of solution. Obviously, such a reorientation of educational policy can only be initiated carefully and step by step; at best, it will be a decade before it bears fruit. The strongest opposition today will be the 'educational patent,' which has become almost a self-evident matter in respect of the accoutrements of social status in all social layers and parties. However, if we are unsuccess-ful in limiting the ranks of those entitled to higher education to those who are capable of studying, higher education will have to introduce its own entrance examinations. But that would break with a more than 200-year-old German tradition, and would place an appreciable additional burden on higher education, especially in the initial phase. Anyone who knows the higher education landscape in Germany knows that there has always been a lot of talk about this 'emergency brake,' but it is highly unlikely that anyone will pull the handle.

To eliminate the 'overload,' sanctioned for a number of years now by the state, a flanking measure is also possible – namely, the abolition of the central office for assigning places of study in Dortmund. It is in any event a centralist element that exists in a relation of tension with the federalist structure of our education system. If the autonomy of higher education is to be strengthened, and the flood of students rolled back, in the future every higher education establishment will have to decide itself how many students it wishes to accept and who they shall be. The Chairman of the Science Council, Dieter Simon, spoke out in favor of such an autonomous selection in 1991. He saw this to be the first step in the right direction. Only in this way will we be able to reduce the number of students, diminish the overload, and at the same time improve considerably the study situation in higher education.

To sum up:

1 The financial situation of the federal government and the states requires a reorientation of German higher education policy. At the same time, in the recommenced expansion of higher education in the five new states there should be a rethinking of the further development of German higher education overall, with the objective of restoring 'internal unity.'

2 The secular trend of a steady increase in the number of students is no natural occurrence but rather the consequence of an 'unrealistic' turn in educational policy in the 1960s, the intention of which was to disengage the education system from the employment system.

3 The proposal of the Conference of College and University Rectors to expand specialized higher educational establishments, develop new areas of specialization, and redirect the flood of students away from the university and into specialized higher education will bear little fruit. Although any expansion of specialized higher education is thoroughly to be welcomed, the objective is unrealistic. A number of specialized colleges will find it difficult to maintain their present status in the future. Above all, the major specialized higher education establishments want to be placed on an equal footing with the universities, and they have some valid reasons for this. Just as the technical colleges were placed on an equal footing with universities in 1990, by the year 2000 some of our specialized higher education establishments will obtain the right to offer masters' and doctors' degrees, and some will become universities. Professional academies and so on will then rise to fill these gaps.

Our reflections lead us back to our starting point: Will the reorientation called for by Dieter Simon in 1991 become a reality, or will a growth-oriented muddling-through remain the maxim of German higher education policy? Our universities will almost certainly be unable to bring about this reorientation, as evidenced by the plan put forth by the Conference of College and University Rectors on the development of higher education in Germany. Only the state can do this (i.e., the federal government and the *Länder*). The parties must also rethink their higher education policy. Perhaps, with tenacity and patience, we will be able to bring the crowd of 'growth advocates' to an objective view of the situation.

NOTES

German text © 1993 Christoph Führ. 'Die deutsche Universität – im Kern gesund oder verrottet?' Original manuscript. Translated with permission.

1 C. H. Becker, *Gedanken zur Hoxhschulreform*, Leipzig, Quelle and Meyer, 1919, p. 17.
2 Karl Jaspers, *Erneuerung der Universität. Reden und Schriften 1945/46 mit einem Nachwort von Renato de Rosa*, Heidelberg, Lambert Schneider, 1986, p. 95.
3 *Gutachten zur Hochschulreform. Vom Studienauschuß für Hochschulreform.* Hamburg, 1948. On this point, see Franz Latzelter's important commentary *Abneigung gegen Veränderungen* in DUZ, no. 23, 1983, p. 12. On overall development see: Franz Latzelter, *Die Wissenschaftlichen Hochschulen und ihre Verwaltung*, in *Deutsche Verwaltungsgeschichte*, vol V, edited by Jeserich, Pohl, and von Unruh, pp. 654 ff. and 1284 ff. Stuttgart, Deutsche Verlagsanstalt, 1987.
4 Hermann Heimpel, *Probleme und Problematik der Hochschulreform*. Göttingen, Otto Schwarz, 1956, p. 7. On this point, see: Hartmut Boockmann, *Der Historiker Hermann Heimpel*, Göttingen, Vandenhoeck and Ruprecht, 1990, pp. 38 ff.
5 *Der Spiegel*, vol. 50, 1991, pp. 52 ff.
6 Hartmut Boockmann, *Der Historiker Hermann Heimpel*, op. cit., footnote 143. But, the text by C. H. Becker mentioned in that footnote dates from 1919 and not from 1920.
7 Niklas Luhmann, *Universität als Milieu*. Kleine Schriften. Edited by André Kieserling. Bielefeld, Haux, 1992, p. 74.
8 See note 5.
9 Konzept zur Entwicklung der Hochschulen in Deutschland. Einstimmiger Beschluß des 167. Plenums der Hochschulrektorenkonferenz. Bonn, July 6, 1992. Dokumente zur Hochschulreform, no. 75, 1992.
10 Ibid., pp. 7 ff. and 28.
11 Ibid., p. 28.
12 Ibid., p. 34.
13 Ibid., pp. 30 ff.
14 A short outline of the history of higher education may be found in my introduction to the *German Manual on Higher Education 54*, revised edition, 1992, Stuttgart, Raabe, pp. lxxiiff.
15 Thomas Nipperdey, *Nachdenken über die deutsche Geschichte. Essays.* Munich, C. H. Beck, 1986, p. 40.
16 On this point, see Christoph Führ: 'Die unrealistische Wendung. Rückblick auf Bildungsreformkonzepte der sechziger Jahre,' in *Zeitschrift für Erziehungs- und Sozialwissenschaftliche Forschung*, 2nd ed., 1985, vol. pp. 259–81; *Schulen*

und Hochschulen in der Bundesrepublik Deutschland, Vienna, Böhlau, 1989 (Studien und Dokumentationen zur deutschen Bildungsgeschichte, vol. 39); 'Die Kalkulierbarkeit der Zukunft: Gremien, Pläne und ihre Schicksale – Geplante und Ungeplante Entwicklungen im Bildungsbereich 1970–1990,' in *Deutsche Gesellschaft für Bildungsverwaltung: Bildungsplanung für die Neunziger Jahre*, Frankfurt am Main, 1992.

17 Ludwig Erhard, *Wohlstand für Alle*, 3rd ed., Düsseldorf, ECON-Taschenbuchverlag, 1990, p. 361.

18 Hermann Lübbe, *Freiheit statt Emanzipationzwang*, Zürich, Edition Interfrom, 1991, p. 112.

19 Walter Rüegg (ed.), *Die Johann Wolfgang Goethe-Universität* 1964, Annual, 1966, introduction.

20 See note 7.

21 Cf. note 10.

22 Adolf Löwe, 'Das gegenwärtige Bildungsproblem der Deutschen Universität,' in *Die Erziehung*, vol. 7, 1932, Leipzig, Quelle und Meyer, p. 1.

23 Hermann Heller, 'Universitätsreform,' in *Die Neue Rundschau*, Berlin and Leipzig, S. Fischer, 1931, p. 685.

24 Ibid.

25 Cf. note 22.

Part II
Standards and assessment

6 Schooling standards in England and Germany: some summary comparisons bearing on economic performance [1986]

S. J. Prais and Karin Wagner

INTRODUCTION

This article is written from an economist's point of view; it asks: are there any clear differences in the schooling systems of two advanced industrialised countries such as Britain and Germany which are likely to bear on their economic performance? The question follows from our previous comparisons which drew attention to the much greater extent of vocational qualification in Germany; this – rather than the number of university graduates – was the main difference between the 'productive quality' of the labour forces of these countries (60 per cent of the German labour force attained apprenticeship or similar intermediate-type examined qualifications, compared with 30 per cent at the most in Britain). German vocational training appeared particularly ahead in those occupations where mathematics, or even basic arithmetic, was involved – complex circuitry for electricians, book-keeping for office workers. It is thus necessary to ask: (1) whether the German schooling system is more effective on the whole in preparing pupils for the requirements of subsequent technical and commercial training; and (2) whether Germany has a particular advantage in school attainments in mathematics. Looked at from the point of view of critics of British schooling, the latter question asks whether mathematical schooling is backward – not simply when judged by some absolute or ideal standard (a question often asked, but which lacks teeth) – but when judged by what is attained in practice in another industrial European country, Germany; and, if so, whether there are implications for educational policy.[1]

As is familiar, considerable difficulties arise in making educational comparisons between countries. In some ways these are as difficult as – though not necessarily more difficult than – those routinely faced by economists in comparing standards of living between countries which may have different climates, different price structures and different social values. Such a very large proportion of national resources is devoted to education that even approximate comparisons of schooling attainments should be of help in encouraging wiser resource-disposition, notwithstanding methodological reservations: evaluations cannot be avoided simply because they are difficult. It must however be said at the outset that there is clearly scope for more detailed work.

The article begins by outlining the German system of tripartite selective schooling. It then describes the standards of education aimed at by the three main types of school, and compares the proportions of pupils reaching those standards with those in England. Special attention is given to attainments in the middle and lower half of the ability range, from which many pupils go on to apprenticeship and vocational training; it is in the education of this stratum that the greatest differences are found between Germany and England. The results and implications are brought together in a concluding section. Appendices deal with more detailed matters: comparisons of attainments in mathematics in the two countries in sample tests today (Appendix 6.1) and twenty years ago (Appendix 6.2).

THREE TYPES OF GERMAN SCHOOLS

The German selective system of education differs not only (and obviously) from the present British comprehensive system, but also from the previous British selective system. There are three main types of secondary school in Germany: the middle type, the *Realschule*, is perhaps the most interesting for the British reader, and may be considered as lying between the two previous British main types, the grammar and secondary modern schools. The middle type has more than tripled in numbers of pupils in the past twenty years; at the beginning of this decade it became the most important type in terms of numbers of pupils reaching the corresponding school-leaving standard.[2]

Selection of type of secondary school to be attended by a pupil takes place at ages 10–12 on the basis of guidance given to parents by teachers, having regard to the pupil's ability. The move towards comprehensive schools has made very limited progress in Germany. These schools need not detain us here though we should note that, where they have been instituted, they run in parallel to the selective schools; a parent may be advised to choose a secondary modern, rather than a comprehensive, school for his child because it offers smaller and more suitable classes. There are subsequent opportunities to move from one type of school to another in the light of progress, or lack of it.

At the end of their schooling, pupils who attain the prescribed leaving-standard for the type of school attended are awarded the appropriate certificate. A pupil at one of the higher types of school who does not attain the prescribed leaving-standard may be awarded a certificate corresponding to a lower type; someone who does sufficiently well in a lower type of school may subsequently attain the equivalent of a higher school-leaving certificate at an evening or continuation school. Details of the regulations governing schools and examinations vary amongst the *Länder*;

to keep this study within the limits of our resources (and within readable limits), in what follows we concentrate on Berlin, where the minimum school-leaving age is 16, as in Britain – elsewhere it is usually 15. We shall however occasionally refer to conditions in other *Länder*.[3]

The numbers of pupils in a recent year leaving each type of school, and the numbers receiving certificates of completion of schooling to the corresponding standard, are summarised in Table 6.1. It will be seen that there is a substantial difference between these two sets of numbers, reflecting the possibilities of moving from one grade of certificate to another. This flexibility is of great importance in making a selective system work in a politically acceptable way. Every parent wants the best type of school for his child: but he does not wish to opt for too difficult a type of school, since his child might be obliged to repeat classes if he does not reach the requisite standard at the end of each year. In considering reasons for higher school standards, the discipline exerted by the reality of the threat of having to repeat classes must be kept very much in mind; it is normal practice in German (as well as French) secondary schools, but virtually unknown in English state schools today.

The three main types of school in Germany are known as: *Gymnasium, Realschule*, and *Hauptschule*; the details are as follows.[4]

Gymnasium

This type corresponds to the English grammar school with a sixth form,[5] and prepares for university entrance: the curriculum is broad and has a classical leaning; two foreign languages are obligatory, and a third is possible (with Latin, and sometimes also Greek, as options).[6] The final leaving certificate is known as *Abitur* or *Hochschulreife*: this gives legal rights of entrance to universities, subject only to limits on the number of places available in costly departments, such as medicine, which operate a *Numerus clausus*. In 1982 a total of some 210,000 pupils attained university entrance requirements of this type.

A more or less equivalent but more technically based certificate, the *Fachhochschulreife*, was awarded by technical or vocational full-time upper schools (schools similar to our colleges of further education or sixth form colleges) attended by 17- to 19-year olds who have attained a school-leaving certificate of a lower level; this certificate permits entry to courses at *Technische Hochschulen* (technical universities), and was awarded to some 70,000 pupils in 1982.

In relation to the average population in the age group 17 to 19 (1.03 million), we may say that a total of some 28 per cent attained German university entrance requirements in 1982; this was over double the proportion a decade earlier.

Table 6.1 Broad summary of the German selective system of schooling and school-leaving standards, 1982

Type of school		School-leaving standard		% of German pupils	
English approx. equivalent	German name	English approx. equivalent	German name	Leaving these schools	Attaining this standard[a]
Grammar school with 6th form	Gymnasium	A-levels for university entry	Abitur[b]	24	28
Secondary: O-level type	Realschule	5 O-level passes	Realschulabschluß	26	34
Secondary modern	Hauptschule	5 CSE passes	Hauptschulabschluß	41	29
Comprehensive	Gesamtschule	(As above)	(Various – as above)	4	—
Special school	Sonderschule	Leavers without certificate	Abgänger ohne Abschluß[c]	5	9
				100	100

Source: Bildung und Kultur (Fachserie 11/1, 11/2). Statistisches Bundesamt, 1982
Notes:
[a] Including school-leavers from other full-time schools who attained this standard (see text)
[b] Including *Fachhochschulreife*
[c] Three-quarters of pupils from special schools leave without a certificate: the remainder mostly attain a *Hauptschulabschluß* (see text)

Realschule

This type of school also has selective entry, dependent on ability. It has an explicitly modern and applied curriculum, with a scientific rather than a classical leaning: a foreign language, usually English, is obligatory (Latin is not available, even as an option, at these schools). In some ways these schools are similar to the English technical and central (commercial) schools, as they were before the move to a system of comprehensive schools. Teaching is provided till the age of 16, and the final standard aimed at may be taken, for the moment, as roughly that of GCE O-level. In 1982 some 420,000 pupils of full-time schools attained the *Realschulabschluß* (sometimes known as *Mittlere Reife*), the intermediate school-leaving certificate aimed at by this type of school.

The majority, 240,000, came from these *Realschulen*; another 80,000 came from full-time vocational schools (mainly *Berufsfachschulen*) which cater for those from the lower type of school (the *Hauptschulen* described below) who wish to continue or extend their general or vocational education; a further 40,000 were pupils of *Gymnasien* who left early or for other reasons did not attain their final leaving standard; and the remainder came from a few *Hauptschulen* with optional upper classes, and from comprehensive schools. Deducting the 85,000 who went on to obtain higher-level certificates (*Fachhochschulreife* and *Abitur*) we arrive at a net total of 340,000, or about 34 per cent of all school-leavers in 1982, who attained this intermediate certificate as their highest level of general schooling.

Hauptschulen

These are the main general schools, and correspond to the English secondary modern schools. A total of 420,000 pupils left these schools in 1982, of whom 78 per cent attained the requisite school-leaving certificate, the *Hauptschulabschluß*. A further 10 per cent of leavers attained the higher level of *Realschulabschluß*, and were included in the preceding category.

The *Hauptschulabschluß* is usually the minimum certificate required for all except unskilled jobs. A pupil leaving without such a certificate may subsequently attain an equivalent certificate at day-release schooling, or at evening classes, or in various forms of vocational full-time schooling. Including those from higher types of schools who were able to attain only this lower level, and those from vocational schools, a total of some 370,000 pupils attained a *Hauptschulabschluß* as a result of full-time schooling in 1982. As above, we must reduce this total to allow for those who go on to take higher certificates at full-time continuation schools (*Berufsfachschulen*), who numbered 80,000 in 1982 as mentioned above.

The total leaving their full-time schooling with *Hauptschulabschluß* as their highest certificate was thus about 290,000, or 29 per cent of the age group.

No satisfactory school-leaving certificate

Those leaving without any satisfactory school-leaving certificate totalled 100,000 – about 10 per cent of the age group – of whom 50,000 came from *Hauptschulen*, 40,000 from special schools (catering for the educationally disadvantaged) and the remaining 10,000 from comprehensive and higher types of school.[7]

It is clear that there are great difficulties in comparisons with England, where 90 per cent of all secondary school pupils now attend comprehensive schools.[8] A gradual move from a selective schooling system took place in Britain over the preceding two decades – though we need not go back very far to find a system much closer in its broad features to that of present-day Germany. In 1965, for example, 26 per cent of all secondary pupils in England and Wales are at grammar schools (including direct-grant schools), about 5 per cent in technical and selective central schools, 49 per cent in modern schools, about 12 per cent in comprehensive and multilateral schools (and 8 per cent in private schools);[9] note, however, the narrowness of what might be regarded as the intermediate sector in technical schools.

Given the present-day differences in schooling structures of the two countries, the simplest way to compare attainments between them seems to be to take the number of pupils attaining particular levels at final examinations in Germany, and to estimate the number of pupils attaining approximately corresponding levels in England.

NUMBER ATTAINING UNIVERSITY ENTRANCE STANDARDS

We begin our detailed matching of schooling attainments at the top of the academic tree with requirements for entry to 'higher education'. In Germany, as mentioned, this is the *Abitur* or equivalent examination, usually taken at the age of 19–20 by those completing the *Gymnasium* type of school.

In England entrance requirements vary with the subject to be studied at university: broadly speaking, passes are required at GCE A-level in two or three subjects at appropriate grades. The total number attaining at least three A-levels (including those of the lowest grade, E) from schools and FE colleges was about 80,000; and at least two passes were obtained by 117,000, corresponding to about 15 per cent of the age group. It is however usually not possible to gain admittance to most university courses with only two passes at the lowest grade; a 50/50 chance of acceptance probably occurs at about five points on the UCCA scale, which corresponds to approximately 10 per cent of all school-leavers.[10]

In Germany, as noted above, some 28 per cent attained school-leaving certificates entitling them to admission to a German university. In *nominal* terms it appears therefore that Germany prepares two or three times the British proportion for university entrance. Before arriving at any judgement on the *reality*, we must consider the scope and level of the school courses leading to university entrance in the two countries, the numbers admitted to universities, and the numbers ultimately gaining university degrees.

Until 1972 the German *Abitur* award was based on achievements in about nine subjects; there was some choice, but it is important here to notice that *mathematics was obligatory for all pupils till the age of 18* (the 'twelfth class'), and study of the native language, science and a foreign language were obligatory for a further year. Thus a broad common core of subjects continued to be obligatory for all German pupils in that age group. Written final examinations were set in three subjects – usually German, a foreign language, and mathematics or a second foreign language; satisfactory course-assessments were required in other subjects. These examinations were set separately by each school, subject to central approval. Remarkably enough, there is no wholly externally set examination at this level as there is in Britain, and as for the *Realschulen* in many *Länder*, as considered below.

The broader scope of the German syllabus as compared with the two or three subjects passed at A-level required in England might be expected to entail a lower standard in each of the subjects at school-leaving level in Germany. Such differences are well illustrated by the results of the *International Study of Achievement in Mathematics*, an investigation carried out in 1963–4 which administered similar test papers to samples of students at various ages in a dozen countries.[11] One of the sets of comparisons ('population 3a') related to school pupils in their pre-university year who specialised in mathematics; in England the sample included those science students taking an A-level mathematics course, and in Germany it included those at *Gymnasium* who had chosen scientific options rather than languages or classical options. The English sample attained an average mark in mathematics of 35.2, which was only slightly below the highest average mark in the sample of a dozen countries of 36.4; while the German sample reached only 28.8. Equally important: the English advantage was obtained despite an average age in the sample nearly two years below that of the German sample – 17 years 11 months compared with 19 years 10 months. British A-level mathematics thus seems fairly clearly to have been in advance of the German *Abitur* level.

But this advantage applied only to those who specialised in the sixth form in mathematics or sciences.[12] For the majority of pupils, those who were not mathematical specialists in their final school-year ('population 3b' in the above study), the ordering was reversed: the English sample averaged only 21.4 points, while the Germans – with their obligatory mathematics courses for all students at that level – averaged 27.7 points.

The latter mark was only marginally below that attained by German mathematical 'specialists': the reason for this similarity was, as explained above, that the German *Abitur* course did not involve a great deal of specialisation.[13]

There is no obvious way of deciding whether the English narrower curriculum taken at a higher standard is, in any general way, 'worth' more or less than the German broader curriculum taken at a lower standard. But from our particular point of view, that is, our interest in the role of schools in providing preparation for life and work in a technically complex economy, it is worth emphasising that *the majority of those entering university had a higher mathematical competence in Germany* than in Britain. The cost of this broader curriculum was substantial, and is reflected in the two-year later age of completion of upper secondary schooling.

As from 1972 there has been a somewhat greater degree of specialisation in German 'sixth forms' in the final years, that is, at ages 18 and 19. Final written examinations in two major and two minor chosen subjects (instead of 'a common core', as previously) are now the usual requirements for the *Abitur*. The breadth of the taught curriculum and the associated school assessments in other subjects have not appreciably contracted in scope; irrespective of a pupil's plans for subsequent specialisation at university, mathematics and the native language remain obligatory at school till the age of 18.[14] It is thus important not to overstate the extent of recent changes.

In 1982, 210,000 German students entered university, equivalent to some 22 per cent of the relevant age group.[15] In the UK in 1981–2 there were some 75,000 new full-time (home) university students studying for a first degree,[16] equivalent to some 8 per cent of the age group; for comparison with Germany, it is probably correct to add the approximately 46,000 who entered polytechnics and other institutes of further education in England for full-time degree courses, so bringing the proportion to 14%.[17]

The proportion entering higher education in Germany is thus roughly half as great again as in Britain, that is, an additional 8 per cent of the age group reach that level. It must however immediately be said that the student 'drop out' rate is considerably higher in Germany, with the ultimate result that the number of graduates with first degrees emerging from the German university system is very similar to that in Britain.[18]

Germany's advantage thus lies at the level just below the top – in bringing more pupils up to university *entrance* requirements, and in allowing more of them to start a university course; after that there is a greater element of 'selectivity' than in Britain. In Britain, the selection can be thought of as taking place before university entrance; once accepted by a university, a student is normally expected to be able to proceed to a degree. Within the same broad total of graduates, the Germans nevertheless seem to have an advantage from an economic point of view, in that the mix of subjects of study has a greater practical and vocational emphasis – especially on engineering and technology.[19]

REALSCHULABSCHLUß AND GCE/CSE EXAMINATIONS

Let us now move one step closer to education for the world of work and commerce. We saw in the second section (p. 96) that about a third of all German pupils leave school with an 'intermediate' school-leaving certificate (the *Realschulabschluß* – sometimes termed *Mittlere Reife*) which was provisionally described there as roughly equivalent to O-levels in Britain. These qualifications are usually taken at age 16 + in both countries. We here consider in a little more detail the requirements for this certificate, so as to be able to select the nearest English equivalent, and estimate the proportion of pupils in England that reach it. This is done most simply in relation to those German *Länder* where central examinations are set at this level (Baden-Württemberg, Bavaria, Saarland, Schleswig-Holstein); standards amongst these and other *Länder* are kept at a more or less comparable level by negotiation at the Federal level, and with the help of the Schools Inspectorate. (The latter, incidentally, has a much more active role in Germany than its counterpart in Britain; it is specifically concerned with assessing the performance of *individual teachers*, and not just in assessing 'teaching' as a whole – the vaguer task assigned to the Inspectorate here.)

A core of three subjects – mathematics, German and a foreign language – is usually obligatory in the final written examinations for the *Realschulabschluß*, together with one or two optional subjects (depending on the *Land*) in which the final tests may be written or oral. There also have to be satisfactory class-achievements in the remaining subjects of the curriculum; a total of some ten subjects enters the final assessment. The qualification is thus similar to, but rather broader in scope than, the earlier English 'matriculation level' which required passes (or 'credits') in five or six subjects – of which English, mathematics, science and a foreign language often formed an obligatory core (requirements varied amongst the examination boards). The German examination is of the type called in Britain a 'group' examination, and differs markedly from the present British GCE and CSE examinations, which are based on single subjects.

Whether a candidate attains the *Realschulabschluß* depends on his *average* attainment in the various subjects. He need not quite reach a 'pass-mark' (a mark of 4, corresponding to about 50 per cent correct answers) in every subject, but there is the restriction that an outright 'fail' (a mark of 6) is not permitted in a core subject: a 'near fail' (a mark of 5) is tolerated in no more than two subjects, and only if compensated by above average marks in other subjects (the regulations vary). Those who fail these requirements are permitted to repeat the final school class and then re-submit themselves for the qualification; but re-sitting of the examination is permitted *only once*, and all subjects have to be assessed at the same time – again differing from England, where individual subjects can be taken in different years. Not everyone who has been awarded a *Realschulabschluß* has thus necessarily passed (a mark of 4 or better) his final examination in mathematics – though perhaps nine out of ten pupils normally do so. In any event, it remains important that every pupil in his final year is obliged to take a mathematics course, knows that his leaving-certificate as a whole depends on his mark in mathematics, and knows he dare not fail completely in this subject. All this is bound to affect positively the incentives to persevere in this subject, and thus provide more pupils with a foundation for subsequent vocational training, whether in technical or in commercial occupations.

If we were to ask simply what proportion of pupils left school in England with an O-level pass (that is, at levels A–C, and treating a CSE grade 1 as equivalent) in three comparable 'core' subjects – English, mathematics and a modern language – we would find only 12.2 per cent of all school-leavers reached that standard in 1980–1 (this relates to pupils leaving school without A-levels). If we added a science subject, making a core of four subjects, the proportion passing falls to 10.5 per cent; a similar proportion (9.6 per cent) passed in five or more subjects, taken without restrictions as to their composition.[20] In addition we might add here a proportion of the 3 per cent of pupils who left school with just one A-level pass and who probably obtained some O-level passes. It would be unusual for pupils to be permitted to stay on for A-levels if they had not passed four subjects at O-level, amongst which mathematics might well have been included: perhaps two-thirds of this group may be added here for comparison with Germany.[21] Some allowance might also be made for those who made up their O-levels after finishing school by attending colleges of further education and the like: another 1 per cent might be allowed for this group.[22] In total, therefore, it appears that something like 14 per cent of British pupils leave full-time schooling with a good intermediate level of attainment, that is, with less than two A-levels, but having passed O-level examinations in a core of subjects to some extent comparable in scope to the German *Realschulabschluß*.

This is less than half the German proportion – a gap which seems surprisingly large. Are the German examinations perhaps of a lower standard, though taken at much the same age? We took specimen examination papers for two 'core' subjects, French and mathematics, and asked secondary school teachers in each country to compare them (attainments in English and German were not compared, since the native language of the one country is of course the foreign language in the other). By taking both GCE and CSE papers in England – that is, tests set for 16-year olds at two levels of difficulty – we were able to ask where in that range the corresponding German *Realschule* examinations should be placed.

Tests in French

We compare examinations in French first, since they more readily illus-
trate important differences between the two countries in the breadth of
attainments tested by their respective examinations. The German assessor
thought the level of the CSE paper more suitable for 14-year olds than
for final year pupils at *Realschule*; for example, part of the CSE test was
based on a French passage and required answers in English to questions
set in English – whereas in the *Realschule* test the questions and the
required answers were in French. The *Realschule* test also included an
essay to be written in French (100 words on, for example, my first day at
school), a reply to a French letter (asking questions on familiar topics –
80 words about your family, home, and so forth), and a simple oral test.
The GCE O-level papers were judged by the German assessor as suitable
for 16-year olds at *Realschule*, though parts of the examination were
appropriate to pupils one or two years younger (especially the listening-
comprehension tests, which required answers to be ticked from a multiple-
choice list).

The English assessors found the standard of difficulty of the *Realschule*
tests in French somewhat below that implied in *some* of the O-level
questions: one of the translations from French in the O-level paper was
of a higher standard and clearly influenced this judgement.

In arriving at a judgement of these views, the important points to
remember are that the German education system is largely based on
selection by ability, and that classes may be repeated by slower pupils:
hence a more uniform standard is attained in the final year than in
Britain. The English O-level examinations cater both for those who leave
school at 16 and for those who hope to go on to A-levels and then to
university. Consequently, O-level questions need to cover a wider range
of difficulty than the *Realschule* test, which is designed specifically for
those leaving school at that age. A pass-mark at GCE O-level, it was
thought by the German assessors, would not require a standard higher
than that required to pass in the final year at *Realschule*; but this is not
inconsistent with the O-level paper also serving the purpose of showing
which pupils came into the 'high-flyer' category.[23]

Tests in mathematics

We turn next to a comparison of mathematics examinations; as mentioned, this is of special interest because of long-standing concern in
Britain as to the standards of mathematics taught in its schools. Surprisingly enough, when an official Committee of Inquiry was eventually set
up in 1978 to consider the teaching of mathematics in schools in England
and Wales, it devoted scant attention to standards abroad – there seem

to have been no comparisons of examination papers or indicators of attainments at various ages in other countries.[24]

Our exchange of test papers yielded conclusions both on the scope of the syllabus, and on levels of difficulty.[25] The scope of the syllabus in the *Realschule* tests was narrower on balance. There were no calculus or matrices – topics included in recent British O-level papers, though they are of more interest to those proceeding to higher levels of mathematical study. On the other hand, more solid and co-ordinate geometry was covered in the German papers, which is probably useful for those going on to technician courses and practical craftwork (drawing offices, fitters). The British assessor thought that the *Realschule* test, even after allowing for a narrower syllabus, was above O-level in its difficulty – it probably lay somewhere between O-level and AO-level (the Advanced or Additional Ordinary examinations in mathematics passed by about 4 per cent of English pupils).

The German assessor thought that the GCE O-level mathematics paper was quite suitable for final-year pupils at a *Realschule*, but lacked more advanced questions lying within the scope of the narrower German syllabus. The broader British syllabus would be covered by those pupils in the final *Realschule* year who had taken 'further mathematics' as one of their optional subjects (pupils in most of these schools have the opportunity of specialising to a certain extent; other options are, for example, a second foreign language, or an additional science subject).

Putting it all together, we concluded that the *Realschule* mathematics standard was somewhat higher than O-level, but the gap is unlikely to be great.

Within that top stratum, it seems that the very best English pupils, those at grammar schools, did well in comparison with those at *Realschule*. This emerges from the international comparisons carried out in the 1960s by the IEA (referred to above in connection with A-level attainments; further details are in Appendix 6.2). These showed that at age 13 grammar school pupils in England attained an average mark of 41, compared with an average for *Realschule* pupils at that age of 32. The difficulty with this comparison is that the strata of the ability range are not quite the same in the two countries. Grammar school pupils accounted for 20–25 per cent of the *top* of the ability range; whereas *Realschule* pupils came from the stratum just below that. Nonetheless, it needs to be said that *at this very top level* in England, mathematical standards at schools seemed satisfactory according to this comparison.

Proportion of pupils with broad O-level attainments

The above comparisons of test-papers in French and mathematics, it may be reiterated at this stage, have been taken only as examples of the larger number of subjects that are assessed for the *Realschulabschluß*. If we are prepared to accept that they are not untypical of other subjects, we are bound to conclude that the German school system brings a very much higher proportion of its school-leavers up to a broadly based intermediate standard: about one in three of all pupils leaves school at 16 in Germany having attained the equivalent of O-level passes in at least four core subjects, compared with one in seven in England. We have noted in the previous section of this article that Germany also has a considerable advantage in the proportion of pupils staying on till 18–19 and reaching university entrance standards (28 and 14 per cent, respectively). Taken together, the contrast may be put as follows: *over half of all German pupils, compared with only just over a quarter of all pupils in England, attain a standard above or equivalent to a broadly based set of O-level passes.* A similar contrast emerged in comparisons, by Miss Dundas-Grant, between France and England of general schooling attainments at O-level standards.[26]

To summarise our various comparisons of attainments in the curriculum as a whole for the upper part of the ability range: the main difference between the countries lies in the greater breadth of the curriculum in Germany that is assessed for their school-leaving certificates. In other words, the German pupil in the upper ability ranges specialises less at school than does his English counterpart; consequently the cleft between the 'two cultures' (cf. C. P. Snow, the 'arts versus the sciences') is less serious in Germany than here – that cleft is in many ways an especially English problem which has its foundations in the features of the schooling system considered above. There also seems little doubt that something like double the proportion of pupils in Germany than in England reaches standards comparable to O-level passes in a group of 'core' subjects.

STANDARDS OF ATTAINMENT OF THE LOWER HALF

So far we have been concerned with the attainments of those who broadly come in the top half in their school performance: but the importance of schooling attainments for the lower half must not be undervalued. Our earlier comparisons of vocational training have shown that the German system has been very effective in achieving high vocational standards – especially remarkable for those occupations recruiting from the lower half of the spectrum.[27] With growing automation in industrial and office work, and the associated fall in demand for unskilled workers, great attention needs now to be given everywhere to raising schooling standards attained by this section.

A feature common to both countries is the lack of any general external school examination system directed specifically towards this group of pupils (apart from Baden-Württemberg, considered below, and Bavaria). However, the Germans have something approaching it, namely, a leaving-certificate testifying to satisfactory attainments in schools corresponding

to our secondary modern schools: the standards required for this certificate are designed to be within the reach of the great majority, but not
quite all, of such pupils. There are strong incentives for pupils in such
schools to avoid being amongst the minority of 'failures'. There are also
other significant differences in schooling practice which seem likely to
bear on subsequent attitudes to work. We shall focus here on differences
in, first, the breadth of the curriculum; second, attainments in mathematics; and, third, the coverage of vocational studies.

The examined curriculum

In England the GCE/CSE system of examinations at age 16 has been
directed to the top 60 per cent of pupils; the same applies to the plans
so far announced for the new system to come into effect in 1988 to be
known as the General Certificate of Secondary Education. Many below
that level have attempted these examinations but, as has often been
observed, it is clearly unsatisfactory that so many of the examination
questions – and the associated teaching – are bound to lie beyond the
reach of the lower half of pupils, and that those topics which lie within
their reach form part of a syllabus with too academic a slant. Topics of
an applied or vocationally relevant kind are generally better in stimulating
the motivation of those who are less academically inclined, and consequently improve their attainments.[28]

Partly as a result of the introduction of new lower grades of 'passing
qualifications', the proportion of pupils in England achieving some kind
of graded result in a public examination has risen sharply in the past
fifteen years: whereas in 1966–7 some 49 per cent left school without a
graded result in a public examination in even a single subject, by 1982–3
that proportion had fallen to a mere 10 per cent.[29] The main rise however
was in the category obtaining 'lower grade' passes in one or more subjects,
that is, O-level grades D or E, or CSE grades 2 to 5 (those with five
higher grade O-level passes or with A-levels rose only from 23 to 27 per
cent). A CSE grade 4, generally regarded as the notional CSE pass-mark,
in mathematics very often requires – as the Cockcroft Report reminded
us – 'little more than 20 per cent' of the marks, and a CSE grade 5 'is
likely to be awarded to a candidate who scores little more than 20 per
cent of the marks'.[30] The span of ability covered by CSE grades is clearly
very wide, and it is little wonder that employers have not found it easy
to recognise the value of a CSE certificate.[31]

In mathematics, taken by itself, a substantial proportion leaves school
in England without any 'graded result'. According to the DES samples
of school-leavers for 1982–3, 19 per cent did not attempt any public
examination in mathematics and 7 per cent failed; so that a total of 26
per cent did not obtain any 'graded result'. Some 9 per cent obtained
only a CSE grade 5.[32] Thus, it may be said that some 35 per cent of *all*

school-leavers did not attain any useful mathematical standard. If we interpret these proportions in relation to those classes ('streams' or 'sets') of comprehensive schools which cater for the lower half of the ability range, corresponding to the German *Hauptschulen*, these figures must mean that very few pupils in those classes pass a public examination in mathematics. All this must not be regarded as wholly surprising, since the notional CSE pass-mark – a grade 4 – is intended to reflect the level of ability of the *average* 16-year-old pupil. It was only towards the end of 1982 that an experimental series of mathematical tests was announced by the government intended for the lowest 40 per cent not specifically catered for by existing public examinations (reports were expected in 1986).[33]

Turning now to Germany: the *Hauptschulen* – the 'main' schools which educate just under half of all secondary school children – generally have a system of internal examinations on the basis of which a leaving-certificate is issued (the *Hauptschulabschluß*, or Main School Leaving Certificate) attesting to the satisfactory completion of the school course. Seven out of eight pupils who left *Hauptschulen* in 1982 in Germany as a whole attained their certificates. Of those who left without receiving such a certificate, some failed the requirements of their final school year; others may not have reached the top class because they were obliged to repeat previous classes, and left on reaching the minimum school-leaving age.

As at other educational levels described in previous sections, the *Hauptschulabschluß* is based on attainments in, usually, about ten subjects. The curriculum has less choice, and includes mathematics and a foreign language (usually English) as obligatory throughout the *Hauptschule*. There is the restriction of no outright failure (a grade 6) in more than one subject, and a near-fail (grade 5) is tolerated in a second subject only if compensated by above-average marks in other subjects. A *Hauptschul-abschluß*, whether from school or from a college of further education, is often a pre-requisite for subsequent acceptance in anything other than unskilled occupations; these requirements provide pupils in their final school years with practical motivation for attaining satisfactory marks in the curriculum as a whole.

The most important contrast with Britain is that – even in this school stratum which caters for those in the lower half of the ability range – the great majority of German pupils are expected to attain a certificated standard; equally important, the award is based on attainments in the curriculum as a whole. The aspirations and norms of pupils and their schools are thus inevitably different from those of the British system, where only a minority of those in the lower half are expected to attain certificated standards in basic core subjects. To put it more narrowly, a German pupil must try harder to avoid failing in a core subject, such as mathematics or writing his native language, than a pupil in England: a failure in one of those subjects might mean that he leaves without a satisfactory leaving-certificate, whereas in England he might still receive a certificate on passing some other subject.

It must be added that employers' complaints in Germany about the standards of 'present-day' *Hauptschulabschlüsse* seem as frequent as those to be heard in Britain in relation to CSEs: and German employers also often set written tests to those applying straight from school for work in order to obtain a clearer impression of their ability. But this does not of course mean that standards actually achieved, or aimed at, are the same in the two countries. In contrast to Britain, the syllabus for each school is centrally laid down in each *Land*, and only approved text books can be used. While the Federal co-ordination of *Hauptschulabschluß* standards has still some way to go, the extent of variation in what is taught is far from being as large as that which occurs in Britain.

Attainments in mathematics

How do actual school attainments for this section of pupils compare in the two countries? We confine ourselves to mathematics (as mentioned, it is easier to compare across countries than other subjects, and it is particularly relevant to many technical and commercial occupations).

The main differences were apparent from the large-scale comparisons on international educational achievement (the 'IEA' studies) carried out in 1964; in addition to the samples of pupils mentioned in previous sections, samples of pupils were taken by the IEA at age 13 with the intention of representing the full breadth of the ability range. In practice, the choice of those samples for England and Germany met with certain problems which make difficult any simple comparison for the samples as published; however, after making allowances for a difference in the average age of the samples in the two countries (as explained in Appendix 6.2), the sections of the samples relating to the lower half of the ability range – those chosen from secondary modern schools in England and from *Hauptschulen* in Germany – can be compared satisfactorily.

Based on internationally agreed tests, the IEA inquiry yielded adjusted average scores of 12.9 for secondary modern pupils in England, and 22.4 for *Hauptschule* pupils in Germany: a gap of 9.5 points. From that inquiry it also appears that a one year difference in ages is associated with some 4.4 points in average achievements of secondary modern pupils: the difference between the English and German average scores can thus be said to be equivalent to an English lag behind Germany of something like two years of schooling. Another way of expressing the contrast is to note that the German average for the *lower half* of the ability range was close to the average for *all* English pupils (the latter attained an average score of 20.1 after adjusting to the same age),[34] that is to say, the German system had raised the average attainment of its *weakest* 50 per cent of pupils to that of the average of *all* pupils in England.[35]

The IEA tests have been criticised in that much depends on the relation between the coverage of the tests and the coverage of the syllabuses: much depends also on the training and ability of the teachers. In other words, English pupils are not necessarily more stupid than German pupils, nor are English teachers less competent than those in Germany with equal qualifications, experience and tasks. All this may be agreed – but it does not contradict the broad implications of these findings. The investigation was guided by an international committee including an English representative (from the National Foundation for Educational Research); the questions were pre-tested in a number of stages; 'drastic criticism' from England based on the pre-tests was taken into account in preparing the final test. There was no German representative on the pre-test committee. It seems therefore unlikely that English pupils could have been at any substantial relative disadvantage in respect of the relevance of the tests.[36]

The poorer relative achievements of English pupils, it must be emphasised, were confined to those in the secondary modern streams; as noted above and in Appendix 6.2, pupils at grammar schools at ages 13–14, and sixth form English mathematicians and scientists, were ahead of their German counterparts.

Poor performance by the lower half of the ability range in school mathematics in England has been noted in many official reports. The 1979 survey of secondary schools in England by HM Inspectors noted that comprehensive schools (as they had almost all become by that time) had 'particular difficulties' in mathematical provision 'for their less able pupils: in nearly one half of the schools the provision for these pupils was unsatisfactory'. The inspectors made *strong* recommendations[37] for new courses in mathematics in comprehensive schools for 56 per cent of classes catering for less able pupils, while for pupils that were *more* able, new courses were strongly recommended for only 6 per cent of classes.[38] There can thus be no doubt that serious problems continue to surround mathematical teaching for the lower half of the ability range in England.

A bluff insular standpoint characterised the work of the official Cockcroft Committee of Inquiry into the teaching of mathematics in schools (disarmingly it said, 'Our terms of reference have not required us to study the teaching of mathematics in other countries . . .'), and consequently it failed – in our view – to bring home adequately the gravity of the problem.[39] Nevertheless, the Committee's Report devoted five pages (pp. 135–40) to a proposed curriculum – 'a foundation list of mathematical topics' – specifically intended for the bottom 40 per cent of pupils. Because of the decentralised system of education, there is no governmental machinery in England for imposing this or, indeed, any other curriculum on English schools; and the lack of qualified mathematics teachers would in any event present an obstacle.[40] That proposals for a better syllabus for the 'lower half' had to be brought forward in 1982, virtually as if on a blank slate (that is, without referring to any previous syllabus or detailed experience in teaching provision for this section), in itself demonstrates the seriousness of England's schooling problems.[41] The above comparisons add to the concern that public policy has for so long failed to intervene adequately on a matter affecting such a large fraction of the population on such an important issue.

Recent comparisons in mathematics

Our more recent comparisons yielded very similar conclusions. Our broadest comparisons relate to Baden-Württemberg: pupils in a cross-section of *Hauptschulen* there have been awarded their final leaving-certificates on the basis of centrally set tests since 1977, and the new system has become obligatory for all schools there since 1984. The results for some 5,000 pupils in 111 *Hauptschulen* in 1984 were compared with mathematical attainment of English 15–16-year olds, as shown by representative samples of *all* pupils in England tested by the DES Assessment of Performance Unit in recent years. Details are set out in Appendix 6.1 below. The conclusion reached there is again that German pupils in the *lower half* of the ability range have a substantially higher level of attainment in basic arithmetical processes than the average of all pupils in England (for example, 75 per cent of German pupils from their secondary modern schools could answer correctly a sum involving additions and subtractions of decimals compared with only a quarter of *all* English pupils who answered a similar sum correctly).

Preliminary results of the 1981 IEA international comparisons in mathematics show English pupils in much the same relation to the other countries as the earlier studies (below Japan and Hungary, but better than Nigeria, for example); Germany did not participate in this inquiry.[42]

Our other comparisons of mathematical schooling with Germany were more limited in coverage of pupils, but added a realistic touch. A specimen British CSE Mathematics paper was judged by two Berlin teachers of mathematics to be a suitable test of achievements for those in their final year at *Hauptschule*, in that the majority of pupils in such schools would be expected to pass (grade 4 or better). The remarkable point is that the lowest 40 per cent of German pupils is to be found in *Hauptschulen*, while CSE tests are specifically designed for pupils above that level in England. The CSE *Arithmetic* paper – which is set at a lower standard than the CSE *Mathematics* paper – was thought too easy(!) for final year *Hauptschule* pupils, but suitable for those a year younger.

Finally, we showed specimen mathematical questions from the *Hauptschulabschluß* at Berlin to teachers in comprehensive schools in England. From the comments received it was clear that the standard in those schools in Germany was significantly above that in the lower comprehensive streams here. Only one in six of pupils in such a class in England was able to attain the German pass-mark, and then only when provided with working hints.

Vocational studies

We turn to the teaching of vocational subjects and career guidance at schools, the importance of which has risen in both countries with the increased length of compulsory schooling. The detailed attention given to these topics by German schools is not sufficiently known in England; wider purposes may be served by providing here a brief outline of the syllabus in these subjects in Berlin, where compulsory education continues to 16 as in the UK, and where this aspect of studies has been especially well developed.[43]

Beginning at age 13 (the 'seventh' class), four periods a week are devoted to what is called *Arbeitslehre*, that is, 'work tuition'; this rises to eight periods a week at ages 15 and 16 (the 'ninth' and 'tenth' classes), of which two periods a week are devoted to career guidance. The latter includes talks given by personnel officers and visits to local places of employment. Three weeks of work at local places of employment are included in the penultimate year to help in choosing a suitable occupation; further work-spells are possible in the final year if no choice of occupation has been made by then.

The subjects covered in the *Arbeitslehre* classes have been developed well beyond the traditional woodwork for boys and cooking or sewing for girls. There is an initial choice among four main options: mechanical technology, electronics, textiles, and household studies. At ages 12 to 14, all pupils – irrespective of their optional subject – are required to take a general course in basic work-techniques: typewriting, filing systems, reading of technical drawings, consumer information, the role of national production standards (DIN), bank accounts and family budgets.

This is accompanied by specialised instruction in the chosen main option. The course at age 14 for someone choosing the 'mechanical technology option', for example, includes both mechanical work – the use of tools in the school workshop on individual and group projects – and a surprising amount of study of the *organisation* of work – the assessment of potential demand for a specimen product, costing, financing, purchase of raw materials (quantity discounts, checking for rejects), packaging, invoicing. Someone choosing the 'household option' would learn at that age, for example, how to plan a week's menu taking into account nutritional requirements, budgetary limits and the daily timetable; or compare costings of washing clothes at home and of sending them to a laundry.

Further specialisation takes place in the last two years at school. A

114 Standards and assessment

pupil who has decided on industrial optional courses would study at the age of 15, with the help of practical exercises, the following topics: (1) artificial materials (for example, thermoplastic and thermosetting materials and their molecular structure, injection-moulding and hot-forming, artificial fibres and the cleaning of clothing made from them, safety regulations in manufacturing PVC, international comparisons of consumption per head of artificial materials); (2) specifications and testing of materials (for example, the various hardnesses and tempers of steel, testing hardness, examining materials for defects, corrosion resistance, flame-resistance of cloth, the role of testing institutions and specifications); (3) automation (for example, comparisons of painting with a brush, with a hand-held spray-gun, and spraying on an automatic line; methods of controlling an automatic process, the use of punched tape and magnetic tape; productivity, cost reductions from automation, the effects of competition). At age 16 a pupil would be expected to have chosen his occupation, and he spends his final year at school on a course more closely related to that choice. He might then study a sample of manufacturing operations in detail (in the paper industry, for example, machinery and processes in making paper, cutting, printing and binding, relevant DIN standards, the history of printing); or he might study industrial control processes (digital and analogue control, open and closed-loop systems, illustrated by an automatic laundry machine and a refrigerator); the class might design and construct a lighting system for the home to be controlled automatically by the level of daylight.

A pupil choosing the 'household options' studies at age 15: *housing* (practical drawing of room-plans with furnishings, comparison of advantages for different family-types of alternative allocations of given areas of housing space, safety in the home, mortgage finance, legal obligations under renting); *family budgeting* (how to keep household accounts, comparison with statistical average 'basket of goods', hire-purchase agreements); and *'socialisation' of the pre-school child* (assessing the suitability of toys, analysing children's TV programmes, child health, costs of child-rearing). In the subsequent year, at age 16, depending on the choice of occupation, such a pupil might choose between specialised courses on social work, or the distributive trades (for example, the use of punched cards, micro-films, flow-charts, decimal classification, calculators: basic statistical concepts up to simple correlation; legal differences between partnerships and companies).

Throughout these classes there is much emphasis on *planning, budgeting and assessment of results*: these terms have virtually become a slogan, their object being to encourage the habit of thinking ahead, and thinking systematically on practical tasks.

Career guidance provided in these final two years helps the pupil to understand the alternative types of training and qualifications open to him on leaving school, the dire consequences of failing his *Abschluß*, the rights and duties of both parties to a training contract, the value of a broad training in safeguarding against the consequences of automation, how to recognise the early signs of occupational obsolescence (short-time working) and what to do about it (re-train early). Part of the course is devoted to setting up in business on your own.

The above details are not isolated aberrations relating to a particular school, but form part of the framework for the curriculum under which all *Hauptschulen* in Berlin are obliged to operate. The regulations vary amongst the *Länder*, both in the time devoted to *Arbeitslehre* and in its content. For example, where compulsory schooling ends at 15, *Arbeitslehre* may be obligatory for only the last three years; in Schleswig-Holstein a traditionally narrower curriculum still prevails; and in the Saarland the number of periods devoted to *Arbeitslehre* is lower than in Berlin but start a year earlier (two periods a week in the 'fifth' and 'sixth' classes, and four periods in the 'seventh' to 'ninth' classes). Nevertheless, a general move may be detected towards the form of instruction described above for Berlin.

The limited attention given to vocational studies in English schools may be inferred from the survey of secondary education by HM Inspectors in 1976–8.[44] Their observations fall under the headings of careers guidance and craft studies. Only about half of comprehensive and modern schools in the sample provided some form of 'careers education programme' for all pupils in their fourth and fifth forms (that is, at ages 15–16); a few more made such provision 'for some pupils'. *The most usual allocation was only one school-period a week.* In 'successful' schools this involved films, talks by visiting speakers and visits to places of employment. Work experience was provided in a similar number of schools, 'mostly for five days or less'.

In relation to the general field of 'craftwork', the Inspectors mentioned woodwork and needlework but, curiously and regrettably, did not explicitly discuss their importance in the timetable. A subsequent survey relating to the more specialised area of 'technology' indicated that about 20 per cent of schools provided such courses, and almost invariably only as optional subjects – obligatory courses were provided in a negligible 1 per cent of all schools (even then, such courses were obligatory only until the third form, that is until about the age of 14.[45] Nevertheless, examination statistics show that craft subjects are relatively popular options; technical drawing was passed at CSE level (grade 4 and above) by the equivalent of 23 per cent of all boys leaving school in 1981, and it is likely that a similar percentage of boys passed in woodwork or metalwork; domestic subjects seem to have been at least as important for girls in terms of CSE passes.[46] These subjects were more important, in terms of number of CSE passes, than history for boys, or French for girls. In some schools the instruction was undoubtedly exemplary.[47] But for less-able pupils, the Inspectors noted that 'sometimes a considerable choice of practical activities was offered, but with little coherence in the curriculum as a whole'. This lack of 'coherence' is probably the clue to the real difficulty, for the average timetable at English schools suggests that a considerable amount of time is devoted to this subject-area. It seems clear also that the courses were not as relevant as in Germany to the workings of modern-day industry and commerce, nor to the proposed occupation of the pupil after leaving school.

In brief, the main contrast between the two countries is that subjects in the general area of vocational studies are obligatory in Germany for the last 4 years of compulsory schooling and have an explicitly practical emphasis: whereas in England there is a very varied pattern – such courses have a *craft* rather than an *industrial* emphasis, and for less-able pupils (in the view of HM Inspectors) the curriculum was particularly unsatisfactory. Perhaps just as remarkable is the lack of knowledge of what, on average, goes on in schools in this subject area; this reflects the view expressed by an English teacher – and quoted by HM Inspectors as summarising the situation – that 'we have no educational system, we have only schools.'[48]

SUMMARY AND DISCUSSION

We started from the question whether German industry's strengths in vocational training and craftsmanship and productivity originated largely at the 'training stage', or whether its origins to any significant extent could be traced to the 'schooling stage'. The simple answer to that question is: Yes, the German schooling system provides a broader curriculum, combined with significantly higher levels of attainment in core subjects, for a greater proportion of pupils than does the English system. Attainments in mathematics by those in the lower half of the ability range in England appear to lag by the equivalent of about two years' schooling behind the corresponding section of pupils in Germany. German schools also provide more pre-vocational instruction than do English schools, and this has a definite commercial and industrial (and not merely 'craft') emphasis: this difference again particularly affects the lower half of the ability range.

These achievements are accompanied by no higher requirements in Germany in respect of resources (pupil–teacher ratios are similar, and the proportion of GDP absorbed by education appears lower in Germany),[49] but curricula are more sharply focused. There is also a stronger superstructure of links amongst German schools which help to co-ordinate the curriculum and to develop teaching material; and there are stronger links between German secondary schools and subsequent vocational schools than in Britain.

The advantage of other countries in the provision of suitable schooling and training for the *average* person – and not merely for the academically gifted – was recognised by some observers as early as the beginning of this century. It was said then, for example, that: 'It is in the abundance of men of ordinary, plodding ability, thoroughly trained and methodically directed, that Germany has so commanding an advantage'.[50] In the present day, when the scope for unskilled labour is so patently being reduced by advances in automation, the need to raise the level of competence of those of average and of below-average ability has acquired an even greater urgency. The British government's current initiatives will undoubtedly assist in increasing vocational training. But until school curricula in England take on a clear direction, it must seem questionable – on the basis of the comparisons in this article – whether the extent and standards of technical and vocational training can approach those current in Germany.

At a more detailed level, perhaps four contrasts deserve emphasis. First, to understand these very complex issues in a balanced way, we must note that differences at the top of the ability spectrum go the other way: comparative tests in the 1960s showed that those English school-leavers specialising in mathematics at A-level reached standards significantly higher than in Germany and, indeed, not exceeded in any other advanced country at schools catering for those of academic ability. Preliminary results of similar comparisons for 1981 indicate that England's advantage for this specialist group has been maintained.[51]

The strengths of the English grammar and 'public' schools are much admired abroad. Some of these strengths reflect an exceptionally early specialisation in the range of subjects studied; but the bulk of pupils do not specialise in mathematics, and finish their schooling with less knowledge of mathematics and science than their counterparts abroad.

The exceptionally high quality of the very best part of the English education system has probably hindered a proper assessment of the limitations of what is provided for those below the top (grammar school) stratum, who form the majority of the population. As pointed out by Professor Benjamin Bloom, one of the main motivators of the international studies referred to, it seems that 'across the world' differences in attainments by 'the bottom 90 per cent' are much greater 'than amongst the top 5 per cent'.[52] Comparisons solely of *average* attainment, as we have seen in the present study, are particularly inadequate if we are comparing advanced countries: it is necessary to compare explicitly *at various levels of ability* the attainments and breadth of curriculum of representative samples of pupils.

Second, only about a tenth of all pupils in Germany leave school without a certificate attesting to the satisfactory completion of their studies covering the broad range of basic subjects. This contrasts with England, where the bottom 40 per cent have so far been excluded, as a matter of policy, from the provision of an examined qualification which caters for their potential level of attainment. Incentives to high attainments in the final years at school for the lower half of the ability stream are consequently very different in England from in Germany. Further, the school curriculum in England is not prescribed centrally, and the requirements of leaving-examinations for the upper part of the ability range have been the predominant influence on what is taught at schools at all levels; the lack of an appropriate leaving-examination for the lowest group has thus also led to inadequacies in their curricula. Much discussion in England is under way (by curriculum review bodies), and so are teaching experiments for low-attainers (the 'Low Attaining Pupils' programme),[53] but it remains unclear how any positive outcome can be made effective in the present decentralised schooling system as a whole.

Third, in order to qualify for their leaving-certificates in Germany, pupils need to achieve satisfactory average marks calculated in relation to *all* subjects; stricter requirements relate to 'core' subjects, which include mathematics. No certificates are awarded in Germany for single subjects, in the way they are in England. This applies as much to those proposing to enter German universities, who are all required to show satisfactory attainments in mathematics at school till the age of 18, as it does to those in the equivalent of secondary modern schools, who are required to show satisfactory mathematical attainment at about CSE pass-level. Certificates in groups of subjects, presumably including an agreed core, have been proposed in England by the Education Secretary for the revised system of leaving-examinations to come into effect in 1988; these proposals have not yet been accepted.

Fourth, we have noticed the rise to a predominant position in Germany of its 'intermediate stream' of schooling, the *Realschule*, which in the course of many decades – two centuries according to Durkheim's historical study of secondary schooling[54] – developed a curriculum with an orientation towards scientific, technical and business requirements, deliberately contrasting with the academic orientation of the older, classical, secondary school curriculum. The classical tradition to some extent still inspires the German *Gymnasium* (as also, for example, the Dutch *Athenaeum*) and originally catered primarily for those intending to enter the clergy, law, teaching or medicine. The classical curriculum of the English grammar and public schools (it may be remembered that the title 'grammar' referred to Latin grammar) followed similar lines, and was progressively widened in the past century to include the natural sciences. The compromise on educational values reached in English schools in general continues to be heavily weighted by the requirements of university entrants, rather than by the requirements for their life-tasks of *average* pupils of an era of 'universal secondary schooling'. The development in the second quarter of this century in England of technical, and central (commercial) schools – which might have provided a remedy – proved only a brief interlude, and left an inadequate legacy of applied or 'practical' eductional ideals for the ensuing comprehensive system.

The contrast between the *growth* of an intermediate stream of schooling in Germany – with its explicit practical educational objectives and syllabus

– and its *submergence* in England, provides an overriding clue to many educational and social differences between these countries. The highly developed vocational training system in Germany may be seen as a complementary development of the same underlying balance in the purposes of education.

This is not the place to expand on policy options: it is sufficient here to understand that other countries take advantage of 'economies of scale' in organising education, and that this seems to benefit pupils in the lower half of the attainment spectrum – those that at present are particularly at risk of unemployment. A proper discussion of policy for English schools cannot therefore avoid questioning whether its accepted decentralised framework of schooling must remain as it is. For the foreseeable future, detailed guidance on the school curriculum as a whole for different ability strata remains a pressing need in England, as does the co-ordination of syllabuses between successive classes and successive schools. Progress in practice, and not merely in words, on all these aspects must be followed with the greatest concern by those who believe that Britain's productivity ought to be, and ultimately can be, raised to that of its European neighbours.

ACKNOWLEDGEMENTS

This chapter could not have been written without the help of a great many persons in Germany and England who generously gave us their time and attention. In our comparisons based on the studies by the International Association for the Evaluation of Educational Achievement, the Association's President, Professor N. Postlethwaite (Hamburg), provided both encouragement and elucidation. Dr R. Strässer (University of Bielefeld, Department of Mathematical Pedagogics) was helpful in interpreting the German IEA study: and the late Bruce Choppin helped on the English part of that study.

In Germany we are indebted to Professor U. J. Kledzik (Technical University, and Head of the School Inspectorate, Berlin), Herr J. Wöppel (Director of the Education Ministry, Baden-Württemberg), Herr R. Maute (school inspector in Balingen), and to a number of headmasters and teachers of schools in Berlin and Nordhorn. In England, we are indebted to D. D. Foxman (National Foundation for Educational Research) for help with the APU tests, to Dr R. Fogelman and R. Ives (National Children's Bureau) in connection with the longitudinal sample study, and to a great many teachers and school inspectors, many of whom are obliged to remain anonymous. Many helpful comments were received from Dr J. White (Institute of Education, University of London) and from our colleagues at the National Institute. Thanks are due to the DES for permission to reproduce some unpublished APU questions, and Crown Copywright is acknowledged in relation to other APU questions reproduced here. The research was supported by the Economic and Social Research Council.

NOTES

1 This article forms part of a series examining the sources of differences between British and German industrial productivity. Previous comparisons referred to here are: 'Vocational qualifications of the labour force in Britain and Germany', by S. J. Prais, in the *National Institute Economic Review*, No. 98, November 1981; 'Some practical aspects of human capital investment: training standards in five occupations in Britain and Germany', by S. J. Prais and K. Wagner, *National Institute Economic Review*, No. 105, August 1983; 'Productivity, machinery and skills in a sample of British and German manufacturing plants: results of a pilot inquiry', by A. Daly, D. M. W. N. Hitchens and K. Wagner, *National Institute Economic Review*, No. 111, February 1985. An earlier version of the present article appeared in the *National Institute Economic Review*, No. 112, May 1985; permission to reproduce is acknowledged. Our immense debt to the many who assisted us with information, and by commenting on earlier versions, is acknowledged at the end of this article.

2 See Bundesminister für Bildung und Wissenschaft, *Grund- und Strukturdaten 1985/6*, pp. 62–5, and Table I. The rapidly changing balance of pupil numbers amongst the three types of German school may be expected to lead to changes in relative school standards – a matter of the greatest scientific interest and likely to involve further policy changes. As explained further below, there was previously also a 'middle type' in England, the technical and central (commercial) school, but it never attained the characteristic importance that the *Realschule* attained in Germany.

3 Berlin is also somewhat less conservative than other parts of Germany in its approach to educational reform, and a little closer to the English approach.

4 School timetables for the three types of school in Germany are compared with that of the average English school in Appendix C of National Institute Discussion Paper no. 60. The statistics that follow are taken for the relevant years from *Allgemeines Schulwesen* and *Berufliches Schulwesen* (for vocational schools), published by the German Federal Statistical Office in their series *Bildung und Kultur* 11/1 and 11/2; summaries are conveniently provided in the German *Statistisches Jahrbuch* (for example, the issue for 1981, p. 346), and in the statistical handbook of the Ministry of Education (*Grund- und Strukturdaten*, Bundesminister für Bildung und Wissenschaft).

5 For the benefit of German readers it needs to be said that sixth forms in English secondary schools normally last two years.

6 It is of interest that Greek remains obligatory in the 'sixth forms' of classical ('*Altsprachliche*') *Gymnasien* in certain *Länder*.

7 The adjustments made to the published figures in the above paragraphs to avoid double counting, and to yield the numbers attaining their *highest* certificates at the end of full-time schooling, are inevitably approximate. The official publication *Grund- und Strukturdaten 1981/2* (pp. 60–3), shows unadjusted totals for each particular school-leaving certificate, the grand total of which exceeds (by about a tenth) the number of pupils in each age-cohort. The proportionate distribution is however much the same as shown here.

8 Ninety-one per cent in England in 1983, of whom 7 per cent were in 'middle schools deemed secondary' which are usually grouped by the Department of Education together with comprehensives. Statistics are not always available for the whole UK on schooling, and it is necessary here, and below, to refer

occasionally to England alone, or to England and Wales. The sources are *Statistics of Education* (Vol. 1), *Schools* (Vol. 2), *School Leavers CSE and GCE*, and *Education Statistics for the United Kingdom* (HMSO). Since 1980 summary statistics are available in the DES *Statistical Bulletin* (approximately monthly).

9 Based on *Statistics of Education, Schools, 1978* pp. 8–10. The statistics on technical and similar schools have to be regarded as approximate. The official source shows only 3 per cent in technical schools; but a further 7 per cent were in 'other secondary schools, which included 'selective central' schools, together with 'bilateral modern/technical schools and multilateral schools. We have here allocated the latter 7 per cent as 2 per cent with technical schools, and 5 per cent with comprehensives.

10 *Statistical Supplement to the Eighteenth Report 1979–80*. Universities Central Council on Admissions, pp. 16–17 (compare tables E7 and E8). For a detailed distribution of UCCA scores we relied on the results of the National Child Development Study, an unpublished report (section 15.5) kindly made available by Richard Ives of the National Children's Bureau, London (for a published summary of some of the results, see K. Fogelman's paper in *Publishing School Examination Results: a Discussion*, Bedford Way Papers 5. University of London Institute of Education, 1981, pp. 28–9).

11 See Vol. II with that title, Ed. T. Husén (Almquist & Wiksell, Stockholm, 1967), especially pp. 24–5, 69 and 86. Much the same ground is covered by N. Postlethwaite, *School Organisation and Student Achievement: a Study Based on Student Achievement in Mathematics in Twelve Countries* (Wiley, 1967). No one should read these studies without taking a pinch of the salt provided in an exceptionally extensive, critical – but enlightening – review by H. Freudenthal. 'Pupils' achievements internationally compared', published on pp. 127–86 of the journal he edits, *Educational Studies in Mathematics*, Vol. 6(2), July 1975 (Reidel, Dordrecht-Holland); however, the critical aspects are of greater relevance later in this article than they are here.

12 'Population 3a' in England included those in 'science sixth forms' who took mathematics as one of their subjects (see Husén, op. cit., pp. 46 and 172). About a quarter of all A-level leavers were probably covered by this definition (see DES, *Statistical Bulletin*, 11/84, Table 11).

13 The test was not, however, exactly the same (Husén, Vol. II, p. 105). Whilst it may seem obvious, in the above context, that the British system of specialisation was the substantial source of the higher marks obtained by sixth-form mathematicians, the experience of some other countries included in the sample study shows that equally high marks in mathematics can be achieved while taking nine subjects (Israel, 36; Belgium, 35; France, 33), and at much the same age as in Britain (Husén, p. 86; Postlethwaite, p. 110). A notional adjustment (Husén, pp. 116 ff.) for the different fractions of the age group at school at higher ages in the different countries does not change the above conclusions relating to Britain and Germany: the adjustment is based on assuming that the *best* pupils in the country with a higher fraction can fairly be compared with those in another country with a lower fraction staying on to higher ages. The adjustment becomes more problematical in relation to countries such as the US and Sweden where *very* much larger fractions are at school at higher ages: in these, the hypothetical cream of pupils in the survey may well yield a sample of significantly higher ability than in countries where selection is carried out by the schooling system at a lower age.

14 By way of example, some details may be given of present requirements in the sixth forms of Berlin *Gymnasien*. The period of study is 2½ years, with a possible further year if required to achieve the requisite minimum of 28

'credits' (each successfully completed course taken for a half year counts as a 'credit': three school periods a week are required for most subjects, but six periods are required in the two major subjects of specialisation). The full curriculum of 13 subjects is obligatory in the first half year, which is introductory (and does not reach credit levels): thereafter, the following are the minimum requirements: four credits each (which normally implies instruction throughout the remainder of schooling) in German, sciences and in geography/ political history: *two credits each in mathematics*, a foreign language and music/ art. Specialised major fields of study are to be chosen from: language/literature/ arts, geography/history/politics, and science/mathematics.

15 *Grund- und Strukturdaten, 1983/84*, p. 108. It must be noted that because some students change their subject of study, or continue for a second degree, the number registered for the first year of a university course was a quarter higher than the number who were in their first year at university (ibid., pp. 124 ff.).

16 *Education Statistics for the United Kingdom 1983*, p. 24; less an allowance of 10 per cent for overseas students (see DES, *Statistical Bulletin*, 13/80, Table 3).

17 DES, *Statistical Bulletin*, 8/84, Table 4(i).

18 In Germany in 1981, there were 78,000 graduates in all subjects, excluding teaching qualifications and foreign students; in the UK in 1981–2, there were 77,000 graduates, excluding those going on to teacher training and other further education, and excluding overseas graduates who returned home (*Grund- und Strukturdaten 1983/84*, p. 154; *Education Statistics for the UK 1983*, p. 25).

19 See Prais, op. cit., pp. 53–4, for comparisons between Britain and Germany of numbers of first degrees by subject of study. Professor Dahrendorf, in his address to the annual Conference of German University Rectors (Vice-Chancellors) in 1982 (reported in the Berlin *Tagesspiegel* of 4 May), strongly criticised the German university system as unduly expensive per graduate produced.

20 DES, *School Leavers 1981*, Tables C8 and C11.

21 This indirect estimation procedure is necessary since the statistics used here are based on the highest achievements of *pupils* leaving school, measured in the year they left (see the Introduction to the source just quoted). The alternative is to rely on statistics based on all examination results in a particular year, but this is not satisfactory, since pupils may spread their examinations over a number of years. For the sake of clarity it may be added that the pupils who attain university entrance standards (with 2–3 A-levels) are excluded here, since they have been covered above.

22 The DES makes no estimate for this group (see DES, *School Leavers 1977*, p. xxv, para. 43). An approximate indirect estimate can be obtained from the recently published results of the National Child Development Study, which show that 10.1 per cent of 19-year olds have achieved five or more O-level passes, but no A-levels, compared with 9.2 per cent shown by the DES sample of school-leavers. The difference of 1 per cent is presumably largely due to this group; sampling errors inevitably imply that this estimate is approximate.

23 The comparisons of French examinations were based mainly on London CSE and O-level, and on the Bavarian *Realschule* leaving-examination. It perhaps needs to be said again here that standards vary slightly amongst the various examination boards, and the above limited comparisons should not be pressed too closely. It is sufficient for the present purposes that a broad correspondence was found between the standards considered here for the two countries. French is normally the first foreign language in English schools, but in German schools it is usually the second foreign language (after English; the main exception is

the Saarland, where French has priority over English); however, this difference seems unlikely to affect the above comparisons to any considerable extent.

24 See the report produced under the chairmanship of Dr J. H. Cockcroft (Vice-Chancellor of the New University of Ulster), *Mathematics Counts* (311 pp., HMSO, 1982); the Committee had been set up following a recommendation by a House of Commons Select Committee inquiring into the attainment of school leavers in 1977. Only four pages (pp. 236–9) dealt with mathematical education in other countries. No mention was made of the *International Study of Achievement in Mathematics*. The role of tests is at one point virtually dismissed on the basis that 'no one has ever grown taller as a result of being measured' (p. 123). That tests encourage pupils to revise, and help parents and teachers to check progress, seems to have carried too little weight with this Committee.

25 The examinations compared were the London GCE O-level mathematics paper (syllabus D), the London CSE papers in arithmetic and mathematics, and the *Realschule* leaving examination as set in Baden-Württemberg. Papers for Saarland and Bavaria were also considered and appeared of similar standard.

26 V. Dundas-Grant (1982) The education of the adolescent: recent developments in secondary education in France. *Comparative Education*, 10, p. 33; her contrast is however over-stated, since it needs to bring into account A-level leavers.

27 Prais and Wagner, op. cit., 1983.

28 These points are well recognised: cf. generally, the survey of HM Inspectors of Schools, *Aspects of Secondary Education in England* (DES, HMSO, 1979); and Cockcroft, *Report*, pp. 128 *et seq*.

29 DES, *School Leavers 1977*, p. viii, and *Statistical Bulletin*, 11/84, Table 3.

30 Cockcroft, *Report*, p. 131. The term 'other grades' is used in the official statistics to describe what are here called 'lower grades'.

31 The use of 'Mode 3 syllabuses', where the school sets and marks its own examinations, subject only to 'monitoring' by the CSE board, has exacerbated the problems faced by employers in recognising the value of these certificates. See the Schools Council Working Paper no. 68 by D. Bird and M. Hiscox, *Mathematics in School and Employment: A Study of Liaison Activities* (Methuen Educational, 1981), especially pp. 17–18 and 110.

32 Cockcroft, p. 250; and *School Leavers 1981*, Table C25.

33 DES Press Notice, 15 November 1982.

34 See Appendix 6.2 for details of the adjustments.

35 In fact, the German average for the lower half of all pupils was a little higher than that attained by pupils in England; but bearing in mind sampling variability, it is safer to note the *similarity* than the 2.3 points (10 per cent) higher German achievement. The present Secretary of State for Education and Science has adopted as a 'goal ... bringing 80–90 per cent of 16-year-old pupils up to the standard of performance now expected of the average pupil': this was first announced in his Sheffield policy statement in January 1984 (shortly after an early version of this paper was circulated), and appears again in a more recent policy statement *Science 5–16* (HMSO, March 1985), p. 14.

36 See Husén, Vol. I, especially pp. 92, 97 and 98.

37 *Aspects of Secondary Education in England: a Survey by HM Inspectors of Schools* (DES, HMSO, 1979), p. 156.

38 '*Strong* recommendations', in the parlance of HMI, are stronger than ordinary 'recommendations'. The worrying statistics on new courses were relegated to a subsequently published supplement: *Aspects of Secondary Education in*

England: Supplementary Information on Mathematics (DES, HMSO, 1980), p. 44.

39 Cockcroft, *Report* (1982), p. 236; the few paragraphs devoted to mathematical education in other countries dealt only with very general matters. The (House of Commons) Select Committee was very much aware of the lack of detailed knowledge of what is happening in other countries; it noted the DES was not able to provide much help on this, and recommended that the 'DES either initiate or encourage select further inquiries . . .' (*The Attainments of the School Leaver*, Tenth Report from the Expenditure Committee, HMSO, 1977; vol. I, para. 157, pp. xlix-l).

40 'It is clear that at the present time it would not be possible to require all those who teach mathematics at secondary level to hold a minimum mathematical qualification' said the Cockcroft *Report* (p. 232); and a further investigation was recommended!

41 This is not the place to go further into this sad history. The interested reader may consult the report on the Schools Council's 'Mathematics for the Majority Project' which was specifically designed to cater for those of below average ability. It has left very little impact (see P. Kaner, chapter 10, *Evaluation in Curriculum Development*, Schools Council, 1973; and the review by R. Munro in *J. Curriculum Studies*, 1974, p. 175). The consequences of so-called 'modern mathematics' are examined by G. Howson, C. Keitel and J. Kilpatrick in *Curriculum Development in Mathematics* (Cambridge University Press, 1981) who concluded (p. 238): 'It is almost thirty years since the "modern math" reform began . . . the practical results of such an enormous expenditure of labour and commitment have been relatively insignificant. The problem remains – many Johnnys still cannot add!'

42 See Professor N. Postlethwaite's special tabulations of the IEA results, 'The bottom half in lower secondary schooling', in *Education and Economic Performance* (ed. G. D. N. Worswick, Gower Publishing, 1985). That article contains some highly interesting tabulations of IEA studies of attainments in science and reading comprehension for bottom-half pupils in a number of countries: these confirm that the problem of poor bottom-half attainments in England is not confined to mathematics, but extends to other subjects as well.

43 The examples below are taken from the *Rahmenplan für Unterricht und Erziehung in der Berliner Schule* (1981), especially pp. 33, 35–6: and *ditto, Fach Arbeitslehre* (Sonderdruck, 1983), pp. 59–114. For lack of space, the full details on the various options cannot be given here, but it should be noted that cross-options are encouraged between the industrial and domestic courses. Much exemplary material is contained in the detailed teachers' guides on *Arbeitslehre* produced by the Pädagogisches Zentrum Berlin (Uhlandstraße 97); several duplicated textbooks have been produced by groups of teachers for each year and each section of the course.

44 *Aspects of Secondary Education in England, op. cit.* (1979). The quotations that follow are from pp. 14, 24, 40, 230–1, 236, 266–7.

45 DES, *Technology in Schools* (1982). This survey was based on 90 schools which represented 'roughly 10 per cent of secondary schools which were running technology courses at that time' (p. 4). Out of a total of some 5,000 secondary schools, the grossed-up total of 900 schools accounts for just under 20 per cent. Only four of the 90 schools in the sample had obligatory courses (p. 10).

46 DES *School Leavers 1981*, Table C30; for more detail see earlier issues such as *1977*, Tables 24–5. The table for the most recent year is difficult to interpret since, for example, passes in woodwork and metalwork are taken together, leading to double counting of the number of pupils involved. It needs to be stressed that this kind of information has not been made available by the

DES for its sample of school-leavers: we are thus compelled to rely on information from examination boards, based on subjects passed. Some of these passes are from colleges of further education rather than from schools.

47 See DES, *Craft, Design and Technology in Schools: Some Successful Examples* (HMSO, 1980).

48 DES, HM Inspectorate, *Curriculum 11–16* (1977), p. 1. In Germany it is taken as self-evident that pre-vocational school instruction is of value subsequently at work and in the daily business of organising one's life, and is also immediately valuable in stimulating the motivation at school of many pupils who otherwise find 'book-learning' lacking in relevance. Much applied research is carried out there on the links between school and work, as evident from the 1,000-page bibliography (*Forschungs-Dokumentation*) issued three times a year by the Nürnberg Institut für Arbeitsmarkt- und Berufsforschung. An interesting British study of the initial impact of schooling on industrial performance was carried out by the Engineering Industry Training Board; it noted the significant positive benefits on subsequent work-planning and budgeting, especially for technician trainees (D. Mathews, *The Relevance of School Learning Experiences to Performance in Industry*, EITB, 1977). There is much scope for further research on these lines.

49 See Unesco Statistical Yearbooks. The lower proportion of GDP may be related to fewer ancillary staff which, in turn, is related to a shorter school day; there is scope for a detailed comparative costing exercise on these matters.

50 By Professor Sir James Dewar in his presidential address to the British Association in 1902! (British Association, 1903: quoted by L. F. Haber, *The Chemical Industry 1900–1930*. Oxford, 1971, p. 53). The same view was also extensively advanced by Alfred Marshall in his writings (cf. his well-known statement: 'Thus all the world has much to learn from German methods of education', *Industry and Trade*, Macmillan, 4th edn, 1932, p. 130).

51 R. W. Phillips, 'Some preliminary results from the Second IEA mathematics study' (paper presented to the IEA General Assembly, August 1983), Table 4.

52 'Implications of the IEA studies of curriculum and instruction', Chapter 3 in *Educational Policy and International Assessment*, Ed. A. C. Purves and D. V. Levine (McCutcham, Berkeley, Cal., 1975), pp. 78–9.

53 Reports are expected in the summer of 1986.

54 Durkheim's book was based on lectures delivered at the beginning of the century primarily to French students of education; he devoted a highly interesting chapter to the development of the *Realist* stream in continental schooling (see E. Durkheim, *The Evolution of Educational Thought*, translated by P. Collins from the French edition of 1938: Routledge, London, 1977), chapter 23.

55 Department of Education and Science, Assessment of Performance Unit, *Mathematical Development: Secondary Survey Report No. 1*, by D. D. Foxman, R. M. Martini, J. A. Tuson and M. J. Cresswell (HMSO, 1980) and subsequent issues.

56 Initial tests were applied to 4,500 pupils in 70 schools in 1977/8: see J. Wöppel, 'Das neue Abschlußverfahren der Hauptschule', *Lehren und Lernen*, 1979, Heft 10, pp. 2 and 24–36 (see also ibid., 1978, Heft 6, pp. 1–54; 1982, Heft 3, pp. 64–80). For statistics of school-leavers with *Abschluß*, see *Allegemeines Schulwesen*, 1982, p. 27.

57 In Baden-Württemberg in 1982, 41 per cent of all school-leavers came from *Hauptschulen*.

58 APU2, p. 44, question 20H.

59 Unpublished APU questions made available to us for the present comparisons.

60 As explained in the main article, the results of the IEA study were reported

in two volumes edited by Husén, and in a parallel volume by Postlethwaite; for brevity, these are referred to in this appendix as HI, HII and P.

61 HI, p. 158; HII, p. 23. Separate samples were taken for Scotland which yielded a similar picture; for simplicity the exposition here is confined to the English samples (in reality: to England and Wales). The lower German variability is undoubtedly an important factor in promoting higher average attainments in successive classes; lower variability within German classes is clearly related to the widespread practice of grade-repeating (advancement to a higher class depends on mastering material in the lower class).

62 HI, p. 271; P, p. 116.

63 Fortunately, a whole chapter (HI, pp. 163–88) was devoted to a description of the administration of the inquiry in England; only Sweden was honoured at similar length. We do not know what problems arose in other countries: further details for Finland, Japan, the Netherlands and Scotland were published in *International Review of Education*, 15, 1969, no. 2.

64 HI, p. 171, lower half of page. A more detailed report devoted to the English study makes it clear that third-form pupils were chosen for Population 1b, but without explaining how this choice is to be reconciled with that of other countries (D. A. Pidgeon, ed., *Achievement in Mathematics: a National Study in Secondary Schools*, NFER, 1967, pp. 8; and 310.

65 For other countries in which there was an age gap between samples 1a and 1b, differences in the same direction in scores and ages can be detected in the tables shown in HII, p. 72 and P, pp. 116–17. The conclusion in the text above would not really be altered if, using regression techniques, we based the age adjustment on the experience of all countries in the IEA study (as in HII, p. 71). There is a suggestion in a more detailed analysis of IEA data (Population 1b) by the late Professor Choppin that the relation between achievement and month of birth is slightly non-linear; this is probably the result of more older pupils in the age-group 13:0 to 13:11 being in a higher class, and subject to a step-jump in their educational experience, as compared with younger pupils. Since we are here concerned with the average advance of a whole age-group, a linear approximation is not likely to be far out (see B. H. Choppin, 'The relationship between achievement and age', *Educational Research*, 1969, especially p. 24).

66 HI, pp. 148, 153 and 260, Table 14.1B.

67 See the graphs, HI, p. 225 and P, p. 55 (identical).

68 HII, p. 81, Table 3.15.

69 W. Schultze and L. Riemenschneider, 'Eine vergleichende Studie über die Ergebnisse des Mathematikunterrichts in zwölf Landern', *Deutsches Institut für Internationale Pädagogische Forschung*, 34 (1969), p. 4. The numbers in the two sources do not correspond exactly, since those published in the international surveys have been re-weighted to allow for differential response rates in the sub-samples (there seems to have been some over-sampling of *Realschulen*).

70 HII, p. 81.

71 Pidgeon, op. cit., pp. 53, 60, 99.

72 Schultze and Riemenschneider, op. cit., Table 8.

73 We were not able to make an exact conventional adjustment for guessing, since the number not answering each of the questions was not published: accordingly we adjusted by linear interpolation between the published figures (unadjusted, adjusted), for *Gymnasien* (38.2, 33.7) and 'Remainder' schools (29.9, 24.3).

74 For England, Pidgeon, op. cit., p 99, interpolated to provide an estimate at age 13:8; for Germany, Schultze and Riemenschneider, op. cit., and HII, p. 81.

APPENDIX 6.1 SPECIMEN MATHEMATICS TESTS FOR LOWER-HALF PUPILS IN ENGLAND AND GERMANY

To gain an impression of how present-day standards in mathematics amongst pupils in the lower half of the ability spectrum in England compared with those in Germany, we compared specimen test papers for final year pupils in *Hauptschulen* ('Secondary Modern' schools) in Baden-Württemberg, Berlin and Niedersachsen with tests set in England to representative samples of 15-year olds by the Assessment of Performance Unit (APU) of the Department of Education and Science. The object, narrowly stated, was to discover whether the German questions lay within the competence of the corresponding section of the ability range in England. The tests in Baden-Württemberg proved of most interest in that they covered a representative and large number of pupils, and the comparisons are therefore set out in some detail in this Appendix.

The other German *Hauptschule* tests available to us related to individual classes. The tests were usually set in the course of the year and dealt with restricted ranges of topics in each test: final tests for the equivalent *Hauptschulabschluß* at a Berlin evening school were also considered. These tests were of much the same scope and standard, and are consistent with those for Baden-Würrtemberg.

The English APU tests, taken for comparison here, were administered to a cross-section of pupils in England, Wales and Northern Ireland each year from 1978 to 1982. Specimen questions have been published, together with the percentage who gave correct answers.[55] The average age of the English pupils when they took these tests was 15 years and 8 months. Aside from the advantage of having available published pass-rates, an important reason for relying on these APU tests is that they were designed to cater for the whole ability range, including the lowest 40 per cent which – in principle – are below the scope of CSE examinations. As will be clear from the main article, it is the adequacy or inadequacy of attainments in the lower half of the ability range that is of most concern in England.

School-leaving examinations intended for *Hauptschule* pupils in Baden-Würrtemberg have been set to a broad sample of schools by the Ministry of Education of that *Land* since 1977, and have been obligatory for all schools from 1983–4. These centrally set final examinations are in addition to internal tests and assessments; they are set at the end of the 'ninth class', at an average age of just under 16. The vast majority of teachers (95 per cent of those surveyed following initial trials) thought the change to centrally administered examinations had been beneficial: it led to more objective results and better motivation, and consequently an increased number of pupils attained required standards (some 92 per cent leave these schools having attained their *Abschluß*)[56] The tests are marked independently by the class teacher and by an externally appointed examiner, usually a teacher from another school; in case of a substantial discrepancy in marks (more than one 'grade' on the standard German scale of 1–6), an arbitrator intervenes. Separate tests were set for A- and B-streams; the B-stream usually accounts for about a third of pupils. The questions set to the two streams were similar in content; but those for the B-stream were slighly easier (A-stream pupils tend to attain a mark about a grade higher on average despite the slightly more difficult questions). In our comparisons below with the English APU tests we found it easier to match questions with those set to the B-stream (since 1984–5 the same test has been set for both streams).

Our initial comparisons were based on tests set in Baden-Württemberg in 1978 and 1979; after discussions with the educational authorities there, based on our initial comparisons, we were able to make use of their 1984 tests which had been influenced by the questions set in the English APU tests. A finer degree of comparability in questions was thus achieved. The results quoted below are based mainly on the results of 1984 for 5,000 pupils in 111 representative schools. The tests consisted of two papers for each stream: the first paper had ten basic obligatory questions to be answered in 45 minutes; the second paper allowed a choice of 10 questions out of 15 (the school eliminates three of these; according to the syllabus covered) – these questions were more difficult and were to be answered in 90 minutes. Our comparisons relate to the obligatory questions. In total the tests took much the same time as a CSE arithmetic paper: they were also similar in scope and level of difficulty (a little algebra is included as an optional question for the German A-stream, but not for the B-stream).

The CSE papers, it may be reiterated, are not intended for the lowest 40 per cent of the ability range, whereas the majority of those taking the Baden-Württemberg papers came from that part of the ability range;[57] that by itself provides a first indication of the higher standard aimed at in Germany for that section of pupils.

The following comparisons are illustrative of the general impression, and are chosen from those where a fairly close match proved possible. No calculators were used in the tests.

The first German question for the B-stream consisted of additions and subtractions of decimal numbers:

$$389.59 - 83.64 + 529.5 - 712 = \ldots$$

A similar question was set in the English APU test:[58]

$$2.6 - 4.12 + 6.3 - 0.44 = \ldots$$

It was slightly easier in that it involved fewer digits, but probably sufficiently similar for the present comparison. The German question was answered correctly by 66 per cent of pupils (the corresponding question set to the A-stream had more digits, and was answered correctly by 83 per cent of pupils). The English question was answered correctly by only 24 per cent of *all* pupils throughout the whole ability range. An analysis of the response to the English question according to level of ability in mathematics (kindly made available by the National Foundation for Educational Research) shows that only the top fifth of English pupils – 62 per cent of whom got this question right – came close to the German percentage attained in the *Hauptschulen*; of the lower half of English pupils, only 4 per cent were able to provide the correct answer.

Division of fractions appears in the following German question:

$$18\tfrac{3}{5} \div 7\tfrac{3}{4} = \ldots$$

which was answered correctly by 69 per cent of pupils. A corresponding English APU question,

$$1\tfrac{1}{3} \div \tfrac{8}{9} = \ldots$$

was answered correctly by 40 per cent of English pupils in the *whole* ability range, and by a mere 13 per cent in the lower half of the ability scale. The English question is easier, in that it involves only single digits after converting the first number to an improper fraction.

The next German question required the division of a decimal number by another decimal number:

$$543.75 \div 12.5 = \ldots$$

This was rather more difficult than the nearest English APU question:

$$40 \div 0.8 = \ldots$$

The German question was answered correctly by 59 per cent of B-stream *Hauptschule* pupils, and the English question by 35 per cent of *all* pupils, and probably (on our interpolated calculations) by only some 10 per cent of English pupils in the lower half of the ability range.

The following two German questions dealt with rates of interest: the B-stream was asked:

What is the interest payable after half a year on DM 16,000 at 4.5%?

The A-stream was asked a similar question, marginally more difficult:

What is the quarterly interest payable on DM 120,000 at 5.5%?

These questions were answered correctly by 44 and 63 per cent of pupils in the respective streams. An analogous English APU question was:[59]

The simple interest on £480 at the end of two years is £72. What is the annual rate of interest?

This was answered correctly by 13 per cent of *all* pupils.

Another APU question in this field was:

A man invested £1,500 for nine years at the rate of 7% simple interest per annum. What will be the interest over the nine-year period?

This was answered correctly by 30 per cent of all pupils, and by 11 per cent of the lower half of the ability range.

For the present purposes there seems no need to proceed to further detail. Others may wish to examine relative attainments in topics such as: calculations of volumes, weights of solids based on densities, areas of sectors of circles, and calculations involving percentages: these topics are given much importance in the German *Hauptschule* syllabus. What should be included in the syllabus has become an issue of great interest in England following the proposal by the Cockcroft Committee on the teaching of mathematics (1982, especially paragraphs 455–9) that a 'foundation list of mathematical topics' needs to be developed, working 'from the bottom upwards' intended to cater for the lowest 40 per cent in the range of attainment. Much is to be learnt from German experience in this field.

By way of summary it may be said that nothing is done in German schools which is in any way completely out of the scope of the English syllabus; but, perhaps by concentrating on a narrower range of topics that have more of an applied nature, it seems that the level of attainment of the *lower half* of pupils in Germany has been brought well above the *average* level of attainment in England.

APPENDIX 6.2   THE IEA COMPARISONS OF MATHEMATICAL ACHIEVEMENT AT AGE 13 BETWEEN ENGLAND AND GERMANY

England and Germany were amongst the twelve countries included in the extensive international comparisons of educational achievement in mathematics, conducted under the direction of Professor Husén (of the University of Stockholm's School of Education) in 1964 with the support of UNESCO. Many of the essential differences in the approach to schooling in the two countries have not altered in the intervening twenty years, and the contrasts revealed by that wide-ranging inquiry remain of great interest today. The main lessons from the mathematical comparisons should have been apparent to those concerned in England many years ago; the lessons were not drawn at the time, and it remains to set them out in detail. That is the task of this Appendix. Comparisons were carried out for 'sixth-form school pupils (in the language of that study: pupils in the 'academic stream' who were in their pre-university year), and for the full cross-section of pupils at age 13. The comparisons at age 13 met, unhappily, with certain mishaps in relations to the English and German samples: these need to be examined in detail in order to draw the most valuable inferences from that study.[60]

The main comparison for 13-year olds published in that study was that the average German pupil attained a score of 25.4 points compared with 23.8 for the average English pupil. These results were based on tests administered to 4,580 pupils in Germany and 3,200 pupils in England, chosen from 161 and 182 schools respectively in each country. In addition to a higher average score in Germany, scores were significantly more uniform amongst German pupils than amongst English pupils (standard deviations of 11.7 and 18.5 respectively).[61] The average scores for the full sample of a dozen countries ranged from under 20 to over 30 (for Japan and Israel), out of a possible maximum of 70.

The difference of 1.6 points between German and England is relatively small. But, as we shall see, there are two qualifications which considerably increase the gap. We need to consider, first, the average age of pupils in the British sample; and, second, the various types of schools included in the samples – more particularly, the gap between schools catering for the lower half of the ability range.

How old are British 13-year-old pupils?

As said, one of the aims of the IEA inquiry was to compare the achievements of 13-year olds. For most countries this was done in two ways. One sample – 'Population 1a' – consisted simply of pupils who were 13 years old; the other sample – 'Population 1b' – was supposed to consist of those pupils who were in the class in which the *majority of pupils* were aged 13, though individual pupils might have been above or below that age. Germany co-operated only on the latter basis, and our comparisons between Germany and England thus need to be based on samples defined for Population 1b. The average age of the German pupils was 13 years and 8 months, just a little above the median for all countries of 13 years and 6 months; but for the English sample the average age, astonishingly enough, was 14 years and 4 months.[62] The German pupils thus seem to have attained a higher average score despite a substantially lower average age.

Something clearly went wrong in the English sampling procedure; but this was mentioned only briefly.[63] After describing three possible component groups of pupils that might be included in the sampling scheme, we learn that 'repeated changes made in the definitions of the component groups . . . resulted in an error in the English numbering – groups 1 and 2 changing places'.[64]

Can we adjust the English score to allow for the age gap? This can be done by considering the alternative English sample based on Population 1a: the average age of this sample was 13 years and 6 months – as is to be expected if pupils are evenly distributed between 13:0 and 13:11. The English sample 1a was thus 10 months younger than the English sample 1b. The average score attained by the English sample 1a was 4.6 points below that attained by the English sample 1b: that is to say, 10 months' additional schooling yielded a rise of 4.6 points in the scores in these tests. This suggests that an English sample with the average age of the German sample 1b (namely, 13 years and 8 months) might be expected to have an average score of 20.1 (that is, 23.8 less eight-tenths of 4.6).

The gap between England and Germany, after adjusting in this way for the age discrepancy, is thus raised to 5.3 points.[65] We infer on the same basis (that is, that an increase of 10 months in schooling leads to a 4.6 points rise in scores) that the *average* English pupil's achievement in mathematics at age 13 lagged about a year behind the average German pupil (we shall see later in this Appendix that the lag is greater for those in the lower part of the ability spectrum.

The German sample of schools

We must next examine the selection of schools for the German sample. Only two *Länder* in Germany co-operated, Hessen and Schleswig-Holstein; and the schools were selected from 'those known to be co-operative' rather than by a random process as in other countries. It appears that 9 per cent of the schools in the sample were 'selective academic'; none fell into the IEA 'selective vocational' category (nor were there any comprehensive schools in Germany at that time); and 91 per cent of the schools came from those that 'receive the remainder' of all pupils after selection.[66]

The treatment of *Realschulen* was not straightforward. It appears from a graph that *Gymnasien* and *Realschulen* were both treated as 'selective academic' schools, and considered as a single group which accounted for some 33 per cent of all pupils at age 13 in the population.[67] It is not explicitly stated to what extent the sampled schools in this group consisted of one type or the other, though the distinction is obviously important since pupils in *Gymnasien* are of higher academic ability than in *Realschulen*. However, from a table in another part of the study[68] a different story emerges: this table gives average scores for different class-sizes and – important for our present purposes – for different types of school. The number of sampled pupils shown there as being in 'Remainder schools' – 3,800 out of the total sample of 4,500 – is consistent only with *Realschulen* having been included in the 'Remainder' category, and not in the 'Selective Academic' category (as suggested by the table mentioned above). This is confirmed by the separate report on the German part of the study which shows 1,700 pupils in the sample came from *Hauptschulen* and 1,800 from *Realschulen*.[69]

Differences for the lower half

The above discussion has been a necessary preliminary to a more refined issue that is of central interest here: how do the results for German *Hauptschulen* compare with results for the corresponding part of the English sample, that is, for pupils in secondary modern schools? These types of school catered, roughly speaking, for the lower 50–60 per cent of the ability range in each country. If we relied simply on the comparisons for pupils in the 'Remainder' schools as published in the international survey edited by Husén[70] based on 3,800 pupils in Germany and 1,800 in England, we would conclude that the IEA inquiry found an average German score of 24.4 against a British score of 16.3; that is, a truly monstrous gap of some 8 points – in addition to which the lower average age of the German sample of pupils has to be taken into account.

Because of the importance of the issue, it is necessary to attempt a more precise comparison based on pupils solely in German *Hauptschulen* (excluding *Realschulen* that were added to the 'Remainder' category) and on pupils solely in English secondary modern schools; the relevant information is to be found in the original national reports for each country, subject to certain adjustments.

For England we learn that secondary modern pupils in Population 1a – namely 13-year-old pupils with an average age of 13 years 6 months – attained an average score of 12.2; and those in Population 1b – third formers with an average age of 14 years and 4 months – attained an average score of 15.9 points.[71] There was thus an increase of 3.7 points in ten months of schooling, or 4.4 points a year. To match with the German pupils who were aged 13 years and 8 months, it may be inferred by interpolation (as above) that English pupils at that age might be expected to attain 12.9 points.

The German sample of *Hauptschule* pupils attained an average score of 28.1 points – an astonishing contrast.[72] Careful reading elucidates however that these scores were before adjustment had been made for 'guessing' in multiple-choice questions, whereas the English scores were published after such adjustment (as were the scores published in the international survey). Most of the questions in those tests offered five possible answers; the average adjusted score for these German schools (calculated by interpolation) is about 22.4.[73] There is thus an adjusted gap between English and German average scores of about 9.5 points, equivalent to an English lag of some two years of schooling at the rate of progress made in these schools at that age (4.4 points a year, as noted in the preceding paragraph).

Though German attainments seem to have been substantially ahead in the lower educational streams, it is worth noticing that in the upper ability streams England appears to have had an advantage: the sample of pupils in grammar schools in England attained a score of 41.2, compared with 33.7 for pupils in German *Gymnasien* and 32.0 for *Realschulen*.[74]

7 Assessment in German schools [1991]

David Phillips

It is like tearing plants out of the soil again and again in order to see whether they have taken root.

Detlef Glowka (1989: 322; see pp. 140–58 in this volume) quotes this graphic description – dating from the *Reformpädagogik* movement – of the German system of assessment (*Notensystem*) in his incisive account of Anglo-German perceptions of education which subjects recent English studies of the German school system to close analysis. Glowka concludes that the particular system of continuous assessment which still prevails in German schools is damaging to a worrying degree:

> If there are now ... some British educationists who recognise certain advantages of the German assessment arrangements, they should also consider that even if these arrangements are 'effective' to some degree, this is only so at the expense of enormous psychological damage. It is no exaggeration to say that the majority of adolescents in Germany leave school with their self-esteem permanently damaged.

Assessment in the German school system is regular, systematic and officially controlled. Since education is a matter for the *Land* ministries, it is the *Land* which produces the legislation that determines the assessment procedures in its schools. It must be remembered that through a process of jurisdiction (*Verrechtlichung*) much day-to-day procedure in schools, as in other state institutions, is codified in a legal framework which allows no real deviation. Since this framework is familiar to all those concerned with education (including parents and pupils), there are norms of expectation which reinforce the uniformity of approach which the *Land* legislation presupposes.

The award of school marks by the teacher, on the basis of oral performance in class, or written homework, or the regular classroom tests, becomes in fact a formal administrative act.

This need not be quite as problematic and alarming as it sounds. Routine in assessment as in other areas becomes so established that it remains for the most part unquestioned. Pearce *et al.* (1985: 2) report puzzlement on the part of German colleagues they questioned about the marking system: 'What, we were asked, could be so strange about it?' Indeed, many German observers, while envying the traditional freedoms enjoyed in our system, find it very curious that pupils have not been legally, or at least formally, required to take tests of any kind. Critics of the German approach, however, feel that it intrudes too much in the learning process to be educationally defensible. I shall return to the problems; first it is necessary to describe the assessment procedures.

In October 1968 an agreement was reached by the Education Ministers of the eleven West German *Länder*, meeting in the *Kultusministerkonferenz* (KMK), that the already familiar six-point scale would be used in state report forms on pupils' progress and in all other internal school assessment procedures. At the same time definitions were confirmed for each of the grades, ranging from 'very good' (1) to 'very poor' (6). (Ingenkamp 1985: 177). The English translation of the descriptors is quoted in an HMI paper on education in the Federal Republic (DES 1986: 7):

> *sehr gut* or 1 = very good, to be given when the performance is well above the required standard.
>
> *gut* or 2 = good, for a performance that fully meets the required standard.
>
> *befriedigend* or 3 = satisfactory, for a performance that on the whole meets the required standard.
>
> *ausreichend* or 4 = adequate, for a performance which, though showing deficiencies, on the whole still meets the required standard.
>
> *mangelhaft* or 5 = poor, for a performance that does not meet the required standard but indicates that the necessary basic knowledge exists and that the deficiencies could be removed in a foreseeable period.
>
> *ungenügend* or 6 = very poor, for a performance that does not meet the required standard and indicates that even the basic knowledge is so fragmentary that the deficiencies could not be removed within a foreseeable period.
>
> ['Inadequate' would be the proper translations of *mangelhaft*, and 'unsatisfactory' of *ungenügend*]

From this scale of marks (*Notenskala*) it is clear that grades 1–4 indicate an acceptable performance when pupils' progress is assessed against the knowledge and skills they should be able to demonstrate at particular stages in their schooling. Syllabuses, of course, are centrally determined (within the *Land*) and are issued in published form, and so teachers and pupils are fully aware of what ground has to be covered at what stage and that it will be assessed at regular points in the year. Grades 5 and 6 indicate unacceptable standards, but grade 5 still indicates that there is a chance of improvement 'in a foreseeable period'.

An immediate problem in this kind of approach will be apparent: the interpretation of the six grades by individual teachers is bound to be subjective. The difference between 'satisfactory' (*befriedigend*) and 'adequate' (*ausreichend*) can be very fine indeed, particularly in arts subjects. The KMK has itself issued further guidance on the interpretation of grades inasmuch as it has encouraged teachers to take into account the type of school – there are four basic types of secondary school in the western *Länder* – and the age of the pupil. But it is the classroom teacher who in effect defines the standards, who has at the end of the year to help determine whether the individual pupil has reached 'the goal of the class' (*das Ziel der Klasse*). The extent to which one teacher's grade 4 in geography is 'the same' as a colleague's grade 4 in that subject – or in history or biology for that matter – will remain doubtful; the same doubt has to be expressed, *a fortiori*, about consistency from school to school, let alone from *Land* to *Land*. (The HMI team (DES 1986: 8) found that with the exception of assessment for the *Abitur* and vocational qualifications 'there has not been marked concern about seeking consistency between *Länder*'.)

The *Notensystem* constitutes a mixture of criterion- and norm-referencing: in so far as it is designed to record whether pupils have reached a clearly predetermined standard it may be described as criterion-referenced; but the individual teacher's decision as to what constitutes, for example, 'satisfactory' in a particular class, can only depend on a process of norm-referencing. Pearce *et al.* (1985: 2) put it this way: 'the system employs norm-referencing within a criterion-referenced framework'.

Pupils' assessment finds its formal expression in the issuing of reports twice a year, the half-year report (*Zwischenzeugnis*) giving an early warning of the likely outcome at the end of the year and so indicating the areas where improvement is necessary. Each subject teacher records a summative grade on the *Notenskala*, based on individual marks that have been accumulated during the period under review for homework, regular school tests (*Klassenarbeiten*), and oral tests (which take into account not only subject knowledge but also linguistic ability).

In the early years of schooling pupils are familiarized slowly with the system by which they are going to be assessed for the rest of their school career. In the first year of primary school (*Grundschule*) no numerical grades are formally awarded, for example, though verbal reporting will be based on the teacher's notional assessments on the six-point scale. By the time pupils transfer to a secondary school, they are fully accustomed to the grading system and its implications.

The implications can be very serious. As we have seen, grade 4 is the lowest acceptable indicator that a satisfactory standard has been reached. Pupils are allowed to notch up *one* average of 5 in their end-of-year report; a 6 or more than two 5s will in most cases result in their not being allowed to move up to the next class. A class may only be repeated once; thereafter, if the formal requirements for promotion to the next class are again not satisfied, a pupil will have to transfer to another type of school (from the *Gymnasium* (grammar school) to the *Realschule* (intermediate school), for example; or from the *Realschule* to the 'main' type of secondary school, the *Hauptschule*). Schools will advise pupils and parents against repeating a whole school year where there is little hope of a successful outcome the second time round.

The final school-leaving qualification, the *Abitur*, is awarded on the basis of written examinations and oral assessment in basic (*Grundkurse*) and specialized courses (*Leistungskurse*). A complex arithmetical marking system is used, with appropriate weighting being given to the *Leistungskurse*. These marks are then translated by means of a nationally agreed table into a grade (calculated to one decimal point) in the six-point *Notenskala*. Students have the right of access to university education once the *Abitur* has been awarded, except in those subjects where there is a restricted entry (*Numerus clausus*). In those subjects decisions can rest on a difference of only one decimal point. (Full details of the *Abitur* formalities are given in the 1986 HMI report.)

It has been estimated that an average of five million marks were awarded each day in the (pre-unification) Federal Republic (*Frankfurter Rundschau*, 19 December 1977). While there is a general acceptance of the system in Germany and some enthusiasm for it among foreign observers (including the HMI team), there is a vast literature containing much criticism of its effects on pupils and teachers. There are obvious problems when teachers are constantly involved in giving their pupils marks which could have serious consequences for their future; when pupils' rights are (quite properly) enshrined in law, so that teachers have to be vigilant about following procedures to the very letter; when pupils resort to every trick to gain advantage; when an important factor in the seriousness with which a particular task is approached will depend on whether it is to be formally assessed; and when, as with all close control of what happens in classrooms, freedom is curtailed, resulting at best in lack of initiative in teaching, at worst in curricular stagnation. Glowka (1989: 322) puts it thus:

> [The] pupils suffer from the permanent pressure to perform well, and from the daily recurring situation of being assessed. . . . It is not surprising that obtaining a good mark – through whatever means and whatever the subject of learning – appears to pupils to be the main purpose of school attendance. Thus they shake with fear several times a week, faced with tests as a means of control, the results of which not infrequently inflict great misery on individuals and families.

On the other hand it is argued that the *Notensystem* provides an immediately understood indication of attainment at all levels and in all types of school, that it imposes a proper degree of uniformity of approach, and that, as the HMI team put it, it works:

Ultimately . . . the system works because virtually everybody involved seems determined that it should do so. Teachers at one school may sometimes grumble about standards achieved by pupils arriving from, or going to, another; one *Land* or university may have views about the standards of students arriving with an *Abitur* gained in another part of the country . . . But nobody in the chain refuses to recognise a certificate which conforms to the KMK outline agreements or, internally, the *Land* pattern. It is, as much as anything else, an article of faith.

(DES 1989: 34)

Comparativists are always wary about assessing the lessons to be learnt from the study of other systems or parts of them. In their 'home' contexts many procedures will appear to work well, but their success often depends on long traditions and attitudes and on hard-fought debates of long ago. Transplanting 'alien' procedures to other systems is rarely advisable; they often serve better as warnings against moving in a certain direction than as incentives to do so. In the case of the German *Notensystem* I suspect that it is the negative lessons to be learnt from the German experience that will prove most valuable to us in designing approaches to assessment that are consistent with what remains of the freedoms traditionally enjoyed by British teachers in their classrooms.

REFERENCES

Department of Education and Science (1986) *Education in the Federal Republic of Germany – Aspects of curriculum and assessment* (an HMI Report) (London: HMSO).

Glowka, Detlef (1989) Anglo-German perceptions of education. *Comparative Education*, 25 (3).

Ingenkamp, Karlheinz (1985) Erfassung und Rückmeldung des Lernerfolgs. In Dieter Lenzen (ed.) *Enzyklopädie Erziehungswissenschaft*, Vol. 4: *Methoden und Medien der Erziehung und des Unterrichts*, eds Gunter Otto and Wolfgang Schulz (Stuttgart: Klett-Cotta).

Pearce, J., Goodman-Stephens, B. and Robinson, C. (1985) *Assessment in West German Schools* (Huntingdon: Education Department).

8 Anglo-German perceptions of education [1989]

Detlef Glowka

APPROACH AND PREMISES

The recent developments in the British education system present a fascinating spectacle to observers from the Federal Republic of Germany (FRG) which they follow with mixed feelings. They perceive the dismantling of elements seen as patterns of British liberality and democracy and which could be quoted effectively as excellent examples in Germany. They also notice with astonishment that this process of transformation is occasionally commented upon with reference to the allegedly excellent state of the education system in the FRG, which is regarded as exemplary. The observers sympathise with the infuriated reactions of their liberal colleagues in Great Britain and their protest against Thatcherism in education. Nevertheless, at the same time observers from the FRG cannot but regard this annoyance as a manifestation of an 'insular' limitation of their horizons – at least in respect of some items in the Thatcherite reform programme, the aims of which appear in various ways to represent a moderate and liberal version of what is taken as a usual feature in other democracies, and which are coped with properly. The positive references to Germany, however, cause irritation; for they are obviously selective, and their motives have to be examined in detail.

In an analysis of recent British references to the education system of the FRG, we must not only consider the phenomena used for comparison but also pay attention to their context. A comparison of education systems is based on descriptions which must be as accurate as possible; but alongside those descriptions, evaluative criteria have to be adduced – otherwise the comparison remains lifeless and boring. This evaluative element must play a stronger part if one is speaking about comparisons already carried out. Such judgement ought also to be allowed by educationists, provided that it is frankly presented and clearly recognisable as such to the reader. The following remarks are written from an evaluative point of view.

Perhaps it should be assumed that the British education system is held in high regard in the FRG. A great number of studies and articles (H.

Schmidt counted more than 900 titles) have made known principally those phenomena which have been regarded here as exemplary, like teachers' centres, the Open University, community education, the great variety of curriculum developments, the establishment of the comprehensive school, and, above all, the development of the primary school as well as the concept of open education. These topics have exerted a strong influence on the pedagogical and political commitment of various groups in education, even if they have rarely produced demonstrable results in which British models could be recognised. The British education system as a whole, however, has attracted only little attention in the FRG; comprehensive descriptions of education in Great Britain, which would meet scholarly standards and at the same time be accessible to a wider public, are virtually non-existent. This may be due to the fact that the development of comprehensive schooling in Great Britain has not been taken as a model in the FRG, where the tripartite system has outlasted the reform period of the 1960s and 1970s. First of all the system of government and administration of the British education system is extremely alien and difficult to grasp for Germans; those difficulties cause a barrier to a comprehensive understanding of the education system in Great Britain. It is significant that the most recent developments and the Education Reform Act (1988) have hardly attracted any public attention yet. At the same time, however, the German conservatives would certainly be keen to hear that their esteemed traditional German education system has now achieved an unexpected reputation under the Thatcher government. A political camp like the Free Democrats (FDP) would certainly like to import some features of the British reform developments into the FRG, if public support could be gained for this idea.

The present British interest in the education system of the FRG has one distinctly recognisable motive. Peter Raggatt (1988) describes this at the beginning of his article included in this present volume (pp. 176–204):

> In recent years economic need has again emerged as the major principle of educational policy. Numerous documents and ministerial speeches have declared that Britain is losing the competition for world markets and have argued that 'education' must serve the economy better than it has in the past.

And he quotes the DES: 'The comparison which counts is that with our overseas competitors and that is to our disadvantage'.

The following reflection is based on three documents which reveal British interest in the education system of the FRG. Among these is the HMI Report of 1986 (DES 1986); it includes a careful description of essential features of the system of general education in the FRG and deserves particular attention because of its distinguished authorship. The Report holds back from making judgements, but even in the presentation of facts, the selection and nuances involved reveal which specific features the observers found particularly fascinating. The authors make no attempt to conceal their generally positive impression:

> The Federal Republic's system sets out to provide qualifications for all its pupils. It is not wholly successful in this, but its achievements are impressive. Within its differentiated system of education and training it appears more successful than we are in retaining a large proportion of pupils in general education or in education and training until 17 or 18 years of age; in providing attainable goals for them to work towards; and in not hiving off different groups of pupils in ways that cut them off from the mainstream of general education.
>
> (p. vi)

Prais and Wagner's (1986) study is intended to provide a thorough and scientific comparative appraisal of the level of performance attained in the schools of both countries. The results have found expression in several concise statements such as the following:

> In *nominal* terms it appears . . . that Germany prepares two to three times the British proportion for university entrance.
>
> (p. 9)

> Taken together, the contrast may be put as follows: *over half of all German pupils, compared with only just over a quarter of all pupils in England, attain a standard above or equivalent to a broadly-based set of O-level passes.*
>
> (p. 14)

> the German system had raised the average attainment of its weakest 50% of pupils to that of the average of all pupils in England.
>
> (p. 17)

The third study by Peter Raggatt (1988) also presents a summary description of the school system in the FRG; in contrast to the other studies it includes a description of the vocational education system as well as a comparison of the two parts. In spite of the unavoidable simplification in such a concentrated presentation, the study gives a very full, clear and accurate description of the circumstances in the FRG. Following previous studies Raggatt starts with the topic of 'how key elements in the vocational education and training policies in the Federal Republic of Germany, the United States and Japan underpin their economic competitiveness' (p. 164). Against the background of the German vocational education system – which appears to some extent to be an ideal one – the author deals with the Youth Training Scheme (YTS) and the Technical and Vocational Education Initiative (TVEI), whose drastic deficiences are revealed.

All three studies themselves include references to further similar analyses in Great Britain. Evidently there are many in Great Britain at the present time, the Secretary of State for Education and Science among them, who, when arguing a case, make comparisons with other countries, and, especially, with the Federal Republic of Germany. Never before – that is the impression one gets – has any reform in the British education system been so informed by a consciousness of international associations.

The various aspects of the education system in the FRG described in the works in question can be grouped into a set of five categories: (1) the continuous assessment of pupil performance; (2) the compulsory nature and breadth of the curriculum; (3) the wide distribution of school-leaving qualifications and the systematic correlations between them; (4) the developed and systematic paths towards accredited vocational education; (5) the regulating force of central guiding and controlling authorities. It appears that in these five areas something could be learnt from the Germans. At the same time these areas are central features of the Education Reform Act of 1988.

THE DUBIOUS NATURE OF THE GERMAN EXAMPLE

I shall deal with these five aspects in turn and subject them to the following questions: 'Are the conditions in Germany being adequately assessed? Is it actually worthwhile learning from the German example?'

Assessment and accountability

Obviously the British observers have been particularly impressed by the fact that German pupils are permanently subjected to checks with regard to their performance, and that teachers are able and ready to perform these checks:

> It is worth recalling and emphasising that we asked to be shown good practice in assessment procedures and that we were impressed by much that we saw.
>
> (DES 1986: 37)

> The element of continuous assessment offers a reasonable check on progress and heightens pupils' awareness of having to qualify before the final examination itself is taken.
>
> (ibid.: 36)

> Oral examining is an important feature of all examinations . . . ; . . . [this] could provide useful material for discussion amongst teachers here.
>
> (ibid.: 36–7)

> [Teachers] have themselves been taught systematically how to undertake this assessment.
>
> (ibid.: 36)

>... the system works because virtually everybody involved seems deter-
>mined that it should do so.
>
>(ibid.: 34)

In fact, the majority of teachers and presumably an even greater majority
of civil servants of the supervising education authorities can hardly
imagine a school without a system of continuous assessment by means of
marks. But a great number of pupils take a different view. These pupils
suffer from the permanent pressure to perform well, and from the daily
recurring situation of being assessed (which adult would tolerate being
given a mark for his professional ability every day that could affect his
staying at his place of work and his career?). It is not surprising that
obtaining a good mark – through whatever means and whatever the
subject of learning – appears to pupils to be the main purpose of school
attendance. Thus they shake with fear several times a week, faced with
tests as means of control, the results of which not infrequently inflict
great misery on individuals and families ('stress at school is a frequent
topic of press articles', ibid.: 38).

Of course, the dubious nature of the assessment of learning performance has been shown in Germany as well as elsewhere in the world.
The objections against assessment of performance are especially valid
with regard to the peculiarities of children's learning (developing personality and gaining a general education) and the assessment by teachers
(the person doing the assessing being himself deeply involved in the
learning situation). There are plenty of studies which prove the insufficient
relevance and lack of objectivity of the assessment system (*Notensystem*)
of German schools (most recently among them, for example, that of the
two renowned educationists Hellmut Becker and Hartmut von Hentig
(1983): 'We hope that we shall reduce the superstition about the "truth"
of marks by means of this publication and that we can at the same time
offer some alternative ways for everyday school life'). However, it is not
the mental pressure on the pupils nor the insufficiencies of the procedures
(which psychometric specialists still believe can be perfected) which form
the main objections in the recent literature. The system is fundamentally
inconsistent with pedagogical principles. Even one of the education ministers (W. Remmers, in Lower Saxony) once quoted with approval a metaphor handed down from the period of progressive education: 'It is like
tearing plants out of the soil again and again in order to see whether
they have taken root.' Educationists of the most different theoretical and
ideological backgrounds find common agreement in the view that school
has to be more than a learning factory, and that one dimension of learning,
which is a priori beyond marking assessment, has to play a central part
in schooling: the development of personality.

I shall have to return to the reason why the *Notensystem* has persisted
so obstinately in the school system in the FRG despite the widespread

disapproval of it shared by nearly all educationists. In the search for alternatives they often looked admiringly towards the British example; it seemed that under the less controlled circumstances there, pedagogical common sense could actually blossom. If there are, now, contrariwise, some British educationists who recognise certain advantages of the German assessment arrangements, they should also consider that even if these arrangements are 'effective' to some degree, this is so only at the expense of enormous psychological damage. It is no exaggeration to say that the majority of adolescents in Germany leave school with their self-esteem permanently damaged.

The compulsory nature and breadth of the curriculum

The British observers rightly concluded:

> There is a long history of detailed development work on the curriculum guidelines for individual subjects at all ability levels, both within the traditional tripartite system and for the comparatively few comprehensive schools. These guidelines exert a strong influence on what is taught and on the manner in which it is taught and, to some extent, upon how it is assessed. [And they add:] But there was no questioning the benefits of or a need for the guidelines.
>
> (DES 1986: 35)

> A German pupil must try harder to avoid failing in a core subject, such as mathematics or writing his native language, than a pupil in England.
>
> (Prais and Wagner 1986: 16)

Every German school has curricula which it is obliged to adhere to. These curricula define subjects, their content matter, attainment targets and the prescribed numbers of lessons per year. Such a prescription of duties for teachers and pupils is justified by the assertion that this is the only way to ensure the attainment of definite standards and a reasonable sequence of learning. Such an approach is based on elaborate theoretical assumptions; the British liberality with regard to such questions appears negligent from the German point of view.

Since the so-called empirical about-turn of our pedadogy – that is, from the mid-1960s – educationists have collected a host of facts and insights which make the theoretical demands of the curricula appear more or less unrealistic. In everyday school life the curricula result in pupils being inundated with material; teachers and pupils feel themselves at the mercy of the pressure exerted by a plan which only grants small scope to their particular interests and abilities. What is given out as a pedagogical structure of the curriculum proves on more detailed examination to be a scarcely rational compromise between competing interest groups (e.g.

associations of subject teachers) the intentions of political leadership and the persistent effects of established conditions.

It was doubt about the rationale for uniform structures which resulted in the decision to introduce elements of choice and specialisation into the curriculum of the *Abitur* in 1972 (Arthur Hearnden (1986) has shown very clearly how little this reform amounted to a convergence with the English model). These elements have recently been largely withdrawn – 'to ensure a wide range of general education'. It is significant that this step provoked vigorous protests on the part of pupils, who joined large street demonstrations, thereby expressing what educationists confirm: that pupils only experience a small amount of the intentions of the curriculum relating to comprehensive education during their everyday lessons; they only reluctantly endure the treatment of ossified subject matter, and their dissatisfaction beyond the primary stage is increasing continuously. Learning in schools is considered a kind of labour: it is done in spite of lack of enthusiasm because its exchange values, the marks and the certificates, are needed; these, again can be exchanged for career progress, and this, in turn, for an improved standard of living.

It is likely that there are similar examples of reluctant school attendance in Great Britain; perhaps they are more obvious in the FRG. Great efforts have been made by educationists and open-minded teachers to place curricula and learning at school on the sort of basis that would make possible learning that was lively and related to experience (like the *Laborschule* in Bielefeld). Also in connection with these efforts, the situation in British schools is widely considered to be exemplary. Recently the school authorities have slackened the reins a little: they allow 'project weeks' and offer supplementary lessons, or permit teachers to arrange part of the curriculum as they like. The system of curriculum guidelines in the FRG is in any case not as unchallenged as it occasionally appears to British observers. Here too the disadvantages of the system have to be endured first and foremost by those who have the least chance of all to attract public attention: the pupils.

School-leaving qualifications and their organisation

It is correct that about 90 per cent of the pupils in the FRG achieve a leaving certificate – according to the type of school attended. The attainment of such a leaving certification appears to be the only real purpose of school attendance. Even at special schools for handicapped pupils there is a standardised leaving certificate. The leaving certificates serve as 'proofs of entitlement', for they regulate transition to other types of school and training routes, and, especially, admission to the civil service. This system has its origin in the last century; today it is kept going by the *Konferenz der Kultusminister* (KMK). British observers confirm this with some surprise:

Nobody in the chain refuses to recognise a certificate which conforms to the KMK outline agreements or, internally, the *Land* pattern. It is, as much as anything else, an article of faith. This wide agreement about education and its assessment is in itself an important message for English education.

(DES 1986: 34)

The system of graded school-leaving examinations – which itself is far more differentiated than the tripartite nature of the school system – is actually supposed to serve the purpose of distributing cohorts of pupils to fields of training appropriate to the needs of society. Today, however, those cohorts of pupils are driven by an uncontrollable inner dynamic. The proportion of those leaving school with the *Abitur* has increased approximately fourfold in thirty years (it is now about 30 per cent); in conurbations it is not unusual for more than 50 per cent of pupils to transfer to the *Gymnasien*, and this tendency is increasing. The *Hauptschule* ('main' school!) has degenerated into a school for the leftovers. Business and industry adapt their demands to the supply: where 15 years ago a leaving certificate from a *Hauptschule* was regarded as adequate, today the *Abitur* is frequently demanded for a job. In many cases a reasonable correlation between school education and vocational training is not recognisable; a pure market economy relationship prevails. Since fewer training places and jobs are available than the number demanded, the bottom group of school leavers is excluded, without any chances. In many cases these are already pupils with a leaving certificate from the *Hauptschule*.

Certainly educationists have examined the question as to what reliability a leaving certificate can have as evidence of a person's ability. As might be expected its value proves to be dubious. Many employers take this into account by setting entrance examinations of their own. If in spite of such doubts the system is still kept in place, then it is because it fulfils excellently an important social function. On their way to the final examination, via numerous less important appraisals, the pupils internalise the perception that the capacity of human beings differs and that it is the task of each individual to achieve the highest target that he is capable of. The qualification finally determines his position *vis-à-vis* admission to vocational training; the pupil is very well prepared to accept that social inequalities are the result of different individual performance levels. In the theory of school – a developed branch of German pedagogy – the function of selection has been emphasised as one of the school's most important tasks. The fact that the system of assessment, which cannot be justified from a pedagogical point of view, is still kept in existence is due to such a function of selection: it satisfies the ambitions of those parents who want their children to gain a proper position in the race (and normally succeed); coincidentally they are the parents who are able to exert great influence on school and policy.

With regard to leaving certificates there were some fundamentally innovative approaches during the past reform period. The most important and remarkable features are those attempts to establish a particular examination for the emerging comprehensive schools, and – more far-reaching – to introduce an *Abitur I*, intended as a final examination for all adolescents aged about 16, and to call the former *Abitur* henceforth *Abitur II*. However, the traditional system has maintained its position. The results attained at comprehensive schools are related by a grotesque procedure of calculations to the 'standards' of the conventional types of schools and are appropriately confirmed with certificates. If British visitors are impressed by all this, then against the background of the criticisms I have indicated a number of aspects could be mentioned in which, as far as examinations and certification is concerned, the Federal Republic could learn something from Britain.

Preparation at school for vocational training

In the field of vocational training Great Britain seems clearly to have fallen behind the Federal Republic of Germany; the self-critical statements prove quite drastic:

> Britain has one of the least trained workforces in the industrial world . . . we have the smallest graduate community compared with our competing nations.
>
> (quoted by Raggatt 1988: 163–4)

> Britain has, as yet, nothing comparable to the Meister system.
>
> (ibid.: 180)

> [Raggatt assumes:] . . . the clues to German economic success lie in the *unitary* nature of the education and vocational system.
>
> (ibid. p. 181)

From the insider's point of view the German system of vocational education proves to have conspicuous deficiencies. The high proportion of pupils who pass the *Abitur* results in correspondingly high numbers of students at universities (about 80 per cent of the pupils who pass the *Abitur* take up a university place; in many cases it is the very intelligent ones who prefer to choose an apprenticeship or training at a *Fachschule* to the university). Many of them choose to begin a university course because after passing through the academic curriculum of the *Gymnasium* nothing else occurs to them. Mass education at the university blunts the mediocre ones; only the particularly bright students are capable of using the relatively liberal set-up, which favours autonomous behaviour, for their own mental cultivation. In comparison with Great Britain we have here a situation opposite to that pertaining to secondary education: British observers normally find it incomprehensible that students are left to themselves with so little curricular guidance and control. Many students do not realise until their final examination or their ensuing search for a job, that is to say at the age of more than 25, that they have chosen the wrong way, and they then turn to the retraining programmes offered by the employment authorities. Unemployment among university graduates is increasing disproportionately. No, university education in the FRG does not prove to be a showpiece if one looks at quality instead of quantity.

I do not intend to discuss the middle sector of *Fachschulen* and *Fachhochschulen* here; in many respects it evidently operates very well. It is the vocational training of apprentices in industry, commerce and crafts, along with parallel school attendance, the so-called 'dual system' (Peter Raggatt has described it excellently), which again and again attracts particular admiration from foreign countries. This system undoubtedly has its advantages and its share in the prosperity of German industry. However, the following aspect restricts it seriously: as a result of the competition for the limited number of jobs a professional training is today absolutely necessary for every young person. Vocational training in the dual system is mainly offered in crafts where apprentices can be used as additions to the workforce; but only a fraction of those trained can get a regular job there. As a result we find that three years after the completion of their vocational training more than 50 per cent of young people are in employment which is different from the trade in which they have received that training.

If we take together the two manifestations of inappropriate qualifications – in the universities and in the dual system – we are able to gain some idea of the waste of national economic resources and of the innumerable cases of individual disappointment and tragedy occurring during the transition into working life. Young people are subjected to extraordinary psychological pressure: never before did they have to cope with such high expectations in regard to training and performance, and never before – during recent decades – have so many of them had to face the experience that society has no need of their abilities (see Mertens 1984). Here again the system serves its purpose of letting the failure of society appear as a deficiency of individual abilities. Whereas a German observer in Britain is impressed by the fact that many teachers and whole schools care about the pupils' future before and after they leave school, German teachers remain quite untouched by such matters. It is their duty to issue or to refuse to issue the leaving certificates; their teaching has nothing to do with the pupils' lives after they have left. The same situation can be found at the universities.

The effects of central guidance and control

British observers of the German school system acknowledge, without doubt correctly, that the advantages noticed by them are interdependent and would not be possible without a system of central direction and control. This Prais and Wagner (1986) end their thorough investigation with the following statement:

> The contrast between the *growth* of an intermediate stream of schooling in Germany – with its explicit practical educational objectives and syllabus – and its submergence in England, provides an overriding clue to many educational and social differences between these countries. The highly developed vocational training system in Germany may be seen as a complementary development of the same underlying balance in the purpose of education.

The authors conclude: 'A proper discussion of policy for English schools cannot therefore avoid questioning whether its accepted decentralised framework of schooling must remain as it is' (p. 24).

Statements of this kind gain weight against the background of the most recent developments in Great Britain which have culminated in the Education Reform Act of 1988, which, an opposition spokesman has calculated, confers on the Secretary of State 175 new powers (*The Times Educational Supplement*, 1987). The management of the education system in the FRG is indeed centrally organised, even if at the level of the *Länder*. Raggatt (1988) rightly states that management primarily operates in accordance with what the law determines (cf. pp. 175 ff.) and he remarks, *inter alia*:

> It is the most comprehensive and detailed regulatory system for apprenticeship training in the Western world.

(p. 175)

Here a subject is raised which has been judged extremely controversial in the FRG. On the one hand the system of management has survived the reform period without serious damage; this topic is no longer under discussion today, because it appears hopeless to take it up again. On the other hand during the reform period the system was subjected to a substantial amount of theoretical criticism whose essence can be predominantly summarised thus: as long as the organisation of management and control remains as it is the education system cannot be improved. Even the *Deutscher Bildungsrat* picked up this topic and published two statements on it: by doing this (and only in this specific case) the committee reached the limits of its ability to reach agreement, and as a result of these two particular statements it was dissolved by the politicians. Even the renowned *Deutscher Juristentag* committed itself in vain to the initiation of a reorganisation of the legal framework of the education system.

Educationists present a different set of arguments, which interpret education in schools as being so dominated by legal and administrative regulations that pedagogical principles perish and school has to be regarded as 'a para-pedagogical institution'.

All of this is not a matter of general political or legal ideas; it concerns the everyday role of teachers in their classes and the feasibility of arrangements in individual schools. The density of regulations is so high that a teacher is unable to keep them all in mind (in a thorough stock reduction the number of valid regulations has been reduced to a fraction, but still more than 400 regulations remain). If a teacher steps outside routine matters he has first to make sure of the legal position; that is why extracurricular activities with pupils or excursions during the school term are avoided so far as possible. To a large extent that is the reason why German teachers are less committed to education and regard themselves as 'teaching civil servants' (*Unterrichtsbeamte*). It is important to make this point when Her Majesty's Inspectors show themselves so impressed by the status of teachers in the Federal Republic (DES 1986: 35).

The circumstances I have described allow little scope for initiatives intended to give a distinctive profile to a state school or even to establish a school outside state control. Educational variety flourishes under these circumstances only to a meagre extent. One can imagine how the advocates of the educational variety in the FRG have until now looked with admiration towards Great Britain.

At the present time those elements of the German education system whose value is judged in the Federal Republic to be controversial or even negative are being considered as good examples in Great Britain. The reader may suggest that the point of view presented here is perhaps that of an over-critical outsider. However, a great mound of books and articles written by educationists can be quoted which takes similar positions (without bringing in extreme points of view, some titles can be mentioned which are representative of the predominant criticism of the education system in the FRG: Lenzen 1982–6; Schweitzer and Thiersch 1983; Bohnsack 1984; Klemm *et al.* 1985; Schweitzer 1986; Müller-Rolli 1987; Tillmann 1987; Dannhäuser 1988; Rolff *et al.* 1988). As a university lecturer it requires a great effort to select one affirmative theory of school out of those offered which could explain to the students why the system operates, given the way it is. Admittedly, this remains so much paper. While the reading of these books creates the impression that the German school system is on the verge of collapse, in practice it continues to exist unflustered and to present itself in the way the HMIs have perceived it.

THE DUBIOUS NATURE OF THE BRITISH SOLUTION

I have indicated to what extent, as I see it, the Thatcher government has dismantled elements of the English education system which have been widely held in high regard in the Federal Republic. This does not mean that British conditions should have been imitated. From the German point of view what is fascinating about the English school system is that something was and is possible there that would simply be considered impossible in Germany. Seen in this way the intention of the Education Reform Act can be interpreted as a move towards reasonable conditions. Compared with the German situation the interventions appear to be moderate. Such a view can be elucidated in several regards; the DES (1989) booklet, *National Curriculum: Theory and Practice*, can serve as a point of reference, for it is here that the Secretary of State put his concrete ideas on the realisation of the Education Reform Act.

From the German point of view it appears plainly reasonable to classify English, mathematics and science as 'core subjects', and there would scarcely be objections to the 'other foundation subjects' (Section 5.3). It is emphasised that: 'The foundation subjects are certainly *not* a complete curriculum' (3.8), so that considerable scope of individual arrangements in schools remains. Nor is there any prescription of the amount of time allocated for particular subjects: 'There are no centrally prescribed time allocations for particular subjects'; the government will restrict itself to 'general assumptions about the amount of time' (4.3). The previous proposal of HMI to regard the curriculum as comprising 'areas of learning and experience' has been positively received (3.7), and several times it is emphasised that: 'curriculum does not mean that teaching has to be organised and delivered within prescribed subject boundaries'.

Such a conception of arrangements for the curriculum would be regarded in German schools as a release into vertiginous freedom. Educationists would hardly deny that pupils need feedback on their progress, and a set of marks – cautiously applied – could undoubtedly be one of the appropriate means. One gains a good impression from the government's intention to restrict the examination of pupils to four key stages. Of course, there is no reasonable control without 'attainment targets and programmes of study', in respect of which individual schools have an important part to play:

> They provide clear objectives on which schemes of work can be based, and to which cross-curricular teaching can be related. . . . They allow for, and encourage, progression whilst also accommodating differentiation. . . . They will specify essential studies which all pupils must undertake.
>
> (4.15)

It sounds convincing when they say:

> The requirements will be far from totally new. Most will be familiar ground to teachers, and will build firmly on present good practice.
>
> (4.15)

The idea of introducing the innovations step by step, so that they are continuously open to revision, and the intention of basing them on good practice, are repeated several times. There is no intention to reduce the assessment of performance to standardised tests:

> Teachers' own assessments are an essential part of the system. They will be able to cover aspects of performance not readily testable by conventional means, and more generally will ensure a place in the assessments for rounded, qualitative judgements.
>
> (6.5)

This seems to go much further than the appraisal of oral performance in German schools. Besides, schools are allowed wide leeway to ask for special regulations for children with special educational needs (cf. 8) or for other reasons (cf. 5.4). The establishment of a new examination aimed at all young people of about 16, the GCSE, reminds us of the German proposal for an *Abitur I*; it seems to be wise to aim at assessing the performance of all pupils, while only in the three core subjects is the taking of GCSE expected as a minimum, since this takes into account young people's different aptitudes. On the whole one gains the impression that the introduction of the National Curriculum with all its consequences could actually result in the kind of positive challenge for all involved envisaged in the document:

> The introduction of the national curriculum seems likely to stimulate a lot of work at local level on aspects of the content of the curriculum and its organisation and to help focus this on the essentials of what teachers and pupils need.
>
> (5.4)

In fact it appears from all this as if the Thatcher government is not only willing to realise something which is educationally reasonable, but also to take what is an educationally reasonable course towards that realisation. Compared with German conditions the whole seems to be pervaded still by the spirit of British liberality.

The British reader will know to what extent the efforts of the government to establish a National Curriculum have been opposed by various objectors, and he will know the arguments used. Reactions from the Institute of Education of London University, an institution with a good international reputation, may probably be taken as representative of the stance of educationists in Great Britain (cf. White *et al* 1981; Lawton and Chitty 1988). That aside, however, some representatives of a liberal or progressive position have clearly advocated some kind of nationwide establishment of the curriculum; like David Hargreaves (1982) (as a staunch supporter of the comprehensive school) or – very early on – John White (1973), who feels he has been duped by the recent developments which have come into place. The objectors to the Education Reform Act have differentiated between two approaches:

> There are two very different approaches to the idea of a national curriculum – the professional and the bureaucratic.
>
> > (*Forum*, 30(1), 1987: 4)

They proposed a long process of consensus-seeking by a National Committee for Education which would have had widely representative membership. This reminds one of the activities and fate of the *Deutscher Bildungsrat*. And against this background the following questions suggest themselves. Had the difficulties not been recognisable long before (cf. McDonald and Walker 1978)? Do not the critics of the current developments recognise that the trend towards a pragmatic and central solution had already begun before the time of the Thatcher government (cf. Tulasiewicz 1987)? Who else other than the government in London could have cut the Gordian knot of pluralistic opinion and arranged a programme of practical implementation arising from discussions? Protest is now expressed with contrasting arguments: on the one hand there are the liberals, the progressives, the democrats, the representatives of children's interests and those of the underprivileged; on the other the conservatives, the reactionaries, the New Right, the centralists. A renowned education reformer such as Torsten Husén (1988) could object to Brian Simon (1988), a representative of one such position:

> He does not conceive of any failings or shortcomings of the pre-Baker system and tends to regard any change as dangerous to it, a strange conservatism in a person with socialist leanings.
>
> > (p. 363)

After pointing out that in other countries, Sweden included, similar tendencies are observable, Husén concludes:

> I do not think that those trying to 'reform' (in Britain or in some other places) are to be perceived as merely conservative or even reactionary or that those who resist change should be seen merely as defenders of progressivism and democracy. The setting is not that simple. What is at stake is the common frame of reference that a system of common schooling can provide in a working national democracy.
>
> > (pp. 368–9)

Even from the German point of view the reform programme appears to be a British version of the internationally manifest problems of school education rather than a result of the ruling party's exceptional narrow-mindedness.

Admittedly this specific British solution must also alienate the German observer – even were he a committed representative of our conservative parties. Those items of the current reform mentioned so far in this chapter are only half the story. A number of additional interventions must be mentioned too: the establishment of school-like courses of vocational education, but outside of the school system itself (Youth Training Scheme); the establishment of City Technology Colleges; the strengthening of the Governing Bodies and the weakening of the LEAs by the opting out of individual schools; the Assisted Places Scheme, etc. Kenneth Bakers' predecessor as Secretary of State had announced: 'This government aims to reduce the share of national resources taken by the public sector' (Joseph 1984: 138), and: 'I continue to ponder ways of increasing the influence of parents' (p. 145).

Not until all these measures and the frankly stated intentions are taken as a whole does the reform gain its special quality, characterised by 'privatisation' and the 'market mechanism'. Thus 'privatisation' goes hand in hand with a policy of 'nationalisation' and centralisation of control. Only when taken as a whole does this reform syndrome explain such spectacular reactions as the *Forum* conference (cf. *Forum*, 30, 1988: 68–73) or the complaint audible since then about the breakdown of consensus (McNay and Ozga, 1985), or, first and foremost, the liveliness of the protest (Haviland 1988).

To German observers the phenomenon of Thatcherite education policy appears very strange. The tendencies towards privatisation and commercialisation of the education system would encounter massive resistance in the FRG and would not be supported by a political majority. School and vocational training are regarded as social tasks which can only be regulated by the state. One of the main duties of the education authorities consists of providing for equivalent conditions in schools within a *Land*. Even in higher education an appropriate expenditure policy allows all universities equal standing. Education in the private (school) sector is strictly limited; it is only permitted on condition that these schools are for the most part in line with provision in the state school system. It is only the Waldorf schools which present a clear alternative to the established school system; the lively interest of parents in Steiner schools or in alternative education has resulted in the number of such schools increasing considerably (from 28 schools in 1964 to 38 in 1974, and 108 in 1987). However, the desire of parents and other groups for variety in the school system operates within severe limits. Most people accept that the school system has to be regulated by state authorities in order to ensure effectiveness and social balance. For this we have the special term *Ordnungspolitik*. To grant parents more influence on the development of the school system would seem inappropriate; parents are primarily interested in giving their children advantages and not in the sensible development of the school system. In the field of education the state can claim to represent public welfare, an important political category. Thus the shift of central government – announced as a 'turning point' – from the Social Democratic to the Conservative parties has not resulted in a remarkable change in respect of the subjects in question. Greater variety within the school system – within the framework of 'public welfare', of course, whatever that may be – would be more likely from a Social Democratic–Ecological coalition today; but definitely not via privatisation and commercialisation. As far as this aspect of education policy is concerned the British conservatives can certainly not refer to a German example.

Neither does the economic motive of Thatcherite policy have any equivalent in the FRG. Admittedly the dual system of vocational training can – as I have mentioned – be regarded as one of the factors which have contributed to German economic prosperity. With regard to general and university education there is no such certainty as to how an economic effect emerges. The general school system only comprises a small number of elements – apparently fewer than in Great Britain – designed to prepare pupils for the working world. This circumstance has been criticised for decades (for a variety of reasons), but, up to now, without any remarkable consequences. During the reform period – which coincided with euphoria for the economics of education and for educational planning – there were tendencies 'to combine' education and the economy as efficiently as possible. However, then the contrasting idea of 'disconnecting' them gained ground. Education should exist on its own terms (of course not in an impractical, academic sense). Because the future demand of industry and commerce for qualifications cannot be anticipated, it is up to the individuals to decide what to learn. Thus the education system goes along with the (individual) demand – with the result, for example, that at least double the number of students are educated than the labour market can make appropriate use of, in terms of the qualifications they offer.

And what is known about the relationship between education and economic success? The British observers quoted here had only examined conditions in the FRG. What about the German Democratic Republic (GDR)? The GDR reached a high level of general education in schools earlier than the FRG; the contents of school education are co-ordinated to the fullest extent possible; the net of performance control is extremely tight; the system of vocational training is in many respects superior to that of the FRG. However, everyone knows how poor the state of the GDR's economy is in comparison to that of Western countries. Which factors make the difference? If one tries to pinpoint the mystery of the FRG's economic prosperity in the education system, one probably has to examine more sophisticated traits than curricula and organisation. As indicated above, the West German school system is apparently very effective in challenging the capacity of pupils' efforts, in holding individual success in high regard, in letting the differentiation of achievement appear just, in transforming people into instruments which work effectively even when reluctant, in satisfying parents' striving for success which they project on to their children, and in passing it on to them. It is less a substantial education which will later serve the needs of the economy than the acquisition of a disposition, of a set of habits. This achievement-oriented character is formed at considerable psychological expense, and it is in all likelihood connected with what in other countries occasionally leads to the image of the 'ugly' German.

CONCLUDING REMARKS

In what I have presented above I have hopefully been able to make clear that the current British interest in Germany is quite selective. In reality the circumstances in the FRG are inconsistent and contradictory. Values like work, achievement and economic success are losing their traditional worth for many people and this trend is evidently increasing. They are subordinated to the question: how do we really want to live our lives? In West Germany a consciousness is growing that the rising and more efficient production of material goods and so-called services is not our real problem. It is our real and difficult duty to preserve or to develop a humane culture under shifting and only partly controllable circumstances. This is an ecological rather than an economic task. In Great Britain today economic engagement seems to be prevalent. Nobody can predict whether such a trend will gain more support in the FRG. There is no such indication at present. In any case, when educational policy makers in Great Britain refer to the situation in West Germany as a model the motives are transparently clear: they are simply adding a further stanza to the old song of international comparison as a means of legitimating already established political goals (cf. Zymek 1975). It has little to do with learning from other countries. At the same time both nations could – with their rich cultures – learn a lot from each other.

REFERENCES

Becker, Hellmut and Hentig, Hartmut von (eds) (1983) *Zensuren, Lüge – Notwendigkeit – Alternativen* (Stuttgart).
Bohnsack, Fritz (ed.) (1984) *Sinnlosigkeit und Sinnperspektive. Die Bedeutung gewandelter Lebens- und Sinnstrukturen für die Schulkrise* (Frankfurt am Main).
Dannhäuser, Albin (ed.) (1988) *Ist die Schule noch zu retten? Plädoyer für eine neue Bildungsreform* (Weinheim).
DES (1986) *Education in the Federal Republic of Germany: Aspects of Curriculum and Assessment. An HMI Report* (London, DES).
DES (1989) *National Curriculum Theory and Practice* (London, DES).
Hargreaves, David H. (1982) *The Challenge for the Comprehensive School: Culture, Curriculum and Community* (London).
Haviland, Julian (ed.) (1988) *Take Care, Mr Baker!* (London).
Hearnden, Arthur (1986) 'Comparative studies and curriculum change in the United Kingdom and the Federal Republic of Germany', *Oxford Review of Education*, 12, pp. 187–94.

Husén, Torsten (1988) 'From consensus to confrontation in educational policy', *Oxford Review of Education*, 14, pp. 363–9.

Joseph, Sir Keith (1984) Speech at the North of England Conference, Sheffield, on Friday 6 January, *Oxford Review of Education*, 10, pp. 137–46.

Klemm, K., Rolfe, H.-G. and Tillman, K.-J. (1985) *Bildung für das Jahr 2000* (Reinbeck).

Lawton, Denis and Chitty, Clyde (eds) (1988) *The National Curriculum* (London).

Lenze, Dieter (ed.) (1982–6) *Enzyklopädie Erziehungswissenschaft. Handbuch und Lexikon der Erziehung*, 12 volumes (Stuttgart).

Liell, Peter (ed.) (1988) Special Bulletin. Education Reform Act 1988, *The Law of Education*, 9th edn (London).

McDonald, Barry and Walker, Rob (1978) 'Die Curriculumreform-Bewegung in England: eine kritische Bilanz', *Zeitschrift für Pädagogik*, 24, pp. 581–99.

McNay, Ian and Ozga, Jenny (eds) (1985) *Policy-making in Education. The Breakdown of Consensus* (Oxford).

Mertens, Dieter (1984) 'Das Qualifizierungsparadox. Bildung und Beschäftigung bei kritischer Arbeitsmarktperspektive', *Zeitschrift für Pädagogik*, 30, pp. 439–55.

Müller-Rolli, Sebastian (ed.) (1987) *Das Bildungswesen der Zukunft* (Stuttgart).

Prais, S. J. and Wagner, Karin (1986) 'Schooling standards in England and Germany: some summary comparisons bearing on economic performance', *Compare*, 16, pp. 5–35.

Raggatt, Peter (1988) 'Quality control in the dual system of West Germany', *Oxford Review of Education*, 14, pp. 163–86.

Rolff, Hans-Günther *et al.* (eds) (1988) *Jahrbuch der Schulentwicklung 5* (München).

Schmidt, Heiner (1981) *Vergleichende Erziehungswissenschaft. 1945–1980. Bibliographie des deutschsprachigen Schrifttums . . .* (Duisburg).

Schweitzer, F. and Thiersch, H. (eds) (1983) *Jugendzeit-Schulzeit. Von den Schwierigkeiten, die Jugendliche und Schule miteinander haben* (Weinheim).

Schweitzer, Jochen (ed.) (1986) *Bildung für eine menschliche Zukunft. Solidarität lernen – Technik beherrschen – Frieden sichern – Umwelt gestalten* (Weinheim).

Simon, Brian (1988) *Bending the Rules: the Baker Reform in Education* (London, Lawrence & Wishart).

The Times Educational Supplement (1987), 4 December, p. 5.

Tillman, Klaus-Jürgen (1987) *Zwischen Euphorie und Stagnation. Erfahrungen mit der Bildungsreform* (Hamburg).

Tulasiewicz, Witold (1987) 'The development of the education system in England and Wales under the Conservative administration of Mrs Thatcher', *Zeitschrift für internationale und sozialwissenschaftliche Forschung*, Sonderheft, pp. 189–219.

White, J. P. (1973) *Towards a Compulsory Curriculum* (London).

White, John (1982) *The Aims of Education Restated* (London).

White, John *et al.* (1981) *No Minister. A Critique of the DES Paper 'The School Curriculum'* (London).

Zymek, Bernd (1975) *Das Ausland als Argument in der pädagogischen Reformdiskussion* (Ratingen).

Part III

Vocational education and training

9 Vocational education: a success story?[1] [1985]

†*Günther Kloss*

INTRODUCTION

West Germany's vocational education and training system has been praised internationally and admired by her neighbours. OECD examiners, looking at it in connection with youth unemployment, called its underlying strategy 'eminently sensible',[2] and a mixed Anglo-German research team stated that 'it seems beyond dispute that Germany's successful economy has been well served by its highly developed vocational training system'.[3] This provides compulsory, part-time vocational education for all 15- to 18-year olds who are not in full-time general or vocational education and vocational training for about 54 per cent of all 16- to 19-year olds;[4] only a very small percentage of those not in full-time education receive no training at all. Thus in 1983, 74 per cent of the 15 to 16 age group[5] entered into a new vocational training agreement, and by September 1984 707,000 of these had been concluded, 29,000 more than the previous year, and only 4.9 per cent of applicants failed to secure an apprenticeship with, as always not inconsiderable, regional variations. The drop-out rate, too, is relatively low for such a young age group. Whatever the statistical inaccuracies associated with these figures (they relate, for example, to the actual number of those still seeking a place), this is an impressive achievement, especially so since the demand for places has been increasing steadily (with the exception of 1981). The increase from 1983 to 1984 alone was 5.5 per cent.

West Germany's vocational training system has been commended and envied because, at least potentially, it is forward-looking in that it raises the level of skills of the labour force generally and thus contributes to higher productivity and improved performance of the economy; because it keeps down youth unemployment both during and after completion of training – the unemployment quota in the Federal Republic of people with completed vocational training is 5.6 per cent (1983), compared to 17.4 per cent of those without;[6] and because it is a well-established system in which governments, employers, and trade unions collaborate and take pride.

Paradoxically, inside West Germany, vocational education and training is considered inferior to general education, it occupies the lowest position in the hierarchy of educational sectors within the system, and it is probably its most neglected branch, both in terms of resources and structural reforms – notwithstanding the 1969 *Berufsbildungsgesetz* (Vocational Training Act) and the 1981 *Berufsbildungsförderungsgesetz* (Vocational Training Promotion Act), a large number of reform proposals, and the efforts of the former SPD/FDP coalition in Bonn to raise its status to one of greater equality with general upper secondary education in the *Realschulen* (intermediate secondary schools) and *Gymnasien* (grammar schools).

Vocational education and training has in recent years moved more into the centre of the educational stage not because of a genuine desire for improvement but because of the fear of unemployment and the pressure of numbers. Whilst rolls in the general schools are falling they are still rising in the vocational training sector. This is also true of higher education, but there the public has lost interest, whereas the fate of 15- to 18-year olds still concerns people. In addition, vocational education is one of the few areas in education where the Federation has some competence – namely to regulate vocational training programmes – and therefore can be active, and can be seen to be active, without, in fact, having to spend a large amount of money itself, at least since 1983, when pupil grants were abolished.

SHORTCOMINGS OF THE SYSTEM

What are the deficiencies of the present system and are they serious enough to question its effectiveness? Most of vocational education takes place in the so-called 'dual system'. This combines regulated training, usually for a period of three years, for a recognised occupation in an enterprise – this may be a large company or a small handicraft firm – under an individual training contract with a modest allowance, with more theoretical education (general as well as training programme-oriented) in the *Berufsschule* (vocational school), usually on a day-release basis for one 8-hour day per week. The responsibilities for the two halves of the system are split three ways: the Federal government, through its various competent ministries, lays down a framework for the training programme for each of the approximately 430 occupations through issuing training regulations. These contain minimum requirements, for example, the basic skills required, skeleton curricula, and examination requirements. The individual enterprises in industry, commerce, agriculture and craft trades then voluntarily carry out the training according to their own schemes under these Federal regulations. The self-governing chambers of trade and industry, the craft chambers and other competent bodies supervise and co-ordinate the practical training and are responsible for the final examinations. Finally, the *Länder* within their general responsibilities for educational matters, look after the *Berufsschulen*, including their curricula.

At all levels of this complicated, interlinking system, from the Federal Training Institute, which prepares the training regulations, downwards to *Land* and local level, representatives of employers and employees collaborate on a statutory basis with Federal and *Länder* government representatives. It is an extremely complicated system but inevitably so, in view of the federal structure of West Germany. In fact, vocational training is unique in that it is the only area within the entire West German education system where the Federation has an original curricular responsibility and where there are consequently uniform, national framework curricula. The system depends on mutual goodwill and compromise. It is true that employers and employees do not always see eye-to-eye over vocational education questions – the possibility of imposing a training levy on all enterprises has been a perpetual point of dispute – but collaboration has been reasonably good, at least as long as the status quo is not endangered. The tripartite administrative organisation of the system, therefore, tends to prevent changes of a more fundamental and innovative nature and favours a conservative outlook.

The majority of the 15- to 18-year olds not in full-time general education are in this dual system. However, adolescents in growing numbers attend full-time vocational schools, sometimes before, sometimes after completion of vocational training. This is a significant development, brought about entirely through changing demand, for these schools frequently lead to qualifications which, though vocational in nature, are considered to be equivalent to general education qualifications. An example is the *Berufsfachschule* (full-time vocational school), for certain careers which invite a more school-like training, like nursing, commerce, home economics and certain industrial/technical jobs. This type of school was attended by 404,000 young men and women in 1983. Its organisation and entrance requirements vary enormously from one *Land* to the next, but most of these schools exempt their pupils from industrial vocational training and many lead to the *Realschule* leaving certificate (others have this as an entrance requirement). There is a *Berufsaufbauschule* (vocational extension school), which follows on from the *Berufsschule* and is part-time or full-time and also leads to a certificate equivalent to the *Realschulreife*, the *Fachschulreife*. Both this and the *Fachoberschule* (upper secondary technical school), which admits pupils with the leaving certificate of the *Realschule*, or its equivalent, lead on to more advanced education in the tertiary sector.

The creation and expansion of these kinds of school has introduced a small degree of flexibility, a small bridge between the otherwise rigid division between general education on the one hand and vocational education and training on the other. This is the most characteristic feature of the German education system and presents, indeed, the greatest obstacle facing the development of vocational education in the country. It is a reflection of the dichotomy between *Bildung*, that is, forming the whole individual personality through academic study, and *Ausbildung* (practical training). Humboldt established the *Gymnasium* as purveyor of *Bildung*, especially through the study of classical Greek and Roman civilisation and culture. It remained an elitist institution, the preserve of the middle class, and in spite of the many changes that have been made, especially in the course of the past thirty years, it still retains something of this image. Any other education was considered inferior, though useful. Thus the priority of *Bildung* over *Ausbildung*, of *allgemeine Menschenbildung* over *fachliche Bildung* was established. It has bedevilled the development of the entire German education system since the beginning of the nineteenth century and neither such eminent educationists as Kerschensteiner or Spranger or the military occupation authorities after 1945 succeeded in establishing the equality of vocational and general education. It is a goal that has still not been attained.

Vocational education and training in Germany had to develop divorced from the 'proper' school system. In fact, although the present-day dual system has its roots in the medieval guilds, it mainly stems from the second half of the nineteenth century. It was a direct product of the industrial revolution. The practical side was regulated for the whole empire by the 1871 *Gewerbeordnung* (Craft Regulation Act) and its 1897 amendment which confirmed the strong position of the craft sector in vocational training by regulating its training arrangements. For industry and commerce, on the other hand, only very general provisions were made, so that they were left to innovate and develop their own forms of training and, through innovation, gain recognition. Only in 1935 did industry introduce its own examinations for skilled workers. Before that, since it did not have a coherent training system many *Facharbeiter* (skilled workers in industry) took the *Gesellenprüfung* (the craftsman's examination) to gain national recognition, for example in the public sector.

Since no fundamental change occurred in these arrangements until 1969, when the new *Berufsbildungsgesetz* was passed, it is not surprising that the employers both in the craft sector and in industry saw the development and execution of training (for which they, of course, also paid) largely as their responsibility. They resented any interference by the state and did not wish to have their independence restricted. The role of the employers in the German vocational training set-up remains, therefore, a particularly powerful one. It makes modernisation and co-ordination with the rest of the system a delicate task and also accounts for the predominance of the practical side within the overall training scheme.

The genesis of the other side of the dual system, the *Berufsschule*, is quite separate from that of on-the-job training. This type of school grew out of an extension of the *Volksschule* (elementary school). Apprentices could, by local statute, be obliged to attend such a school. Only in 1938 was it actually made compulsory throughout Germany for all those under 18 not in full-time education. Originally instruction in this *Fortbildungs-schule* (further education school) was mainly in religion and civics. Only later did it concentrate on the technical, economic and social aspects of the *Beruf*, thus linking it more closely to the young person's practical training. After the war, the system was re-established along the Weimar and pre-Weimar lines; only now the *Länder* were the education authorities and have retained responsibility for the school side of vocational education ever since.

The *Berufsschule* always took second place behind the practical training in the firm; it merely supplements it. The *Berufsbildungsgesetz*, whose main purpose was, indeed, to put the mechanism of the training side on a proper footing, along the lines described earlier, was also to effect structural changes. These, it was hoped, would lead to an improvement in the co-operation between school and firm, and a better co-ordination between their curricula. In spite of a plethora of committees, whose task this is, it has not happened enough. To a certain extent this is due to under-funding, under-staffing and under-equipping these schools: they have been neglected for many years. The result is, for example, that many lessons are regularly cancelled. But this lack of co-ordination also reflects a fundamental uncertainty about its role: is it merely to provide a theoretical base for what the apprentice learns in the enterprise – a task which is difficult enough in view of the many training occupations, and calls in itself for organisational flexibility within the school half and, for example, regional concentration for classes and for groups of trades; or is to be a major agent of socialisation for the young people it teaches? The fact that its curriculum contains such subjects as German, economics, social studies and religion would indicate the latter. The *Bildungsrat*, the independent Education Council, recommended, and the Comprehensive Education Development Plan of the *Bund-Länder-Kommission für Bildungsplanung* (BLK, Federation-*Länder*-Commission for Educational Planning) stipulated that vocational and general education should be brought closer together in order to achieve true comparability. The BLK actually envisaged a reduction in the attendance at *Berufsschulen*, in favour of other types of school). This has not happened;[7] nor has the quality of instruction improved noticeably. The grouping together of the *Berufschule*-instruction for a whole year in one block of 12 weeks, or two blocks of 6 weeks, would give an opportunity to improve the quality of teaching, but this does not happen enough. Similarly, the full-time *Berufsgrundbildungsjahr* (basic vocational education year) a concept favoured by the governments, has not been greeted with any enthusiasm by industry. It is, in fact, a tenth year of schooling, with a general education element, through the teaching of German, social studies and sport, and an occupation-oriented element, consisting of theoretical and practical instruction in one of thirteen so-called 'vocational fields', like economics and administration or metal technology. The idea is to broaden and deepen the curriculum and to avoid early specialisation. Industry is obliged to recognise this year as the first year of vocational training. It is reluctant to do this, so that pupils often do not find a training place after having completed the year. For that reason not as many youngsters as had been expected opted for this type of education. Only recently numbers have increased (to 132,000 in 1983),[8] chiefly because classes fill up with people who fail to obtain a normal 3-year training contract.

It thus remains a major weakness of the German system that the two 'sides' of education are still separated by this wide gulf. It is the students themselves who now remedy this, in a way which was not foreseen. On the one hand, many more choose the school-form of vocational training because they cannot get an apprenticeship place; this accounts for the larger numbers in the *Berufsfachschule* as well as in the *Berufsbildungsgrundjahr*. On the other hand, the number of young men and women with a qualification higher than the minimum required who want a training place is increasing. This accounts for the overall rise in the number of applicants, since demographically the 15 to 16 age cohort peaked around 1980, and numbers should have fallen. In 1984, 43.6 per cent of applicants held the *Realschule* leaving certificate (this figure was also high in the previous two years) and 13.4 per cent had the *Abitur* or the *Fachhochschulreife* (which entitled them to study at an advanced technical college in the tertiary sector). In 1981, this percentage had been only 6.9.[9] By following this path they obviously hope to increase their chance of obtaining employment later, with or without subsequent study at a higher education institution.

This development is welcomed from the point of view of bridging the gap between the two branches of the secondary level II, and equally so from the point of view of opening up job possibilities as alternatives to higher education, something that is as yet rare in Germany where traditionally four-fifths or more of qualified school leavers enter higher education (for the 1977 group it was still 79 per cent but with several years' delay in the take-up). It does, however, create problems for the *Hauptschule* school-leaver as long as there is a shortfall of places: he or she tends to be squeezed out by better-qualified applicants, especially in the more interesting clerical-type jobs which they prefer. In 1983, for example, around 70 per cent of advertising clerks and data processing clerks, and around 50 per cent of shipping and travel clerks held a higher education entrance qualification.[10] The interest is also great for dental technicians; here, there exists an obvious affinity to a later university course. On the other hand, non-clerical, technical and craft jobs have a low participation rate from applicants with a higher education entrance qualification; for example, only 2.8 per cent of motor mechanic apprentices (the most popular training occupation of all) held a higher education entrance certificate, and there are similar low figures for others. (The 8.7 per cent of joiners is a strange exception, probably motivated by general practical as well as sentimental considerations.) It is by no means certain whether this sort of development presents an advance, for it may lead to a new hierarchy within the training system, with a distinct social class bias.

A further problem is the quality and the content of the training given in the enterprises. It varies enormously, which is not surprising, since some 60 per cent of trainees (*Auszubildende* in the new official terminology) are trained in small or medium-sized firms. Often their equipment is not up to the standard required and the qualifications of the training staff itself are not adequate: in the interest of securing as many places as possible the deadline for qualifying through an examination as *Ausbilder* (trainer) has twice been extended and many staff have been excused the examination altogether. The Federal government can do no more than continue with the task of modernising the training regulations; it has done so for 148 occupations since 1969, replacing 253 old trades, and it is aware, for example, that provision must be made to offer scope for the training in applications of new technologies. It is up to the individual enterprise to adapt training to new technological requirements. This is difficult for many firms which lack the incentive, knowledge, and equipment to make this change. Yet controls seem to be rare. The creation of more places in separate training centres, of which there are not enough, is an obvious solution, and the Federation gives grants to establish such centres.

A question which needs to be asked is whether it is really necessary to have training for so many specialist occupations when technical change happens too quickly and there will be an increasing demand for the multi-skilled. Is there a need for about twenty-five different training routes in textile manufacturing and processing, including hat-making, textile darning and tie-sewing? In fact, very few adolescents are trained in any of these. On the other hand, in 1983, 49 per cent of all male and 69 per cent of all female apprentices trained in just 15 trades, which, however, did not coincide. For men the five most popular trades were motor mechanic (7.7 per cent), electrical fitter (5.4), machine fitter (4.5), joiner (3.7) and painter and varnisher (3.5); for women, hairdresser (9.2 per cent), shop assistant, first stage (8.9), shop assistant in the food sector (6.6), office clerk (6.0) and doctor's assistant (5.8).[11] Furthermore, it is highly unrealistic to train some 27,000 bakers (1983); only a fraction of these will get a permanent job or will even want one in this particular trade, which is not popular because of the unsocial hours worked. It is surely questionable to encourage young people to train in such occupations simply to make them into some sort of skilled person and to provide training establishments with cheap labour. This appears to be a waste of human resource which is bound, in most cases, to lead to unemployment, or, at best, to an unskilled job, with the need for further training or retraining. Conversely, there are not enough applicants for certain apprenticeship trades, notably for the group of bricklaying and associated trades and that of general goods and service clerks.

The permanent employment of young people who have completed their training and are now classified as skilled workers is a very big problem, without an easy answer. Training enterprises are not obliged to employ their former trainees, and many do not. A recent pilot study, limited to about 1,000 young adults who had successfully qualified six months previously in metal and electrical trades, revealed that just over half did not work in their training firm any more, only 40 per cent worked as skilled workers in their trade, and two out of five had never worked in their trade at all since completing their training.[12] It is known that the share of the unemployed is particularly high among qualified skilled workers under 25 in such trades as car mechanic, hairdresser, gardener, petrol attendant, baker or pastry cook. A great deal depends, of course, on the actual trade – a qualified car mechanic must surely be more easily employable than a pastry cook, because he is more flexible in the job he can do; on the numbers involved – at least thirty times as many car mechanics qualified in 1983 than petrol station attendants; and also on the sex – overall the unemployment share of qualified female skilled workers under 25 who had been unemployed for less than a year was higher than that of male workers (10.6 per cent compared to 7.6 per cent), and the discrepancy was particularly marked in such occupations as car mechanic, joiner, and decorator where girls were in a minority anyway, but also in hairdressing, where there were thirty times as many qualified girls than men. Only in a few, mostly clerical occupations, where both males and females had qualified was the share for women lower than that for men. It is difficult to see – in a system which for the purely vocational training and employment part relies on the voluntary efforts of the employers – what the Federal government can do to improve the situation, short of introducing comprehensive manpower planning for the young. However, a greater concentration on training courses which are more relevant to future work rather than encouraging *any* effort to create and find a training place anywhere, in the interest of providing some skills for everyone, may have to be considered if, in a longer-term perspective, waste is to be reduced.

The German vocational training system has other weaknesses. One is its discrimination against women. The much higher percentage (68) of women *Auszubildende* in the fifteen most popular training occupations for girls than in the equivalent fifteen occupations for men has already been mentioned, as has the concentration of women in office/sales-type jobs. The overall percentage of girls entering into a training agreement is only very slowly increasing, from 35.3 per cent in 1975 to 39.3 per cent in 1983,[13] but certain apprenticeships, particularly in the technical sector, are still an almost exclusive male preserve, despite several pilot projects financed by the Federal government. Women find it generally more diffi-cult to obtain a training place – 64 per cent of applicants not yet placed in September 1984 were female; therefore, as the sixth *Jugendbericht* has found, they seek to achieve their career aims via a higher school leaving qualification and/or a full-time vocational school.[14] This may, indeed, explain the high percentage of girls in *Realschulen* and *Gymnasien*, and also in the *Berufsfachschulen* and the basic vocational training year where there has been a recent increase.

Apart from girls, the training of children of foreign workers is bound to become a serious concern. Their attendance at full-time schools beyond compulsory schooling is low; even the number attending the *Berufsschule* is only about half what it should be (still 122,000). But the number of foreign apprentices has increased and in 1983 stood at 45,000, mostly in the craft sector. On the other hand, 13 per cent had failed to secure a contract.[15] The problem in the vocational sector is, of course, bound up with the much wider question of the place of foreign workers in German society. Given the particular problems facing young foreign adolescents in the German school system the route via vocational education may, in fact, be for the time being the best way to provide general education for these youngsters and, at the same time, train them for a job. Much greater efforts than in the past – and the Federal government has by no means been inactive – will be required in the next few years. More resources from both the *Länder* governments (for the *Berufsschule* sector) and the Federal government (for special training programmes) will be required. In this area, too, the collaboration between enterprise, school, and competent authority needs to be improved.

CONCLUSION

Despite its obvious shortcomings German vocational education is an impressive system. It is comprehensive; it complements general education; it provides a framework for raising the general level of competence and for increasing the flexibility of the German workforce; employers and the state, supported by the trade unions, run it and contribute financially to it in a successful, if sometimes uneasy, partnership. Young people accept the system in principle: they clearly regard a vocational qualification as giving them a better start and better prospects in the uncertainties of the labour market. Considering the system from a longer-term point of view, some of its deficiencies, especially its separation from general education, are serious and impair its effectiveness. The danger is that the current concern about finding sufficient training placed for all actual and potential applicants will continue to overshadow the need to improve the quality and the structure of the dual system; and that, when the demand will drop in a few years time, this need will be forgotten and little will change.

NOTES

1 The (unpublished) M.Sc. thesis by J. V. Burch, 'Analysis of developments in the dual system of vocational training in the Federal Republic of Germany', University of Manchester, 1981, provided the author with valuable insights into the problems of vocational training reform in West Germany in the 1970s.

2 OECD, *Youth without Work: Three Countries Approach the Problem* (Report by Shirley Williams and other experts), Paris, 1981, p. 125.

3 S. J. Prais and K. Wagner, 'Some practical aspects of human capital investment: training standards in five occupations in Britain and Germany', in: *National Institute Economic Review*, No. 105, London, 1983.

4 Der Bundesminister für Bildung und Wissenschaft (BMBW), *Grund- und Strukturdaten*, 1984/5, Bonn, 1984, p. 80.

5 For these and subsequent figures see: BMBW, *Berufsbildungsbericht 1985* (= Grundlagen und Perspektiven für Bildung und Wirtschaft, 7), Bonn, 1985, pp. 2 ff.

6 Ibid., p. 57. It is as true for Germany as for any other western industrial nation that the employment rate for young people is higher than for the total labour force (15- to under 20-year olds: 8.4 per cent; 20- to under 25-year olds: 12.9 per cent in 1984, compared to 8.1 per cent of the total labour force, cf. 'Arbeitsmarktanalyse 1984 anhand ausgewählter Bestands- und Bewegungsdaten', in: *Amtliche Nachrichten der Bundesanstalt für Arbeit*, Nr 3/1985, March 1985, pp. 173 ff.) But the situation in the Federal Republic has consistently been better than in other countries. See the analysis by Dieter Cassel, 'Jugendarbeitslosigkeit: Ausmaß, Ursachen, Gegenmaßnahmen', in: *Der Bürger im Staat*, 34/1, März 1984, pp. 43–50.

7 The 1984 *Berufsbildungsbericht* states openly that 'with regard to the equivalance of vocational and general education, at best a start has been made', see BMBW, *Berufsbildungsbericht 1984* (= Grundlagen und Perspektiven für Bildung und Wissenschaft, 2) Bonn, 1984, p. 6.

8 BMBW, *Grund- und Strukturdaten 1984/85*, op. cit., p. 25.

9 BMBW, *Berufsbildungsbericht 1985*, op. cit., p. 29.

10 Ibid., pp. 38 ff.

11 Ibid., pp. 38 ff.

12 Ibid., pp. 57, 140 ff.

13 Ibid., pp. 4, 37.

14 *Verbesserung der Chancengleichheit von Mädchen in der Bundesrepublik Deutschland* (Sechster Jugendbericht), BT Drucksache 10/1007, p. 18.

15 BMBW, *Berufsbildungsbericht*, pp. 86 ff.

10 The German dual system: a heretical view [1987]

Christopher Dougherty

The German dual system of apprentice training has attracted international attention by virtue of the quality of its organisation, the resources devoted to it, and the results obtained. With the aim of at least providing food for thought, and perhaps stirring policy makers into action, a number of recent English language studies have documented it with vigour and clarity (Prais and Wagner 1983, and Hayes *et al.* 1984, have been especially influential). In the process, however, they have projected a somewhat stylised image of the model. The purpose here is not so much to question the thrust of these studies as to bring into clearer focus some features of the system which are crucial to an understanding of its role in the preparation of young people for employment and which have not received the attention they deserve.

The conventional description of the dual system is puzzling in two respects. First there is its comprehensiveness. It is effectively obligatory for all except the college-bound *Gymnasium* students to enter it on leaving school, and typically they do so for 3 or 3½ years. (In practice a shortage of training places has prevented a proportion of school-leavers from gaining immediate entry and programmes have been developed within formal education to accommodate the backlog.) The minimum length of an apprenticeship, for the lowest grade of shopworker, is two years. And yet studies in other countries have concluded that only a small minority of the labour force requires extended occupational training. For example, the United States National Longitudinal Survey of the High School Class of 1972 revealed that 87 per cent of high school graduates needed less than three months of occupational training, and most of the remainder needed less than six months (Sherman 1983). Perhaps, as Prais and Wagner (1983) have suggested in the case of clerical workers, the benefits of such extended training tend to be underestimated elsewhere, but nevertheless there remains a huge gap between the German conception of training and those prevalent in other countries which on the surface can only be explained in terms of the German commitment to training for cultural and social reasons.

The second puzzle relates to the location of training places. Defying conventional notions, the statistics show that apprentices are not dispro-portionately attached to large firms, or to industry rather than to crafts.

As a first step to understanding the solutions to these puzzles, it is necessary to recognise that the dual system is far less monolithic in its structure and operation than is sometimes supposed. Most studies do draw attention to the fact that while the system is regulated at the Federal level by the *Berufsbildungsgesetz* (Vocational Training Act) of 1969 and amendments, this only provides a framework and some variation must be expected in its implementation. But this is still an understatement. The system is in reality highly diversified and decentralised, control residing in the hands of local chambers of commerce tempered by the intervention of the unions at various levels. One important consequence is that the wages of apprentices vary from occupation to occupation, and even from *Land* to *Land*, reflecting the state of the corresponding labour markets.

Another is that the quality of the enterprise-based element of the training can vary widely. The apprentices benefit from day-release, or equivalent block-release, for instruction in theory, which is partly job-related and partly general education. In addition they are supposed to have organised employer-based training. The popular notion is that of a *Meister*, the possessor of an advanced qualification, breathing down the neck of the apprentice on-site and checking the cards recording progress and rotation. The reality may be much more elaborate – many firms indeed have implemented virtually full-time vestibule training – but at the other extreme the training may amount to only a few hours of instruction per week with the *Meister* not being directly involved.

To some extent this variation reflects the differing degrees of commit-ment to training on the part of enterprises and the differing ability of the chambers of commerce to exercise quality control: a chamber responsible for 1,000 enterprises may, like one responsible for only 100, have just one or two staff for this purpose. But it also reflects the fact, acknowledged in practice if not *de jure*, that occupations like baking need only a fraction of the training time required by those in metalworking.

By tradition, wages are relatively flat during apprenticeship (Table 10.1). The natural operation of the labour market is blunted by the fact that in Germany school-leavers have little alternative except to enter apprenticeship. In other countries they have the option of entering the labour force directly, and this exerts an upwards pressure on apprentice wages. As a consequence, in Germany the average apprentice is still earning only 40 per cent of the adult wage at the end of his third year. In Britain, by contrast, the apprentice earns this proportion in his first year. In Ireland and France he reaches 40 per cent in his second year (Koeditz 1981).

The construction trades are exceptional in this respect in Germany, the difficulty of attracting and retaining apprentices being responsible for the relatively high payments received by them. In other trades the insu-

Table 10.1 Apprentice earnings as a percentage of qualified worker earnings, selected industries and occupations, October 1984

Industry/occupation	Year 1	Year 2	Year 3	Year 4
Iron, metal and electrical (NRW)	28	31	34	38
Metal (NWB/NB)	29	32	36	40
Engineering (NRW)	21	24	28	31
Chemical (NRH)	27	32	37	41
Printing (Bu)	21	25	32	38
Construction (Bu)	26	40	51	—
Baker (BW)	18	23	29	—
Baker (NRW)	17	21	27	—

Source: Beicht and Wiederhold 1986: Table I.
Note: Bu = Federal Republic; BW = Baden-Württemburg; NB = Nord-Baden; NRH = Nordrhein; NRW = Nordhrein=Westfalen; NWB = Nord-Württemburg

lation of apprenticeship from regular employment allows the employer to subsidise an apprentice during the early part of the contract in the knowledge that the loss can be balanced by a net profit (output – wage cost – training cost) towards the end.

In principle, therefore, given the flexibility of apprentice wages, one would expect to find an inverse relationship between them and the technical sophistication of the training. From the employer's point of view, the more sophisticated and costly the training, the lower he should set the wage to avoid a net loss overall. And from the apprentice's point of view, relatively low wages under these circumstances are acceptable in view of the relatively high wages he will earn as a skilled worker. Similarly in occupations requiring relatively little training, relatively high apprentice wages should be expected.

The reality, however, is almost exactly the opposite (Table 10.2), and to understand why one must largely abandon the notion of the dual system as a universal training system and recognise that in Germany, as elsewhere, there is only a relatively small core of jobs which need extended training, and that the rest of the apprenticeships represent little more than an extension of the adult labour market.

With some oversimplification, the two parts of the apprenticeship system can be characterised as follows. In a minority of occupations where significant training is needed, apprentice wages are overshadowed by the direct cost of training and variations in them have only a marginal effect on the total cost. Employers prefer to keep wages high to attract good applicants and hope to recoup by inducing them to stay on when qualified, the net cost of training being less than the cost of recruitment through an open labour market. The numbers of such training places is geared to employment prospects and is therefore limited within a narrow range.

At the other extreme in some craft occupations (baking, hairdressing, ladies' tailoring), employers can afford to pay relatively high wages, by virtue of the low cost of training but, at present, flooded by an oversupply

Table 10.2 Average apprentice wages, selected occupations (DM per month), October 1984

Sector	Wage
Industry and trade	
Maintenance mechanic	795
Machinist	545
Toolmaker	622
Average, industrial sector	669
Craft	
Bricklayer/mason	938
Butcher	585
Plumber	578
Mechanic (craft)	523
Carpenter/cabinet-maker	509
Automobile mechanic	499
Baker	483
Electrician (installation)	450
Hairdresser	332
Average, craft sector	525

Source: Beicht and Wiederhold 1986
Note: Trades listed are those with the greatest numbers of apprentices; average is for the sector as a whole

of applicants, are under no pressure to do so, and do not. They become accustomed to having a relatively high proportion of apprentices in their workforce and to hiring only a fraction of them when they qualify.

Why do apprentices take up such training posts, knowing that they will probably not lead to a permanent job with the employer? The alternative is to be stuck in one of the holding patterns being devised within formal education to keep down the open unemployment of young people, and the apprentice qualification does confer a substantial advantage even in an alien job market. The Opel automobile company is said to be the greatest employer of bakers in Germany, taking them on its production line knowing that, although they will need additional training, they can at least be expected to have acquired industrial discipline. More generally, there are a number of industrial occupations characterised by shiftwork or arduous conditions, particularly in heavy industry, from which young people are excluded, and which recruit adults who have completed apprenticeships elsewhere, for the same reasons.

In some occupations, particularly those requiring little capital investment, the risk of not being offered a permanent job by the employer is not a critical factor because the apprentices can strike out on their own. In Berlin one now has the paradox of hairdressers, haunted by the spectre of ever-increasing competition, trying to find a way to raise apprentice wages and thereby restrict the volume of training.

In conclusion, while the volume of occupational training is greater in Germany than in most other countries, the difference is not as dramatic as appears at first sight. In many occupations, the apprentices are effectively part of the main labour force. They do get more training than their counterparts elsewhere and it is of better quality, but it is not realistic to treat the apprenticeship of a florist on the same level as that of a toolmaker. They do have continued access to general education through part of their day-release instruction, but that is a separate matter.

Apart from this, the most significant feature of apprenticeship in those occupations needing little training is the modest level of earnings in the second and third years of training. This is made tolerable by long tradition and the fact that all young people have similar expectations, and recently it has conferred an important benefit for society as a whole. The worst of the youth unemployment threatened by the baby-boom has been averted by an increase of apprenticeships on a massive scale. Some writers attribute this to a response of employers to the national interest, or, less charitably, as a way of averting increased governmental intervention. These explanations may be partly correct, but the observation that the greatest expansion has been recorded for such occupations as shop assistants, hairdressers, bakers, butchers and medical assistants (Alex 1985) suggest that the incentive provided by relatively low apprentice wages has been the most important factor.

REFERENCES

Alex, L. (1985) 'Development prospects of vocational training' (Paper delivered at International Association of Educational and Vocational Guidance, International Seminar, Dubrovnik, Yugoslavia, 23–8 September 1985).

Beicht, U. and Wiederhold, S. (1986) *Entwicklung der Ausbildungsvergütungen von 1976 bis 1984* (Berlin, Bundesinstitut für Berufsbildung).

Hayes, F.C., Anderson, A. and Fonda, N. (1984) *Competence and Competition: Training and Education in the Federal Republic of Germany, the United States and Japan* (London, National Economic Development Office).

Koeditz, V. (1981) *The Material and Social Standing of Young People during Transition from School to Working Life* (Berlin, CEDEFOP).

Prais, S. J. and Wagner, K. (1983) 'Some practical aspects of human capital investment: training standards in five occupations in Britain and Germany', *National Institute Economic Review*, 105, pp. 46–65.

Sherman, S. W. (ed.) (1983) *Education for Tomorrow's Jobs* (Washington, DC, National Academy Press).

11 Quality control in the dual system of West Germany [1988]

Peter Raggatt

In recent years economic need has again emerged as the major principle of educational policy. Numerous documents and ministerial speeches have declared that Britain is losing the competition for world markets and have argued that 'education' must serve the economy better than it has in the past.[1] The policies that have followed from this assessment have sought to align the education system more closely with the economic system through a variety of structural and curriculum initiatives which are summarised in the term the 'new vocationalism'. These initiatives have affected virtually every level of education omitting only the nursery schools. They include, for example, the Technical and Vocational Education Initiative (TVEI), one of numerous schemes that link schools and industry,[2] the Youth Training Scheme for young leavers, 'new blood' appointments in universities (which were overwhelmingly in technology and science) and various adult training schemes.

Economic comparisons, used to chart the decline and the gravity of the problem, combined with the argument that inadequacies of the education system are responsible for economic failures, have in turn led, as they did in the second half of the last century, to international comparisons of education and training systems.[3] 'The comparison [of vocational education and training provision] which counts is that with our overseas competitors and that is to our disadvantage' (DE/DES 1986: 2). Comparisons have been concerned both with the quantity and the quality of the skilled workers being produced in various systems. The Youth Task Group Report (MSC 1982), for example, states that: 'Britain has one of the least trained workforces in the industrial world . . . in recent years . . . our training performance has tended to get worse not better', a view confirmed by the very low proportion of 16- to 19-year olds in full-time education or training which Britain has compared with other advanced European countries. A similar judgement has been made about higher education; Lord Gregson, a member of the House of Lords Select Committee on Science and Technology, provides a succinct and telling comment:

[Britain has] the smallest percentage of children proceeding to higher education of any of our major competitors; we have the smallest graduate community compared with our competing nations and within that small graduate community we have the lowest percentage of technologists and of that tiny fragment of our population that we are training to be technologists in order to earn our living in the world, they have the poorest level of qualification.

(Gregson 1986: 9)

Most such reports have confined their analyses to factors within education and training, foregoing the more complex and sensitive examination of external factors that encourage young people to leave at their earliest opportunity.[4]

A number of research studies have been undertaken with the express purpose of learning what it is that makes some other countries more effective in producing the human resources required by their economies. The countries selected for study are, not surprisingly, those with the most successful economies. Thus *Competence and Competition* (NEDO/MSC 1984) examined, 'the nature, scale and direction of vocational education and training in Germany, the US and Japan', selecting these countries 'because they are Britain's major competitors in world markets'. The introduction by the authors underlines the point: 'This report describes how key elements in the vocational education and training policies in the Federal Republic of Germany, the United States and Japan underpin their economic competitiveness, and how they support their effective response to changing markets and a rapidly changing economic environment' (NEDO/MSC 1984: iv). The report of a study visit by HMI to Bavaria and North-Rhine Westphalia *Education in the Federal Republic of Germany* (HMI 1986) offers a similar justification. The report first stresses the economic role of education in preparing young people for working life within a context of declining manufacturing industry, technological changes and high youth unemployment. In such circumstances, HMI explains, 'we should look at how other countries appear to do things more effectively than we do; and what . . . useful lessons . . . we might take to heart and make use of' (1986: v). In common with many other reports HMI's concern is exclusively with the workings of the educational system; no attempt is made to study the cultural factors and the linkages between the educational system and its social context that were a feature of Michael Sadler's authoritative reports when he was at the Board of Education.[5]

This paper continues the exploration of education and training in the Federal Republic of Germany. The main purpose is to explore what it is that makes the system work. The paper focuses on a feature of the German system of vocational education and training that has been the subject of particular interest – the dual system – examining a number of mechanisms, internal and external to the system, that sustain quality control. The paper then notes some of the weaknesses in the system. The concluding section offers some comments on two recent developments in Britain. First, however, a brief introduction to the system of education in the Federal Republic is necessary.

THE SCHOOL SYSTEM

Education in Germany starts at 6 and is compulsory until the age of 18. From 15, or 16 in those federal States (*Länder*) in which full-time education has been extended to ten years, it can be part-time. Pupils transfer from the primary school to one of three types of secondary school at 10: the *Hauptschule* (main school), the *Realschule* (middle school) or the *Gymnasium* (grammar school).[6] The decision on the type of secondary school a student will attend is made on the basis of grades in the primary school and parental choice.[7] In all *Länder* the first two years following the primary phases are regarded as an observation period during which there is a continuing assessment of whether students have been placed in a school that is suited to their ability. Transfers are almost always from the *Gymnasium* to the *Realschule* or to the *Hauptschule*.

The *Hauptschule* provides education to 15 or 16. Students follow a broad core curriculum and work towards the Main School Leaving Certificate (*Hauptschulabschluß*). Courses in English and Mathematics are provided at two or three levels to take account of different aptitudes. Students who wish to obtain the *Realschule* certificate and who have the appropriate level of qualification can stay on for a tenth year though this is not an opportunity available in all *Länder*. Both the certificates are group certificates and depend largely on school-based tests. Most graduates of the *Hauptschule* go directly into work or to a vocational training programme.

The popularity of the *Hauptschule* is in sharp decline. Numbers fell from about 60 per cent of the age cohort in 1960 to about 40 per cent in 1985. In Berlin the numbers are below 30 per cent while in North-Rhine Westphalia in 1985 fewer students were recruited to *Hauptschulen* than to the *Gymnasium*. The decline may be attributed in part to the devaluation of the *Hauptschulabschluß* in the training market and the preference of parents for other types of schools. Falling rolls are exacerbating the trend [Bendelow 1986: 7]. From being the Main School the *Hauptschule* is now frequently called the 'school for the leftovers'.

The *Realschule*, or Intermediate School, also provides education to 16. The curriculum is more demanding than that of the *Hauptschule*. Elective subjects and differentiation within subjects enable the schools to cater for the relatively wide range of academic and vocational interests and abilities of the students. Vocational orientation is not timetabled in the *Realschule* but takes place in elective courses. It places less emphasis on the practical than the *Hauptschule* does. Most of the students take the Intermediate Certificate (*Mittlere Reife*). Mathematics, German and a foreign language are obligatory for the final written examination together with one or two optional subjects which may be written or oral. Satisfactory achievement in other subjects where a form of continuous assessment is used is also required. The *Realschule* certificate is obtained by 35 per cent of the age group (Statistisches Bundesamt 1984). It confers the right to attend the *Gymnasium*, though in practice only those who do particularly well are able to do so. Most graduates of the *Realschule* start apprenticeships, take jobs or enter full-time vocational schools.

In recent years the popularity of the *Realschule* has been increasing at the expense of the *Hauptschule*. Numbers in the *Realschule* more than doubled, from 13 to 27 per cent in the period from 1960 to 1985. In part this is because of the higher market value of the leaving certificate and its appeal to lower social groups seeking advancement. The *Realschule* certificate is not only valued more highly because it has status with employers but also because of the educational opportunities it provides for apprenticeship or further education.

The *Gymnasium*, which provides education to 19, concludes with the *Abitur*, a qualification which entitles holders to enter any university. The *Abitur* is also a group examination. Like the other examinations it is based on a common core curriculum. All students are examined in four subjects – three in written examinations and one oral. These subjects must be drawn from across the curriculum, for example, physics, mathematics, English and economics. Examination scores are added to scores attained during the previous four half-year periods or semesters. In 1986 27.9 per cent of the age group obtained the *Abitur*. In the large cities the percentages are particularly high – in Hamburg it was 40.9 per cent and in Bremen 37 per cent.

Curriculum

The German curriculum has been developed according to encyclopaedic principles since the beginning of the last century. It provides a broad core of subjects and electives (see Table 11.1 in Appendix 11.1 for details). Clear curriculum guidelines are established for all subjects. These include statements of objectives and an indication of the standards expected are issued by each state. The programme in the *Hauptschule* is more practical than either of the other school types or levels and now includes work preparation (*Arbeitslehre*), a combination of introductory economics and careers guidance. Teaching tends to be very traditional in style. Written tests as required by the curriculum guidelines must be set in German, English and mathematics. They are graded on a 1–6 scale and contribute towards the leaving certificate (1 is the top score). Six tests are set in each year for each subject and in each type of school.

Sixty per cent of the age group leave school at 15 or 16. Most, about 90 per cent, hold the Main School Leaving Certificate or the Intermediate Certificate and either enter a full-time vocational school (30 per cent) or an apprenticeship lasting for 2 to 3½ years depending on the occupation (60 per cent). For those students without qualifications the prospects are poor. Some enter unskilled jobs and have few chances of improving their marginal position in the economy (Schober 1984; Williamson 1983). Others enter the *Berufsgrundbildungsjahr* (BGJ), the basic vocational year, where they receive training in one of thirteen occupational fields (*Berufsfelder*). This has two forms – a cooperative form in which the school has agreements with companies to provide a training place and a school-based form in which the training is wholly at school. The BGJ, particularly the latter form, has a low standing with employers, 'It's worth zero' one employer explained, and though it is supposed to be equivalent to the first year of apprenticeship many young people searching for apprenticeship places hide the 'qualification' from prospective employers.[8]

THE DUAL SYSTEM

The centrepiece of vocational education and training in the Federal Republic is the dual system which currently provides education and training for 1.8 million young people, about 60 per cent of the young people who leave school at 15 or 16. The term, which has been in general use only since the 1960s,[9] has four meanings. First, and most widely known, it indicates that, in most cases, training involves two different learning venues: the company and the vocational school (*Berufsschule*).[10] Second, it indicates the division of responsibilities for financing training: individual employers are responsible for the costs of in-company training, for any training materials required by the apprentice and for his or her pay, while the costs of the *Berufsschule* are funded by the *Land*. Third, it indicates a separation of legal responsibilities: in-company training is regulated by the 1969 (Federal) Vocational Training Act (VTA) while vocational education in the *Berufsschule* is regulated by school laws which are the responsibility of the individual states. Fourth, it follows that the young person in the dual system has a dual role: trainee (*Lehrling*) and student (*Berufsschüler*).

QUALITY CONTROL

A number of studies have compared the quantity of skilled workers in England and Germany. Some have also compared the quality of workers and control of the quality of training. Most have focused on mechanisms of control *within* the education and training system. Thus Prais (1981) and Prais and Wagner (1983) have discussed the standards of vocational qualifications, and (1985) the schooling standards; Flower and Russell

(1982), Russell (1982), Parkes and Shaw (1983) and Dickenson and Erben (1985) have considered the role of the *Meister* in the dual system and this is a feature to which Prais and Wagner (See Chapter 6, this volume) have recently turned. A rather wider but brief study was contributed by NEDO/MSC (1984) which cited social influences contributing to quality control.

In this section I shall consider five forms of quality control:

- the qualifications held by young people entering apprenticeships;
- the standards of vocational qualifications attained on completion of apprenticeships;
- process control procedures including (1) the regulation of training places; (2) the quality/qualifications of trainers; (3) mechanisms for the development and renewal of the training curriculum;
- historical and legal continuities; and
- collaboration between the social partners.

Entry qualifications

The relative standards of schooling in England and Germany, as indicated by the numbers of pupils attaining similar levels of achievement in the two countries, have been the subject of comparison by Prais and Wagner (1985). They concluded that approximately half of the German pupils achieved the Intermediate Certificate – a standard equal to or above 'O'-level in a broadly based set of 'O'-levels – compared with just over one-quarter of English students with about twice as many German pupils achieving a pass at 'O'-level standard, or slightly higher, in mathematics. Turning to the *Hauptschule* they concluded that the average attainment of the weakest 50 per cent of pupils was equal to the average of all pupils in England while in mathematics English pupils lay behind German pupils by 'something like two years of schooling'. In a detailed examination of mathematics, which they argue is particularly important for subsequent technical training, Prais and Wagner found that 66 per cent of German pupils in the lower half of the ability range could answer correctly a sum involving addition and subtraction compared with 4 per cent in England and that these students had a substantially higher level of attainment in basic arithmetical processes than the lower half of students in England.

Summarising their findings they argue that:

> the German schooling system provides a broader curriculum, combined with significantly higher levels of mathematical attainment, for a greater proportion of pupils than does the English system; differences are particularly marked at the lower half of the ability range. Attainments in mathematics by those in the lower half of the ability range

in England appear to lag by the equivalent of about two years of schooling behind the corresponding section of pupils in Germany.

(1985: 68)

The qualifications of young people entering apprenticeships have been steadily increasing in recent years. In 1986 60 per cent of the 732,000 applicants for training places held the *Mittlere Reife*. In addition there has been an increase in the numbers of *Abiturienten* (holders of a university entrance qualification) entering the dual system. Almost two-thirds of those entering the dual system thus have a qualification equal to, or higher than, 'O'-level. Moreover, the qualification is broadly based. A related feature is that the age of the entrants to the dual system is rising.

One consequence of the rising educational threshold is that graduates of the *Hauptschule* although still able to obtain apprenticeships are experiencing greater difficulty in getting places in the more favoured occupations; their choice of career is increasingly restricted to manual occupations – carpenters, car mechanics, office and sales assistants. In contrast graduates of the *Realschule* and the *Gymnasium* enter technical and lower-level managerial occupations. The situation has been exacerbated with the handicraft trades' initial scepticism that holders of the *Abitur* were suitable recruits now replaced by enthusiasm and a drive to recruit holders of the *Abitur* and particularly girls. A second consequence is that the 10 per cent of young people without qualifications, which includes the majority of the children of non-German migrant workers, are unable to get apprenticeships and are increasingly marginalised. Moreover, those that do find places often do so in firms with low standards of pedagogical care and very rigid discipline (Braun 1987). Research studies by the Federal Institute for Vocational Education and Training indicate that the trend of rising educational thresholds will continue with the employment market increasingly calling for young persons with good school qualifications.

Vocational qualifications

Studies of the respective vocational qualifications of the labour force in Britain and Germany have been undertaken by Prais (1981) and Prais and Wagner (1983). The earlier study reported that a much higher proportion of the German workforce is formally qualified; some 60 per cent hold intermediate vocational qualifications compared with, at most, 30 per cent of the British workforce. The latter study confirmed that Germany had substantially more skilled workers in the same occupations than Britain did[11] and after examination of five occupations, concluded that the standards attained in Germany were as high, and on the whole a little higher, than those attained in Britain by the smaller proportion of qualified workers. In seeking explanations Prais and Wagner concentrated on assessment in the two countries and concluded that the formal examination process used to assess competence at the end of apprenticeship is a better guarantor of quality, especially at the lower end of ability, than the largely time-serving apprenticeship system that was used in England.

The examination procedure is set down in the training regulations which are specified for each recognised skilled occupation and craft and outlined in individual training contracts signed by employers and apprentices. The examination includes both written and oral tests and for technical occupations apprentices must prepare work-pieces or samples of work under supervision. They may, for example, be required to make a metal product using the given material, tools and a blueprint. The product is assessed for precision and craftsmanship. The written portion is commonly in multiple-choice format (Hamilton 1987). A pass must be achieved in all areas and examinations may be repeated twice. It requires factual recall and knowledge of procedures. Commercial apprentices may be expected to demonstrate their abilities in a social interactive situation or in an oral examination which may tap knowledge and skills developed on the job and at school.

Process factors

The training contract

Training is controlled by the 1969 Vocational Education Act (*Berufsbildungsgesetz*) and subsequent regulations which set out the minimum requirements for each occupation. These are published each year by the Federal Ministry of Education and Science in the *Index of Recognised Skilled Occupations*. The regulations specify the length of training in each occupation, the outline content and order of training content, the examination requirements and the obligations of employers. Further details on training are provided by the company and are included in the contract which employers and apprentices sign at the start of each apprenticeship.

Contracts must specify:

- the skilled occupation description (which specifies the required knowledge and skills in the occupation);
- the outline training plan (which sets out the content and the sequence of training);
- the starting date and length of training;
- the training arrangements outside the company (for example in a *Berufsschule*, another company or a shared training centre);
- the examination requirements (including the areas to be covered by the examination and the weightings attached to the different parts).

All in-company training costs are borne by the employers, including the costs of any teaching materials, clothes, equipment and social security benefits. Apprentices receive salaries based on collective agreements between employers and trade unions. These vary by age of trainee, year of apprenticeship and occupation, ranging from about £75 per month (dressmaking apprentices) to about £350 per month (mining mechanic). This works out at between 20 and 40 per cent of a skilled worker's starting pay. There is a considerable variation in the costs of training between sectors and between the years of apprenticeship because the value of the productive work of apprentices differs between sectors and increases sharply from year to year of the apprenticeship. In the industrial-commercial sector the average net costs are a little over £3000 per trainee per year (Noll *et al.* 1983; Wiederhold-Fritz 1986). In the craft sector the net cost is about £2,000.

All training contracts must be registered with the local 'competent authorities', usually the chambers of industry, commerce, agriculture, the professions and crafts. The Chambers, which are self-governing bodies, are responsible for ensuring that the quality of training is satisfactory and for the final apprenticeship examination. They employ training advisers who monitor the quality of training through the examination of the training plans submitted to the Chambers by the companies, visits, by reference to the trainees' record books and through the mid-term formative examination which is taken after about two years. They act as advisers to both companies and trainees. For companies they provide advice on any improvements needed in training methods, teaching materials, relationships with trainees, equipment needs and so on. To discharge these duties they make periodic visits to companies, but visits are also triggered by poor examination results and complaints by trainees. Thus if the examination performance of trainees in a company is poor the training adviser will discuss the problem with their training manager and may move the trainee to another company or arrange for interplant training. They follow up complaints from trainees about their training – a more common occurrence in craft training than in industry and commerce where trainees would normally complain to the works council – provide advice on trainees' rights and obligations in particular training contexts, any queries about the training contracts and the possibilities of lengthening or accelerating the training period. Training advisers also organise the examinations at the end of the training period.

Apprenticeship, however, is not simply about developing technical competence within an occupation; it is also about socialisation into work and organisational culture. Several mechanisms contribute to this. Most noticeable is the training log book which all trainees must maintain. This is regularly checked and signed by a responsible trainer and it provides a focus for counselling on work skills and on behaviour, relationships with fellow workers and so on. In a Durkheimian sense it stresses both organic and mechanical solidarity. The log book is also required by the examination board. A second feature is the clear structure of progression of qualifications, esteem, responsibility and pay within the workplace – from apprentice to skilled worker to part-time instructor to *Meister*. It is a progression which most trainees view as a realistic personal goal.

More immediately there is the goal of skilled worker status and, in industry, the probability of a job with the company – provided the trainee's behaviour in the workplace is satisfactory, i.e. provided he or she is a punctual, hard-working, reliable and cooperative workmate, a job as a skilled worker is likely to be offered – some 80 per cent of apprentices in industry stay on at the company where they trained on completion of their apprenticeship (Institute for Vocational Training, Berlin, 1985) – and at a salary two to three times higher than he was earning as an apprentice. In the normal context of employment opportunities motivation to conform is considerable, in the context of relatively high unemployment at 19 + the socialisation pressures are particularly powerful and effective. The successful end of apprenticeship is marked by a formal presentation of the certificate. It is a ritual confirmation of transition not simply of apprentice to skilled worker, but also from youth to adulthood, from novitiate to full citizenship in a society in which skill attracts esteem and status.

The trainers

Notwithstanding all the formal regulations controlling the content and organisation of training the quality of that training is powerfully affected by the competence of in-company trainers. This is a matter of both technical and pedagogical skills. Who may train is tightly controlled. Companies and small businesses may only employ and train apprentices if they have suitably qualified trainers. The qualifications established follow the traditional qualifications held by the master craftsman – occupational competence, experience, teaching (pedagogic) competence and respectability.[12] Specifically trainers must:

- be skilled workers, i.e. have passed the final examination at the end of the apprenticeship in the trade in which training is being given;
- have appropriate experience;
- be at least 24 years of age;
- have passed an examination that tests their technical *and* pedagogic competence;
- be a master craftsman (*Meister*).

The role of the *Meister* in the dual system is pivotal. This is not the place to discuss it or the training process leading to *Meister* status in detail (see Flower and Russell 1982; Raggatt, in preparation) but some further comment is necessary. Most workers do not attain *Meister* status until they are about 30 years of age.[13] To get there the *Meister* will first have become a skilled worker developing theoretical and practical capabilities in his or her occupation both on-the-job and at vocational college, extending his general education in German, social studies, economics, and possibly religion, politics, sport and a foreign language, and, at the same time, is socialised into the work norms and organisational culture at the plant. After some years' experience as a skilled worker an aspirant *Meister* can ask, or may be encouraged, to help with the practically based component of apprenticeship training as on-site instructors. To become a *Meister*, however, the skilled worker must take an examination to demonstrate advanced occupational, pedagogical and managerial competence.

In most instances workers follow courses which are run by the competent authorities. They are available on a full-time and part-time basis and provide around 1,000 hours of instruction. The full-time course lasts about 9 months while the part-time course is spread over 2 or 3 years. The latter requires attendance for two evenings a week plus Saturdays.

The pedagogical component of *Meister* training has four strands; structure, organisation and contribution of the dual system and the role of the trainer; planning and implementing a training programme – vocational curriculum, training methods and assessment; the young person in training covering psychological and sociological aspects of training; and the legal basis of training – *Land* law and Federal Labour law. The examination covers all strands. It is multi-choice, short essays and a sample training session given to the examination board which is followed with an oral.

The courses concerned with business and management emphasise economics, business organisation and personnel management, industrial and social law, principles of industrial and social relationship and negotiation and there is a considerable difference between the content of courses depending on whether the trainee is working towards a *Handwerkmeister* or a *Industriemeister* qualification. At the end of this time candidates take written, practical and oral examinations. Certificates are awarded formally, often at a dinner held for *Meister* or at annual dinners organised by the Chamber or Guild. Here, too, then the ritual confirms entry to a new and more prestigious group. On qualifying the *Meister* will enjoy the high level of occupational and social esteem and respect accorded to a master craftsman. In the craft trades it enables him to open his own business and in industry and commerce it brings an income about two-thirds as much again as unskilled workers and 40 per cent more than skilled workers.

By the time that he or she – more women are now training as *Meister* than was the case some years ago (Flower and Russell 1982) – qualifies he or she will have had some fifteen years of socialisation into work and organisational values, norms and procedures stressing business efficiency, cost and quality control as a process, and other business considerations. This pattern of *Meister* training, as has been pointed out elsewhere (Flower and Russell 1982; Dickenson and Erben 1985), enables the

Meister to operate effectively at the intersection of two occupational cultures – that of shop floor and management. Moreover, it is a role that has cultural continuity:

> The *Meister* role is a social role that does not separate work culture from family culture. It is a role which is affectual, patriarchial, traditional, hard-working and skilled. Clearly then for many parents and young people the role of the *Meister* will not appear to deny family values but rather to formalise them in a work setting.
>
> (Flower and Russell 1982: 17)

The numbers passing the *Meister* examination have grown steadily over the years with some 43,000 qualifying in 1985 (see Table 11.2 in Appendix 11.1). In Berlin alone each year some 1,000 skilled workers follow courses at the Chambers of Crafts which lead to *Meister* status. About 80 per cent are successful.

The routine business of training in industry is shared with skilled workers who have had additional training. In 1985 almost 775,000 qualified persons were registered as instructors with the competent authorities. Of these about 46,500 were full-time instructors working in company training centres, group training workshops, practice firms and centres serving a number of businesses. On average instructors are responsible for two or three trainees. The number of registered instructors in all branches rose by about 24,000 over 1984 and by 52,000 over 1983 (Schultze 1986).

The occupational curriculum

Rapid technological and economic change brings with it a need for a more mobile and flexible workforce. This places specific pressures on curricula. On the one hand there is a demand for workers with a good general education, workers who have developed a broad range of knowledge and skills and who are better able to understand the economic, social and technical changes taking place, the corresponding need to alter organisational and work practices, to learn new skills and have the confidence to do so. It is a matter both of cognition and attitude. On the other hand rapid technological and economic change places considerable pressure on the content of the occupational curriculum. Constant effort and effective mechanisms are needed to update the curriculum and to ensure that it provides the necessary content leading towards a range of occupational qualifications. The need is for a polyvalent curriculum that leads to a number of occupations with specialisation coming towards the end of training.

Earlier sections have noted that the recruitment threshold for the more desirable apprenticeships has been rising. *Hauptschüler* find increasing difficulties in getting apprenticeships in the more popular occupations. System level changes increasing the level and amount of general education post-16 are also evident with attendance at vocational school increasing to 1½ or 2 days. The extra time is given both to general education, e.g. foreign languages, and to extended theoretical studies relating to the apprentice's occupation.

The occupational curriculum is outlined in the training regulations for each of the 429 skilled occupations. The regulations, as we have seen, set out the knowledge and skills required in the particular occupations, the outline training plan, which provides the timing and structure for content areas, and the examination requirements. Initiatives for changes in the regulations usually come from employers' associations, the central organisations of the Chambers, the Guilds and the trade unions. The key agency, however, in establishing a new curriculum is the Federal Institute for Vocational Education and Training (BIBB). The Institute, which is directly responsible to the Federal government (which exercises legal supervision through the Federal Ministry for Education and Science) engages in research into vocational education and training (including adult training), evaluates pilot projects in company training practice, advises the Federal government on matters of vocational education and training and participates in the preparation of training regulations, orders and other legal regulations. It is the last of these tasks, its involvement in the preparation of training ordinances, establishing the objectives and content of vocational education and training and adapting vocational education and training to technical, economic and social development, that makes it the central agency in the development of the occupational curriculum – although the regulations themselves are published by the competent Ministry.

Much of BIBB's efforts since it was established in 1970 have been concerned with reducing the numbers of skilled occupations. This has been a deliberate policy of the Federal government and in the period from 1970 the number of skilled occupations has fallen from over 600 to 429 (Munch 1984). This has been accompanied by a shift towards polyvalent training in which the first part is general to a number of occupations. This is well illustrated by the current reorganisation of training regulations in the metal working industries involving 42 occupations. These regulations cover a range of qualifications and a wide range in trainee numbers within occupations – 48,000 trainees who are preparing to be machine fitters, 22,000 toolmakers, 13 makers of diamond-tipped drawing dies and so on, numbering 155,000 training places in all. The new regulations define six skilled occupations which have a common broad-based foundation. On top of this the occupations are broken down into sixteen qualification profiles. The first broad-based phase for all lasts 12 months, the next 6 months is spent training in a specific occupational cluster and six months' training in the specialised area plus 1 year's further differentiated training.

Modular approaches to training have also been developed in which trainees follow a core or foundation curriculum and take modules specific to a particular occupation.

Tradition and the socialisation of young workers

The dual system is rooted in the apprenticeship system developed in the craft guilds in the Middle Ages. The basic pattern is a familiar one. A young boy (very few girls were ever admitted), German, and from a respectable family, would enter an apprenticeship with a master crafts-man. As an apprentice he lived with the *Meister*'s family and learned the skills of the craft, the knowledge required and the values of the small businessman. At the end of his apprenticeship training the young man became a journeyman travelling from town to town plying his trade, honing his craft skills and developing his personality. After a minimum period of five years he could be formally accepted into the Guild and set up a business. Admittance to the Guild required more than good, even excellent, craft skills. A *Meister* was required to be a mature person of good repute, to have a broad understanding of the world and the values of a small businessman. The Guild controlled the credentialling process and through that controlled the curriculum. Strict regulation of entrance to the Guild and the maintenance of a code of practice for Guild members – members could be expelled from the Guild and this effectively removed their livelihood – were functional factors in the high status and esteem accorded to the *Meister*.

From the sixteenth to the latter part of the nineteenth century the craft guilds and apprenticeship training were in decline (Taylor 1981; Munch 1984). In the nineteenth century apprenticeships were badly affected by increasing industrialisation and the spread of economic liberalism. The former reduced the demand for the products and services of the craft trades while the latter turned apprenticeships, in practice, into private (unregulated) agreements between employers and apprentices. The vocational training system deteriorated: too many apprentices were engaged as cheap labour, training was inadequate and apprenticeships were frequently extended over long periods.

Towards the end of the century, however, the growing concern for the poor quality of products and the need for skilled workers as German industry expanded served to revive and revitalise the Guilds. Though by now the Guilds were mostly ineffectual their history offered a model for controlling the quality of goods by controlling those who could practice and who could train entrants to the skilled occupations. In 1897 the Craft Guilds Act was passed. This restored corporation rights to the Guilds. A further bill in 1908 established that only master craftsmen, examined under state regulations, could train apprentices, and made attendance at the part-time continuation schools compulsory.[14]

Concern about the poor quality of goods was not the only issue that stimulated the development of vocational training and increased the power devolved to the Guilds at this time. The latter decades of the nineteenth century and the early years of the twentieth century had witnessed increasing conflict between the state and the growing Social Democratic movement. In this context the state attached much importance to the political socialisation and social integration of young men. A solution to the state's problem was offered by Georg Kerschensteiner, the Superintendent of schools in Munich, who in 1901 won the Erfurt Academy prize for an essay on citizenship training in which he accorded a central role to vocational education. For Kerschensteiner and later Eduard Spranger, work was central to human development, or, as Spranger put it, 'The way to higher general education is through one's occupation and only by way of one's occupation.' Kerschensteiner's award-winning essay described the relationship of the individual to trade in terms of 'conscientiousness, industry, perseverance, responsibility, and self-restraint', in similar vein vocational education was seen to contribute to the individual's appreciation of the need for self-control, justice, devotion to duty and a strong sense of personal responsibility. In this interpretation vocational education is not simply training for a trade but is education for the full development of the individual. The role of the vocational schools thus extended beyond technical training to include education in citizenship and acceptance of the existing political and social order, and to give support to the privately owned firms in the socialisation of their apprentices (Max Planck Institute 1979: 240).

The success of Kerschensteiner's essay was matched by the success of the trade schools that he developed in Munich. In the training that was provided the *Meister* had an important role both for occupational training and for citizenship training or moral development. Other regions followed by developing the existing part-time continuation schools as vocational schools in which citizenship training accompanied practical trade training and theoretical trade training (e.g. book-keeping). The prototype of the dual system emerged in the craft trades during this period. In the 1930s industry began to adopt similar procedures and legislation was gradually extended in the years that followed.

The idea of socialisation through vocational education and training has persisted. It was neatly caught by George Ware, US High Commissioner in Germany in 1951 who underlined the horizontal linkages between work and community:

> The Germans regard vocational specialist training as necessary . . . because they consider it edifying to be an expert in one field. In addition, in their opinion, apprenticeship is most likely to form the young person in such a way that he best fits into the economic and social structure of the community. Here, more stress is placed on the development of moral virtues such as honesty, loyalty, reliability, thrift,

hard work and obedience than on initiative, independence and personal
freedom.

(Quoted in *Bildung und Wissenschaft* 1972: 2)

The central role of the workplace in the socialisation of young people
remains an important consideration for employers. Despite the relatively
high costs of work-based vocational training employers' organisations
have consistently resisted attempts by the Social Democratic Party and
the trade unions to make vocational training more school-based and paid
for by a levy system on companies. They increased training places by a
half from 1975 to 1984 (Clement 1985), though this was predominantly
in the craft sector. It is perhaps less a matter of the social responsibility
of employers, as Jochimsen (1978) suggests, than a matter of self-interest.
Such an explanation fits comfortably with the increased importance given
to training in companies following the student demonstrations in 1967
and 1968, which in Germany included apprentices, after which training
became a responsibility of a director in many companies (Interview data,
BIBB). An additional factor in employers' decisions about training is a
concern about recruiting a sufficiently skilled labour force. By training
their own apprentices they can guarantee the quality of those they choose
to keep at the end of their apprenticeship, and of course save recruitment
costs and the costs of vocational adjustment (Wiederhold-Fritz 1986; and
interview data). This is, as Clement points out, a particularly important
consideration among big firms: 'The corporate indentity, the reputation
and the relative market power of a firm all correlate strongly with the
existence and defence of a skilled core labour force' (1985: 215).

The law

In 1969 the VTA consolidated much previous practice under one Act. It
is the VTA that provides the legal foundation for all on-the-job vocational
training in the Federal Republic.[15] It covers all apprenticeship training 'in
so far as it is not carried out in the vocational schools', where the school
laws of the *Länder* apply (Art 2, para. 1, VTA); training facilities at shop
floor and company level, group training centres (where several companies
provide training facilities); the qualifications required by trainers; provisions in training contracts; the rights and responsibilities of various
interested parties including works councils and advisory committees at
Land and Federal level. The Act also specifies which agencies are responsible for regulating and controlling training in particular occupations or
occupational areas. It is the most comprehensive and detailed regulatory
system for apprenticeship training in the Western world.

The dual system (and the VTA) is thus based on a long established
and respected system of training which is understood by all. Originally
used in the craft guilds it was extended to industry and carried with it

much of the respect accorded to the *Meister* and the social expectations built around the *Meister* role. This was translated into a 'curriculum' that included practical occupational skills and the knowledge and values of business. This is supported by a system enabling progression (through further study and training) from one level to another, from trainee to skilled craftsman to *Meister*, a formal presentation of a document making successful transition from one level to another, the probability of a job with the company at the end of the apprenticeship and differentials of pay and esteem relating to level of qualification.[16]

The law, then, built on tradition and, as in other areas of social activity, specified in detail the role, responsibility and obligations of the various participants in relation to training. This follows the views of Kant, Hegel and other German thinkers who equate the law with freedom for the individual or, as Goethe put it, 'Only law can give a freedom'. This stands in sharp contrast to the English approach. Whereas in Germany the law is regarded as guaranteeing rights, in England legislation is viewed as restricting rights. Hence where the role, responsibilities and obligations of the participants including structures for cooperation in the dual system are set out in law there is very little comparable legislation in England. The law then functions as a primary source of quality control in Germany. The system established in law provides continuity with the past, building on established models and traditions.

The social partners: cooperation and co-determination

A feature of the German approach is the assumption of cooperation between the employers and trade unions in vocational training. At *Land* and federal level the third of the social partners, the government, is also involved. Cooperation, or more accurately, co-determination of policy, is consolidated in legislation, notably in the VTA, the Works Constitution Act, 1972 and the Vocational Training Promotion Act, 1981.

Vocational training is formally the responsibility of the Federal Ministry of Education and Science. The Ministry administers the VTA and is responsible for vocational education and training policy. For this it maintains and is advised by the BIBB which also has a major role for curriculum development concerned with training programmes and regulations. The institutional pattern of cooperation in vocational training policy is well illustrated by the BIBB which has a central governing body comprising eleven representatives each from employers' organisations, trade unions and the *Länder* and has five representatives from the Federal government who have eleven votes.

In similar vein each *Land* has a Committee for Vocational Training on which the social partners have equal representation. This committee is advisory to the *Land* government on all vocational education and training matters and has particular responsibility for coordinating school-based and in-company training.

Responsibility for supervising the implementation of in-company training, for monitoring the quality of training and for examinations, rests with the competent authorities. Each has a vocational training committee, as required by the VTA, with six representatives from employers' organisations, six representatives of employees (proposed by local trade unions and independent associations of workers) and six representatives of vocational schools who have an advisory role. The chair of the committee normally alternates on an annual basis between employers and trade union representatives. The vocational training committee makes recommendations to the competent body but it is also a decision-making committee having responsibility for deciding the legal regulations for implementing vocational training. It is responsible for the examinations. Here, too the chair normally alternates, although in some cases the chair is taken by the representative from the *Berufsschule.*

The same principle of co-determination operates at company level where vocational training matters are within the purview of the works council. According to the Works Constitution Act, 1972, both the employer and the works council are responsible for promoting vocational training and for ensuring that all employees are given an opportunity to participate in vocational training inside or outside the establishment (including opportunities for older workers). Employers are required to consult the works council about in-company facilities and provision for vocational training. Furthermore under the implementation of in-company measures it is laid down that the works council 'shall participate in decisions relating to the implementation of in-company training measures' (Article 97); and 'can oppose the appointment, or request the removal, of a person charged with carrying out in-company training if that person lacks the necessary personal or technical qualification, in particular the pedagogic aptitude for giving training in the occupation . . . or neglects his duties' (Article 98).

The rights of young workers are legally guaranteed and they have a system that allows for grievances to be heard. Moreover they may apply to the works council for the introduction of new training measures.

There is then, at all levels of the dual system, a structure that brings the social partners together for decisions about vocational education and training. It assumes collaboration in the formulation of policy and its implementation. It also provides a mechanism for the resolution of differences; for example, disputes between the employer and works council are referred to the conciliation committee and can be taken to the Labour Court by the works council.

WEAKNESSES IN THE DUAL SYSTEM

The main purpose of this paper was to explore the mechanisms that make the dual system work. There are, however, a number of weaknesses in the system that should be acknowledged.

Fitting training to labour market needs

Much has been made of the efficiency of the dual system in providing the skilled workers needed by industry. Close inspection, however, suggests that the fit is not that good. The problems are both structural and regional. Government pressures on companies to increase the number of training places achieved greatest success in the craft sector where the overheads are low, training is on-the-job and trainees quickly contribute to production. In contrast training opportunities in the white-collar occupations, which are increasingly popular with young people, and in the industrial sector, where training costs are substantially higher, continued to be limited to the number of skilled workers which the companies estimate will meet their own needs. Thus in 1980 some 40 per cent of training places were provided by the craft trades, yet this sector of the economy employed only 17 per cent of the working population.

A consequence of this differential expansion is that training has become concentrated in relatively few trades, 36 per cent of trainees in just ten skilled trades – the expansion was predominantly in trades such as painting and decorating, bakery, butchery, hairdressing and sales assistants (Braun 1987). Moreover, it is in these trades that there are both vacant training places and a high risk of unemployment on completion of training. It is then not surprising that a survey of 10,008 young people transferring from training to jobs, which was commissioned for the 1986 Vocational Education Report, revealed that no more than half were actually practising an occupation related to their training (*Bildung und Wissenschaft* 1986). The unemployment level varied between individual trades with 18 per cent salespersons and 17 per cent of motor mechanics still without a job six months after completing their apprenticeship. Substantial numbers of trained young people take semi-skilled and unskilled jobs or time-limited contracts. It appears that in Germany the problem of youth unemployment experienced by most industrialised countries has been transferred to the 20- to 24-year olds, a conclusion supported by Tessaring (1986) who points out the unemployment rate for the 20 to 25 age group increased from 6.5 per cent to 14 per cent between 1975 and 1985.

There are also regional difficulties in matching young people with training opportunities. In 1987 nearly 40 per cent of vacant apprenticeships were in Bavaria (mainly in the building trade or motor mechanics trade) which was not much good to an unplaced boy or girl in Hamburg.

But perhaps the major problem is that training places are geared to existing jobs or to jobs that are in decline. There are few training opportunities in the future employment market, in the high-technology areas. Here then there is a sense of a problem deferred because of the short-term success of the dual system in keeping youth unemployment low.

Training quality

The considerable expansion of training places in the crafts has also resulted in some deterioration in the quality of the training that is provided. Training in small shops often leaves much to be desired.

The demands of production can easily override the trainees' needs for a regular and organised curriculum and the training is often company-specific with few skills transferable to other companies. The gap is especially large if the trainee subsequently seeks to move, as many craft trainees must do at the end of the training, to a large industrial company where production processes and practices are different. Not surprisingly then these young workers often must take semi-skilled or unskilled jobs.

Access to training

A further but closely related problem is the increase in competition for the most favoured training opportunities. This has resulted in an inflation of entry qualifications for training places. Young people who have performed poorly at school have little chance of getting training places in the more desirable occupations and often drift into an occupation in which they have little interest or talent. Quite substantial numbers of young people in this group fail to complete their training (Braun 1987) and together with other young people who have failed to get a training place are increasingly pushed into a peripheral position in the economy.

Other access problems include the difficulty of providing diversified training opportunities in regions which have a narrow economic base; in establishing a sufficiently close relationship between the curricula offered in the *Berufsschule* and on-the-job training and experience (Mitter 1986) and providing equal opportunities for girls who typically work in occupations characterised by limited promotion prospects and limited job security, and for the children of migrant workers.

BRITISH INITIATIVES

The last few years have witnessed a number of initiatives in Britain which have been intended to strengthen vocational education and training. Two are very briefly considered in these final paragraphs: the Youth Training Scheme (YTS) and the Technical and Vocational Education Initiative (TVEI).

The Youth Training Scheme

YTS is intended as a high-quality youth training scheme. It was born out of collapsing confidence in the Youth Opportunities Programme and a recognition that a permanent training scheme for young people was needed.[17] YTS was introduced in haste and while significantly better than YOPs it continues to have a number of quality control problems. Many of these problems arise from the political and operational compromises that had to be made in order to meet the deadline set by the MSC – the Youth Task Group charged with producing the plan had less than three months to complete its task. But particularly interesting in light of the discussion of quality control, given above, was the way in which the CBI backed away from the model provided by the dual system and chose an employer-led scheme. This aspect of YTS's development has been analysed by Ewart Keep (1986) in an excellent and entertaining study.

The CBI was initially enthusiastic for a scheme along the lines of the dual system. However, this enthusiasm withered as detailed understanding of the system developed. The absence of an effective existing local or regional mechanism similar to the German Chambers was one difficulty and the CBI did not wish to see the development of a major new role for rival representative organisations such as the Chambers of Commerce (Keep: 21). A larger problem was the very strong opposition to a trade union role in YTS similar to that which the German trade unions had in the dual system. It strongly rejected the notion of co-determination in the field of vocational training. The CBI was in a powerful bargaining position on this because it was clear that the YTS would rely on the participation of small employers many of whom, it was argued, would not participate if unions were involved, a particularly likely outcome in view of the use by some employers of previous training schemes as an opportunity for job substitution. Nor was the CBI prepared to countenance a statutory framework underpinning youth training as used in Germany where training contracts are legal documents which set out in great detail the rights and responsibilities of trainees and employers. The CBI was consistently anti-legislation, arguing for a voluntary system in line with their policy of freeing industry from Government intervention. A further difficulty with the German model was that it was very clearly founded on different attitudes on the part of employers. In Germany employers provided the financial support for training; in Britain employers insisted on government funding (and opposed an effective system of monitoring).

In summary the CBI insisted on an employer-led scheme with the work-experience element being completely controlled by employers. Their preferred model was based on the WEEP element of YOPs – which had the added attraction of an early contribution to production by trainees. And with the overriding priority of obtaining sufficient training places, the CBI was able to resist an effective mechanism for monitoring the new scheme. Quality control yielded to that need.

Some mechanisms for quality control are now being introduced. Most notable is the establishment of the Training Standards Advisory Service (TSAS) from April 1987. The main role of the TSAS, which is an analogue of HMI, is to assess the overall effectiveness of YTS by carrying out comprehensive evaluations of individual schemes, and to use the findings to influence changes in central policy (Tinsley 1987). It is also seen as a mechanism through which good practice can be identified and spread more widely. It is too early to judge the effects the TSAS may have and the curious decision not to publish TSAS reports on YTS, unlike HMI reports on schools, but to give them instead to the MSC and to the managing agent, has not made the task any easier. There are, however, already indications that a number of YTS schemes, including those in very large and well known companies, have been strongly criticised by TSAS inspectors. Many of these companies have already been awarded Approved Training Organisation status by the MSC and there is considerable uncertainty about how to handle the criticisms. In general, however, the critical reports not only confirm the inadequacy of previous monitoring arrangements but also raise major doubts about the overall quality of YTS.

Nor does Britain rate highly on another measure of quality control – the training of trainers. Britain has, as yet, nothing comparable to the *Meister* system and a pilot scheme to introduce it in the gauge and tool industry is struggling to find enough recruits (Evans 1987). And while Accredited Training Centres are working to improve training skills at grass-roots level their resources are very limited.

The Technical and Vocational Initiative

TVEI is a rather different animal. It is intended to provide 'full-time general, technical, and vocational education including work experience' (MSC 1984). Underlying the government's sponsorship of the initiative, which came as a complete surprise to the educational establishment, including the DES, was a belief that strengthening technical and vocational education in schools would improve the education system's contribution to industry by providing a workforce with more relevant skills and improve the employability of young people.

A rather grander aim of TVEI may be to transform the negative social attitudes toward technology, industry and commerce that many have held are at the root of Britain's industrial decline and believe are reproduced in the educational system (Barnett 1979; Finniston 1980; Weiner 1981). Again critical comparisons have been made with other countries which give higher status to 'practical capability' based, in the case of Germany, on the concept of *Technik*. This line was taken by the Department of Industry during the Great Debate:

> The present situation may be partly explained by the influence of British institutions and ways of thinking as they have developed in the nineteenth and twentieth centuries:
>
> (i) Britain has a two culture system based on the distinction between arts and science, whereas continental society distinguishes a third culture in *Technik* (or the art of making things);
> (ii) Partly because of the lack of a separate technical culture in Britain, 'pure' science has a higher status than applied science and academic work a higher status than vocational.
>
> (DI 1977: 2)

The distinction is important and it may be that TVEI will help to blur the boundaries between the two cultures. TVEI, however, in common with other initiatives, continues to miss the key element in the German system that sustains the high status attributed to the vocational side of education. In Germany vocational levels, *by law*, are full equivalents of academic certificates, conferring on those students the same entitlements to progress to higher levels of education including university.

CONCLUSION

The main purpose of this paper was to discuss how the dual system works and how quality is maintained. Political, legal and social influences, including the principle and the process of co-determination and the clarification of rights and responsibilities of employers, trade unions and trainees supported by a statutory framework, are key features. These are absent in YTS and seem to be inimical to employers' participation in the scheme. Other mechanisms for quality control in YTS are only now developing and are weak.

The brief consideration of TVEI introduced another perspective, that of reshaping cultural attitudes and in particular promoting the culture of *Technik*. It may well be that it is from this perspective that contemporary initiatives in education and training need to be judged. If that is the case the clues to German economic success lie in the *unitary* nature of the education and vocational system and the opportunities *legally* guaranteed to holders of vocational certificates to proceed to higher (academic) levels of education rather than in the content or structure of the dual system itself.

NOTES

I am indebted to Professor Jack Sislian for his remarks on an earlier draft of this paper.

1 Typical of the genre is the 1987 White Paper *Higher Education: Meeting the Challenge:* 'above all there is an urgent need, in the interests of the nation as a whole, and therefore of universities, polytechnics and colleges themselves, for higher education to take increasing account of the economic requirements of the country' (pp. 1–2) and 'for policies to increase access to higher education to take greater account of the country's need for highly qualified manpower' (p. iv). But see also: DI (1977) *Industry, Education and Management*; DES (1985) *Better Schools*; DE/DES (1986) *Working Together – Education and Training*. See also, Neave (1984) who argues that through the 1970s there was a general trend in Europe to measure educational efficiency increasingly in terms of how far school leavers were qualified for the labour market and not simply in terms of the attainments of the brightest.

2 See Bloomer (1985) for a survey of practices.

3 Then, as now, international comparisons of education and training were undertaken with the express purpose of learning what it was that made the education system of some other countries more productive in producing skilled workers. The 1884 Commission on Technical Instruction (the Samuelson Commission) is a case in point. Its terms of reference were 'to inquire into the instruction of the industrial classes of certain foreign countries in technical and other subjects for the purpose of comparison with that of the corresponding classes in this country; and into the influence of such instruction on manufacturing and other industries at home and abroad.'

4 See for example Steedman (1984) for a more sensitive analysis.

5 Sadler's approach is crystallised in his 'How far can we learn anything of practical value from the study of foreign systems of education?' It is well caught in the following quotation: 'We must not keep our eyes on the brick and mortar institutions, nor on the teachers and pupils only, but we must also go outside into the streets and into the homes of the people, and try to find what is the impalpable, spiritual force which, in the case of any successful system of Education is in reality upholding the school system and accounting for its practical efficiency. We should not forget that the things outside the school matter more than the things inside the school and govern and interpret the things inside.' (Sadler, 1900, reprinted in Higginson 1979: 49.)

6 In Bremen, Hamburg and West Berlin pupils transfer at 12. Just over 4 per cent nationally attend comprehensive schools.

7 Parents have the right to contest the allocation of their children to a particular school, for example to a *Hauptschule* or a *Realschule* when they wanted their child to go to a *Gymnasium*. In these circumstances a trial period is organised to assess whether students can handle the work.

8 Interview data, 1986.

9 The German Commission for Education, 1953–65, in its 'Expertise on vocational training and education' referred to 'dual' training on-the-job and at school following which the term dual system has become generally accepted.

10 Trainees spend about 30 hours per week on in-company training, either on-the-job in the smaller companies or in training workshops in the larger companies, and a day or a day-and-a-half a week in a *Berufsschule*. The largest companies run their own theoretical courses.

11 The numbers of qualified workers in Germany are two or three times as high for mechanical fitters, electricians and building craftsmen, five times as high for clerical workers (to the level of a broadly competent office worker) while

almost no formally recognised training for shopworkers is given in the UK. These figures take no account of the fact that many apprentices in the UK did not enjoy day release and few therefore obtained a further education qualification. The situation subsequently improved but there are still many skilled workers in Britain who went through a five-year apprenticeship but did not attend a further education college and therefore did not take the professional examinations.

12 In practice this means people who have not offended against the Young Persons (Protection of Employment) Act, 1960, 1976.

13 According to Flower and Russell (1982) about one-quarter of skilled workers attain *Meister* status by the age of 30 with some then taking a second *Meister* qualification in a related trade and a few taking a third; Prais and Wagner (1988) claim that about one-quarter of all *Meister* qualify by the age of 25.

14 The 1845 Prussian Trade and Industry Code stated that a person may employ apprentices only if he has produced proof of his competence and is a guild member – but it was not enforced.

15 The 1965 Crafts Code provided for foundation for training in craft trades. This was amended by the VTA to bring it into line with the provisions of the VTA.

16 Prais and Wagner (1983) have pointed out that status on the factory floor is much more connected with qualifications than is the case in England.

17 YOPs had been introduced in 1978. By 1980 it was widely criticised for the low quality of its work placements, for serving more as a source of cheap labour than as a training scheme and for the inadequacy of the MSC monitoring procedures.

REFERENCES

Barnett, C. (1979) 'Technology, education and industrial and economic strength', *Journal of the Royal Society of Arts*, 5271 (February), pp. 120–32.

Bendelow, Paul (1986) 'Secondary moderns lose out in the numbers battle', *The Times Educational Supplement*, 21.3.86, p. 7.

Bildung und Wissenschaft (1972), (1986), (1987).

Bloomer, Gordon (1985) 'Linking schools and industry: a survey of current practice', *Educational Research*, 27(2), pp. 79–94.

Braun, Frank (1987) 'Vocational training as a link between the schools and the labour market: the dual system in the Federal Republic of Germany', *Comparative Education*, 23, pp. 123–44.

Buchaus, Deiter (1985) 'Vocational qualifications and flexible production as demonstrated in the industrial metal working and electrical engineering occupations', mimeo (Berlin, Bundesinstitut für Berufsbildung).

Clement, W. (1985) 'Is the dual system responsible for low youth unemployment in the Federal Republic of Germany?', *European Journal of Education*, 20, pp. 203–19.

Coopers & Lybrand Associates (1985) *A Challenge to Complacency: Changing Attitudes to Training* (Sheffield, National Economic Development Office/Manpower Services Commission).

Department of Education and Science (1985) *Better Schools* (London, HMSO).

Department of Education and Science (1987) *Higher Education: Meeting the Challenge*, Cmnd. 114 (London, HMSO).

Department of Employment/Department of Education and Science (1986) *Working Together – Education and Training* (London, HMSO).

Department of Industry (1977) *Industry, Education and Management: a Discussion Paper* (London, HMSO).

Dickenson, H. and Erben, M. (1985) 'An aspect of industrial training in the Federal Republic of Germany: sociological considerations on the role of the Meister', *Journal of Further and Higher Education*, 9, pp. 69–76.

Evans, Jill (1987) 'Master class which wants more pupils', *Transition*, January 1987, pp. 16–18.

Finniston, Sir M. (1980) *Engineering Our Future: Report of the Committee of Inquiry into the Engineering Profession*, Cmnd. 7794 (London, HMSO).

Flower, Fred and Russell, Russ (1982) *The Industrial Tutor in the Federal Republic of Germany*, Studies in Vocational Education and Training in the Federal Republic of Germany, Number 4 (Blagdon, Further Education Staff College, Coombe Lodge).

Gregson, J. (1986) 'Open learning for national recovery', *Open Learning*, 2, pp. 8–10.

Hamilton, Stephen F. (1987) 'Apprenticeship as a transition to adulthood in West Germany', *American Journal of Education*, 95, pp. 314–45.

Her Majesty's Inspectorate (1986) *Education in the Federal Republic of Germany: Aspects of Curriculum and Assessment* (London, HMSO).

Higginson, J. H. (ed.) (1979) *Selections from Michael Sadler: Studies in World Citizenship* (Liverpool, Dejall & Meyorre).

Jochimsen, R. (1978) 'Aims and objectives of German vocational and professional education in the present European context', *Comparative Education*, 14, pp. 109–210.

Keep, E. (1986) 'Designing the stable door: a study of how YTS was planned', Warwick Paper on Industrial Relations, No. 8

Lauglo, Jon (1983) 'Concepts of "general education" and "vocational education" Curricula for post-compulsory schooling in western industrialised countries: when shall the twain meet?', *Comparative Education*, 19, pp. 285–304.

Manpower Services Commission (1982) *Youth Task Group Report* (Sheffield, MSC).

Manpower Services Commission (1984) *Technical and Vocational Initiative Operating Manual* (Sheffield, MSC).

Max Planck Institute for Human Development and Education (1979) *Between Elite and Mass Education: Education in the Federal Republic of Germany* (Albany, State University of New York Press).

Mitter, Wolfgang (1986) 'Continuity and change – a basic question for German Education', *Education:* a biannual collection of recent German contributions to the field of educational research, 33, pp. 7–23 (Tübingen, Institut für Wissenschaftliche Zusammenarbeit). [See pp. 44–59 of this present volume.]

Munch, J. (1984) *Vocational Training in the Federal Republic of Germany* (Berlin, CEDEFOP).

National Economic Development Office/Manpower Services Commission (1984) *Competence and Competition: Training and Education in the Federal Republic of Germany, the United States and Japan* (London, NEDO/MSC).

Neave, Guy (1984) *The EEC and Education* (Stoke-on-Trent, Trentham Books).

Noll, I., Beicht, U., Boll, G., Malcher, W. and Weiderhold-Fritz, S. (1983) 'The net cost of firm-based vocational training in the Federal Republic of Germany', *Summary of a Survey Report prepared for the Federal Institute for Vocational Training* (Berlin, BIBB).

Parkes, David and Shaw, Gisella (1983) 'Britons take a *Meister* class', *The Times Higher Educational Supplement*, 5 August, p. 12.

Prais, S. J. (1981) 'Vocational qualifications in the labour force in Germany', *National Institute Economic Review*, No. 98, pp. 47–59.

Prais, S. J. and Wagner, K. (1983) 'Some practical aspects of human capital investment: training standards in five occupations in Britain and Germany', *National Institute Economic Review*, No. 95, pp. 46–95.

Prais, S. J. and Wagner, K. (1985) 'Schooling standards in England and Germany: some summary comparisons bearing on economic performance', *National Institute Economic Review*, May 1985, pp. 53–76.

Prais, S. J. and Wagner, K. (1988) 'Productivity and management: the training of foremen in Britain and Germany', *National Institute Economic Review*, No. 123.

Raggatt, Peter (in preparation) 'Training the trainers: Germany and the UK'.

Russell, Russ (1983) *Learning about the World of Work in the Federal Republic of Germany*, Studies in Vocational Education and Training in the Federal Republic of Germany, Number 7 (Blagdon, Further Education Staff College, Coombe Lodge).

Schober, Karen (1984) 'The educational system, vocational training and youth unemployment in West Germany', *Compare*, 14, pp. 129–44.

Schultze, W. (1986) 'Titles and functions of vocational trainers', mimeo (Berlin, BIBB).

Statistisches Bundesamt (1984) *Berufliches Schulwesen 1983 Fachserie 11 Reihe 1* (Stuttgart & Mainz).

Steedman, Hilary (1984) 'Running to stay in the same place: a quantitative comparison of provision for technical education and training of young people in France, England and Wales', *Compare*, 14, pp. 157–66.

Taylor, M. E. (1981) *Education and Work in the Federal Republic of Germany* (London, Anglo-German Foundation for the Study of Industrial Society).

Tessaring, Manfred (1986) 'The employment and earnings situation of young workers in the Federal Republic of Germany', *Social Europe*, Supplement on Youth Pay and Employers' Recruitment Practices for Young People in the Community.

Tinsley, David (1987) 'YTS-quality assurance', *Training and Development*, April, pp. 26–7.

Weiner, Martin (1981) *English Culture and the Decline of Industrial Spirit* (London, Cambridge University Press).

Wiederhold-Fritz, Suzanne (1986) 'Is there a relationship between cost of in-company vocational training and the offer of training places in the Federal Republic of Germany', *Social Europe*, Supplement on Youth Pay and Employers' Recruitment Practices for Young People in the Community.

Williamson, Bill (1983) 'The peripheralisation of youth in the labour market: problems, analyses and opportunities: Britain and the Federal Republic of Germany', in J. Ahier and M. Flude, *Contemporary Educational Policy* (Beckenham, Croom Helm).

APPENDIX 11.1

Table 11.1 The curriculum in German secondary schools

Subject	Year 7 H	R	G	Year 8 H	R	G	Year 9 H	R	G	Year 10 H	R	G
German	4	4	4	4	4	4	4	4	3	5	4	3
Mathematics	4	4	4	4	4	4	4	4	3	6	4	3
Foreign lang.	4	4	8	4	4	8	4	4	6	4	4	6
Sciences	3	4	3	3	4	3	4	4	5	4	4	5
Hist./Geog.[a]	3	4	4	3	4	4	4	4	4	3	4	4
Music/Arts	3	3	3	3	3	3	2	2	2	2	2	2
Religion	2	2	2	2	2	2	2	2	2	2	2	2
P.E.	3	3	3	3	3	3	3	3	3	3	3	3
Arbeitsl.[b]	3			3			3	3		3	3	
Options[c]	2	3		2	3		2	2	4		2	4
Total hours	31	31	31	31	31	31	32	32	32	32	32	32

Notes:
[a] May be offered as Social Studies
[b] *Arbeitslehre* is a form of vocational orientation or work preparation. It is intended to make pupils aware of the world of business and employment. It usually includes introductory economics and technical skills
[c] Compulsory electives, e.g. a second foreign language in the *Gymnasium*

Table 11.2 Numbers passing the *Meister* exams according to areas of training

Area of training	1978	1979	1980	1981	1982	1983	1984	1985
Industry and trade	4,135	4,732	5,154	6,219	7,203	6,979	6,689	6,735
Crafts (and mechanics)	24,836	25,348	27,585	28,331	29,788	29,243	29,296	31,149
Government employees	671	407	185	181	192	160	99	129
Agriculture	2,605	2,752	3,044	3,124	3,564	3,580	3,859	4,349
Others	905	1,213	893	1,031	1,127	1,073	999	915
Total	33,152	34,452	36,861	38,886	41,874	41,035	40,942	43,277

Source: Schultze, 1986 BIBB

12 The genesis and evolution of pre-vocational education: West Germany [1991]

Stephanie Marshall

The guiding principle of working-class training in West Germany is 'utilitarianism'. Today, the utilitarian concept, originally formulated as a fundamental constituent of Enlightenment thought, means that a significant period of the socialization of the majority of young people is determined primarily, and to a high extent, by economic usefulness and profitableness.

(Kunze 1982: 120)

BACKGROUND

Germany has long had a well-respected tradition of pre-vocational education. Georg Kerschensteiner (1854–1932), a leading middle-class educationist of Wilhelmine Germany, was recognised throughout Europe as an innovator in the area of vocational education, offering the notion that vocationalisation can serve social discipline. He believed that

'the masses' did not need 'intellectual schooling', but rather 'consistent training for industrious, conscientious, solid, and neat work'. Working-class youth, he wrote, must be 'steadily and authoritatively accustomed to servitude, unconditional obedience, and faithful performance of duty'. Above all, in Kerschensteiner's view, the task of lower-class training was to produce 'useful' persons.

(Kunze 1982: 125)

'Useful' persons, in this context, were those who would be capable of promoting trade efficiency which in turn demonstrated devotion to the state. This utilitarian interpretation and justification of pre-vocational education continued to influence German educationists up until and including Nazi Germany, when it provided the moral justification for their totalitarian regime. As Hans (1961) states:

the Nazi educational system was divided into two school systems: one for the masses, training them to blind obedience, and the other for the leaders, training them to rule and command as faithful paladins of the 'Führer' . . . the Hitler Youth undertook a nation-wide campaign of vocational training in collaboration with the German Labour Front.

Annual National Vocational Competitions were organised in which about one million German youngsters of 14–18 took part. . . . Besides vocational skill, personality, family record, physical appearance and political activity were taken into account. During the war this vocational as well as military preparedness of the German youth greatly facilitated the 'totalitarian' mobilisation of the nation.

(p. 232)

The above raises the interesting consideration: is mobilisation for war so different from mobilisation for the economy?

POST-WAR RECONSTRUCTION

After the extremes of the Third Reich, both the Germans and the Allies were keen to set up a system which would ensure no recurrence of the events of 1933–45 (see Samuel and Hinton Thomas 1949; Hearnden 1978). The existence of the eleven individual *Länder* (states) of West Germany, combined with the different zones of Allied occupation, led to the adoption of slightly varied educational premises. As the Allies considered the denazification process, restoration of decentralisation of power was to provide the key; thus the eleven *Länder* of the FRG were given great autonomy in all respects, although as Samuel and Hinton Thomas (1949) observed:

The consequence of this lack of uniform policy has already left its mark on the pattern of German education, which in each zone tends to reproduce aspects of the educational principles of the occupying power . . . on the whole, it can be said that a conservative education policy has been followed in large parts of the American zone (in particular, in Bavaria . . .) and the French zone as a whole. A more progressive spirit has been manifest in Greater Hesse (American zone) and Hamburg (British zone).

(pp. 164–6)

Understandably, reconstruction was the major concern of the post-World War II German and Allied occupation educationists. Heimann (1963) perceives the emergent post-war German secondary school system as a direct result of social science research of the Western countries which suggested that the best way to equip the majority with the skills required to meet the needs of the 'dynamic, progressive culture' of the mid-twentieth century was to encourage pupils to draw on their own experience: the notion of praxis. Thus the majority were to be educated in schools which strove to promote skills to prepare youngsters for life after school. The education system, agreed upon by the occupying powers was very much akin to that advocated in Britain's Education Act of 1944: a tripartite system consisting of schools providing for first, the most academically able – *Gymnasien*; second, the technically or practically orientated – *Realschulen*; and, third, for others a basic or general education – *Hauptschulen*. Pre-vocational education at this time thus took on the status of its counterpart in Britain – working class preparation for apprenticeships in, for example, metalwork, woodwork, cookery – and was primarily restricted to the *Hauptschule*. What could have been the ideal opportunity to look to a full revision of the 'traditional' knowledge-based curriculum, which had been in place prior to the Third Reich, was missed. The Max Planck Institute (1983) identify factors accounting for the lack of concern for reforming the traditional curriculum:

> Although the fifties were more than merely a period of stagnation and restoration, it is undeniable that rapid and continuous overall change in education started much later in the Federal Republic than elsewhere . . . the delay of education reform in the FRG was due to the particular constellation of a number of factors . . . (1) the absence in the Federal Republic governmental organization of such legal and administrative structures as are necessary for nationwide implementation of educational policy . . . (2) A further delay . . . [caused by] large reserves of unemployed among both the resident and the refugee populations, and in the following years there was a continuing influx of highly qualified refugees from the GDR. Therefore before the end of the fifties there was no shortage of the educated and trained manpower required by the rapidly expanding West German industry.
>
> (pp. 70–1)

The first obstacle – 'the absence in the Federal Republic governmental organisation' – was overcome by the formation of the *Ständige Konferenz der Kultusminister der Länder* (KMK), the Standing Conference of Ministers of Education and Cultural Affairs, set up by the individual *Länder* as a forum to co-ordinate certain structures, curricula and leaving certificates. The second obstacle – an oversupply of traditionally skilled labour – was minimised as the FRG perceived their greatest resource to be their people, and thus strove to equip their youngsters with a greater range of skills, to include adaptability and flexibility, ensuring the challenges of the future could be met. It is this latter point which leads to consideration of the development of pre-vocational education, *Arbeitslehre* (literally translated as 'work theory'), in the FRG today, and this development can be viewed in three distinct phases – phases which are not so dissimilar to the stages of Britain's Technical and Vocational Education Initiative (TVEI): first, piloting of *Arbeitslehre* in a number of *Hauptschulen*; second, extension of *Arbeitslehre* (described below) to all *Hauptschulen*; and third, general agreement that *Arbeitslehre* should be compulsory for all in the *Sekundarstufe* I, 'Secondary I' phase of education (grades 6–10) or even to include *Sekundarstufe* II, 'Secondary II' students (grades 11–13).

OVERVIEW: THE EVOLUTION OF *ARBEITSLEHRE*

Loosely translated, *Arbeitslehre* as a curriculum subject is about 'the world of work'. The subject emerged in the late 1960s, initially as a result of a recommendation in 1964 by the *Deutscher Ausschuß für das Erziehungs und Bildungwesen*, a consultative committee of education experts set up by the Federal Government in 1953, that the school curriculum should attempt to promote a greater understanding of 'real life'. Their recommendation prompted discussion revolving around the relationship between learning and work, which led to debate regarding the relationship between theory and practice. Kledzik (1988), one of the early forceful and influential advocates of *Arbeitslehre*, recalls that at this stage of the infancy of the subject certain points, particularly questions such as: 'How could meaningful learning occur?' 'Could the relationship between general and vocational education improve?' required clarification. However, policy makers proceeded to consider provision:

1 to prepare for careers and the world of work, as part of general education, in order to facilitate an understanding of career choice;
2 to give an elementary introduction to the interdependence between technology, economy, household, and careers;
3 to give familiarisation of the essential features of today's work in modern production and service, and also regarding household matters;
4 to prepare for the appropriate behaviours for the growth of self-responsibility for each individual;
5 [and finally] the question was posed as to whether in the existing school subjects the introduction of new contents could happen [i.e. could the subject be 'infused' across the existing curriculum or would it have to be a 'new' subject?].

(p. 6)

In a sense, the above deliberations were hijacked by the Employers' Unions who felt that they were in the best position to determine or 'prescribe' any futures-oriented curriculum innovation that was to prepare more adequately youngsters for life after school. Further discussion of the *Deutscher Ausschuß* thus resulted in the idea of *Arbeitslehre*, which at this stage was characterised by about thirty terms, to include such learning areas as: technology, economics, 'work', ecology and instruction and guidance in career choice.

With the debate about the need for a more relevant curriculum taking centre stage, a large-scale discussion of curriculum reform ensued. Subsequently, revision of the 'practical' side of the curriculum began, parallel to the development that took place in Britain almost a decade later, the result being a range of courses which arose out of the traditional craft subjects of woodwork, metalwork, and home economics. In Britain, the move towards Craft, Design and Technology reflected the educationists'

belief that, with the advance of the technological revolution and the need
to develop far greater flexibility of thought and capability for action,
study of the traditional crafts was to some extent outdated. *Arbeitslehre*
reflected the same beliefs in the FRG. West German educationists looked
to the curriculum development models of the USA and Britain in their
attempt to co-ordinate progress, endeavouring to emulate, particularly,
the research, development, and dissemination model as applied in other
western industrialised countries but found that the absence of a central
co-ordinating body such as the Schools Council in Britain greatly hindered
the dissemination process. Instead, 60 regional Pedagogical Centres were
set up in an attempt to co-ordinate innovation. Thus the extent of the
remit of *Arbeitslehre* varied greatly from *Land* to *Land* (as indeed from
school to school) – assuming that a move from the traditional craft
subjects was, in fact, taking place.

By and large, programmes of *Arbeitslehre* in the late 1960s and early
1970s included pre-vocational, technical, human relations and socio-
economic education. It was not conceived merely as a training programme
for employment, nor particularly as a preparation for working life, but as
a form of general education (*Allgemeinbildung*) and practical learning,
which proponents believed to be an essential part of the students' secondary education. Thus the KMK, in providing curriculum guidance for
Hauptschulen in 1968 stated: 'the new *Hauptschule* derives its educational
aim mainly from the modern working world.' (KMK Empfehlung 68),
and the following year provided further recommendations specifically
referring to *Arbeitslehre* in the *Hauptschule*, leaving out all reference to
'pre-occupational basic training' as before, and defined the subject's aims
and objectives as:

> to impart insights, knowledge and abilities in the technical, economic
> and socio-political sectors which constitute essential elements in the
> basic education of every citizen;
> to provide new impulses for co-operation;
> to provide assistance in choosing an occupational area and preparation
> for choosing an occupation, but not to provide vocational training
> itself.

> (KMK Empfehlung 7/69)

There was also a clear emphasis on the creation of personal characteristics
and behaviour patterns necessary for mobile, well-adapted workers:

> The choice of subject-matter to be used should be made mainly accord-
> ing to the criterion that it should allow young people to develop and
> practise fundamental working qualities, like concentration, adaptability,
> co-operativeness, thinking economically, acting according to a plan.
> The learning of fundamental work qualities has priority over the

development of specific work capabilities (concerned mainly with the second task mentioned above for *Arbeitslehre*).

(KMK Empfehlung 7/69)

The recommendations divide *Arbeitslehre* into three areas or phases:

a general orientation on the industrial and working world; the development of 'work habits'; choosing an occupation.

(KMK Empfehlung 7/69)

The exact meaning or interpretation of the term *Arbeitslehre* varies according to the way each *Land* has developed its programme, which is embodied in the *Rahmenplan* (subject guidelines and suggested programmes of study) of individual *Länder*, but it is a unique subject in the curriculum in that it is rarely taught using traditional classroom methods. *Projektorientierung*, the project-teaching approach, is aimed at making pupils understand technical systems, by involving the class (or more usually the class split into two or more groups within the class), in setting itself (themselves) the task of making a certain product (within the guidelines set out in the *Rahmenplan*) or of investigating a certain phenomenon, and carrying out this project over a specified period, systematically following pre-planned procedures. These various stages or procedures have been mapped out by groups of students at the beginning of the project in an action plan and thus 'successful' completion of the theoretical and practical tasks needed to achieve their aim should be ensured. Idealistically, such a method of promoting skills such as negotiation and co-operation are most admirable, but it must not be forgotten that in order to empower students in such a manner requires a fair degree of skill on the part of the teacher, who moves into the role of facilitator rather than imparter of knowledge for successful execution of such a project. In considering the movement towards new forms of teaching and learning in the sphere of *Arbeitslehre*, it is important to remember that most of the teachers entrusted with teaching this new subject were trained as teachers of woodwork, metalwork, or home economics, and herein we find an obstacle which has not, to this day, been fully overcome.

BASIC PHILOSOPHY UNDERPINNING *ARBEITSLEHRE*

The problem of teacher training remained a central problem for the successful introduction of *Arbeitslehre* for many years: a problem only partially overcome in the last decade with the advent of departments of *Arbeitslehre* in initial teacher training institutions. The basic philosophy behind *Arbeitslehre* emphasises the technical-philosophical studies of Tuchel and Dessauer, whereas the historical-materialist philosophy relates to Marx and Engels, among others. This notion of *praxis*, relating the theory to the reality by means of direct involvement in the practice, is central to Marxist epistemology, and central to the view of 'polytechnic education' embodied in *Arbeitslehre*, stressing the belief that individuals learn by acting on natural phenomena, transforming them through direct experience. Therefore the curriculum, in seeking to integrate 'theory' and 'practice' should emphasise the educative value of productive work. It is from the latter that the view of education and development of personality by means of practical work, that is, striving to ensure adequate connection between the society of school and society at large through practical involvement, arises. This is summed up by Ziefuss (1980) as:

The evolution of man's needs and the security of man's existence are oriented to technical development.

(p. 59)

However, Ziefuss elaborates on the dilemma of transferring this notion to provide the central, unifying philosophy of *Arbeitslehre*:

Some specialists demand technics/technology as a focal point within a subject (pre-vocational education or polytechnics) or sphere of learning (work–economy–technology). Others demand technology to be a separate instruction subject which differs clearly from pre-vocational education, economy and professionally oriented instruction. Even the individual *Bundesländer* – despite lengthy discussion and deliberations – have not been able to arrive at a common solution. The more materialistic oriented approaches emphasize the connection between action and thought, work and the formed products of nature, its function and consequence for the individual and society; the more idealistic oriented approaches emphasize the important part technology plays in situations of family life, at school, in public and in professions.

(p. 67)

No matter what focal point courses of *Arbeitslehre* pursue, almost all aim to promote activity and social competence and to relate the applied forms of learning (e.g. confrontation with technology by means of practical work on the one hand or theoretical utilisation of practical experience on the other) to one another and thereby help the development of polytechnological skills which any individual course of instruction cannot convey on its own.

Confronted with the above basic concepts, many teachers being called upon to teach *Arbeitslehre*, despite agreement with the basic philosophy, found they lacked the combination of depth of knowledge and diversity of teaching skills necessary for successful integration of productive work, whether it be practical project work within or outside the classroom, and technological and socio-economic instruction, in order to promote consideration of such questions as the socio-economic impact of advancing technology on changing patterns of production: the basis of polytechnic education.

Thus, in 1973, *Aids for the Hauptschule* was published (KMK Empfehlung 73) stating that 'the aim of *Arbeitslehre* is to enable young people to perceive the interconnection between economic, technical, vocational, social and political matters', moving away from merely a means of careers guidance and instead furthering the 'polytechnic' underpinning of *Arbeitslehre*. However, this document, being a recommendation, failed to offer any constructive practical support. It remained up to the individual *Länder*, and particularly the individual Pedagogical Centres, often in conjunction with teacher training departments of *Arbeitslehre*, to provide the requisite training and advice. In addition to the curricular development of the subject *Arbeitslehre*, these institutions worked together in an endeavour to make good the existing deficiences in both teachers' understanding of the subject and their skills at promoting the students' understanding in an 'active' or student-centred approach. To aid this professional training, the various state institutes for teacher training were given the task of preparing the teachers to face the requirements of the new subject. The lack of teaching material as well as deficiences in teaching strategies and active learning methods led to various public and private initiatives, comparable with Britain's 'Open Learning' packages. Ziefuss (1980) maintains that 'The level of research (into this particular aspect) altogether shows distinct characteristics of under-development' (pp. 90–1).

ARBEITSLEHRE FOR ALL?

Providing further validation for *Arbeitslehre* and serving to stimulate further debate, in 1976 the *Bundesvereiningung der Deutschen Arbeitgeberverbände*, the employers' union, stated that schools should provide guidance on the economy and the world of work, implying that basic social and economic education must be a central task of general education. Furthermore, the task should not be for only the *Hauptschule*, but for all schools involved in teaching Secondary Phase I. This view was given trade union support in the guidance sentences of their statement of 14.2.77 (see *Deutscher Gewerkschaftsbund* (1977)), which stressed that pupils must be given a polytechnic education in the sense that school instruction must be connected with the reality of business to provide students with a comprehensive view of future work and living conditions. The trade unions further this point of view in a refined position paper on *Arbeitslehre* of 1979, and stay with it in their statement of January 1980, in the preamble of which they stress that economics, work, and careers are elementary education – a view reiterated in their statements of 1986 and 1990. Furthermore, adding to the debate, in an article in *Die Welt* (28 February 1986) Paul Schnitker, President of the German Handicrafts (TUS), stated that pupils were not being adequately prepared for work and careers, stressing schools' responsibility to provide more information and education in this area and thus '*Arbeitslehre* should be a compulsory subject for all teachers undergoing their training' (p. 9).

One of the recommendations of the Council of Europe 1983 was that secondary education should lay the preparation for life (Empfehlung Nr. (83)13) which should include a general introduction to theory of work with further understanding gained by work experience (many German educationalists perceive the TVEI programme to be one of the positive and commendable outcomes of these recommendations). Furthermore, the *Memorandum des Europäischen Gewerkschaftsbundes zur aktuellen Bildungs – und Berufsbildungspolitik in Westeuropa* (14–15 June 1984) regarding education and training in Western Europe, was a further attempt to mobilise support for curriculum innovation in this area. This document contained specific demands for better preparation of youngsters for adult life, particularly stressing ways that in secondary education a programme which included co-ordinating of information, and consideration of future orientation could be offered, combined with systematic consultation with youngsters between 14 and 19 about career choice and/ or possibilities of continuing education.

The evidence provided by the various Employers' and Employees' Unions combined with those of the Council of Europe outlined above was considered sufficient for the KMK to discuss and investigate further the claim that *Arbeitslehre* should be extended from the *Hauptschule* population of Secondary I pupils to all pupils of Secondary Phase I. At the KMK's 221st sitting of 29–30 November 1984, a review of the existing state of *Arbeitslehre* took place. It was recognised that the recommendations of 1969, regarding the introduction of *Arbeitslehre* to *Hauptschulen*, had been realised. After consideration of various statements combined with empirical evidence, it was agreed in principle that *Arbeitslehre* should not be restricted to e.g. *Hauptschulen* but should move into all secondary I instutions, as *all* school pupils should have equal access to pre-vocational education which imparted instruction with economic, technical, social and job orientation. A working group, the *Kommission Lernfeld Arbeitslehre*, comprising one representative from each of the eleven *Länder*, was set up to undertake research and to provide recommendations. Subsequently, the commission drew up guidelines regarding the content by identifying certain 'spheres', all under the umbrella theme of 'work'. The relationship between content and teaching methods also was considered. The working group, whose deliberations are well documented by Kledzik (1988), the Berlin representative and Chairperson of the Committee, perceived economic, social, and ecological changes in the present mode of life as making this topic an important component of general education. An investigation into the current state of the subject revealed three different approaches to *Arbeitslehre*, roughly summed up by Kledzik (1988) as the

1 *'integrativ'* – in which it is integrated into the curriculum as a free
standing subject;
2 *'kooperativ'* – in which compulsory instruction has been revised, and it
is realised through fixed available subjects;
3 *'additiv'* – as an addition to each of the conventional subjects.

(p. 8)

Decisions about how it should fit into students' timetables and the terms
of the learning fields were *Länder*-specific, and revealed a great variation
from *Land* to *Land*. Thus, prior to presenting their findings to the KMK,
the working group sought confirmation of the validity of their findings
from representatives of other institutions to include a sample of secondary
schools. Consideration of appropriate materials was included in their final
documentation.

At the KMK's 235th sitting of 8–9 October 1987, the result of the
Commission's work, *Lernfeld Arbeitslehre: Materialien*, was presented as
part of the working group's final documentation to provide the *Länder*
with guidance, stressing not so much the 'training' aspect as pre-vocational
orientation as part of a broader general education. However, two *Länder*
chose not to ratify the recommendations. Endorsement of the extension
of *Arbeitslehre* for all Secondary I students was agreed in principle, but
would not not yet be realised. *Länder* strongly advocating *Arbeitslehre*,
such as Bremen and Berlin, have gone a fair way in extending access,
but generally *Gymnasien* have remained firm in their justification for
taking up no more than work experience. One useful outcome of the
above was that the aims and objectives of *Arbeitslehre* were carefully
considered, refined and mapped out, and are spelled out in the 1987
handbook of the Technical University of Berlin's Institute for *Arbeitslehre*:

The following developmental trends seem crucial:
The influence of science on production is increasing. The time-lag
between scientific discoveries and their technical implementation and
diffusion on the market has become shorter. Government and industry
use the assistance of research institutes and applied sciences for the
solution of practical problems in many sectors of policy. In this respect
not only natural sciences but also economics and social sciences
become more and more important. The aims of *Arbeitslehre* seek to
emphasise two main points:

(i) to introduce (basically) the contents and methods of the sciences
which determine industrial production, the quality of work, marketing;
(ii) to teach methods of problem solving by combining separate subjects and provide a new quality of learning.

... The application of new technologies, i.e. information and communication technologies, computer science, requires special endeavour and

creative flexibility in all sectors of the economy and the social system to improve international competitiveness and national welfare
... Structural changes have become a dynamic element of modern societies
... Many of the skills and knowledge become obsolete by technological innovation.

Two other aims of *Arbeitslehre* should therefore be noted:

(iii) to provide a general education and vocational preparation . . . [enabling] greater flexibility in [students'] profession or vocation;
(iv) to make students aware of the situation of the worker (employee) in industry, trade, and craft as well as at home, and of the consumer, both in the market-place and in his/her household. Ecological considerations are integrated in both categories.

(pp. 13–14)

It is not difficult to draw parallels with the aims and objectives as outlined in the British Training Agency's Mission Statement (1989) for TVEI:

TVEI's role is to help produce a more highly skilled competent, effective and enterprising workforce for the 1990s. It is a bold long-term strategy, unique amongst nations for investing in the skills of ALL our young people 14–19 in full-time education and equipping them for the demands of working life in a rapidly changing highly technological society. It does this by
– relating everything that is learnt in schools and colleges to the world of work;
– improving the skills and qualifications for all; in particular in science, technology, information technology and modern languages;
– providing young people with direct experience of the world of work (work experience, work shadowing projects);
– enabling young people to learn to be effective, enterprising and capable at work;
– providing counselling, guidance, individual action plans, records of achievement and opportunities to progress to higher levels of achievement.

It is readily evident from the above that both programmes stress the need to consider general education as something broader and more comprehensive than merely the traditional academic diet and perceive the need to more adequately equip youngsters for a rapidly changing society. As the Max Planck Institut (1983) notes:

The common denominator of these critical perspectives seems, however, to have gained widespread acceptance in the form of a sensitivity to the need for a new equilibrium of cognitive orientations and standards on the one hand, and expressive/affective and evaluative/moral orientations on the other ... Empirically speaking, one way this search for a new equilibrium manifests itself is in a renewed emphasis on the multi-dimensionality of teaching and learning ... the problem of 'social learning'.

(pp. 81–2)

CRITIQUE

An abundance of critical literature surrounding *Arbeitslehre* was evident in the FRG in the early 1970s. Marxist critiques of *Arbeitslehre* (see Reisen (1972); Groth (1977)) particularly stressed *Arbeitslehre* as a strategy for development and training to suit the needs of the economy, stressing the 'functionalist' or 'utilitarian' and 'social reproduction' perspectives. An examination of the political nature of the course led to the questioning of the laying down, in rank order, what a particular group of students – those populating the *Hauptschule* – should have in terms of knowledge and skills in order that they be equipped to fulfil their role as citizen, group member, working person, and consumer. This subsequently raised the issue of different interpretations of the future as being a factor which militates against such a prescription succeeding. Most critics stressed the reservation that *Arbeitslehre* prepares youngsters for discrimination in that it usually only featured in the curriculum of the *Hauptschule*, thus reproducing what they perceived to be the present set of inequalities. The attack appears to have abated with the movement to first, ensure that all Secondary Phase I students are involved in studying *Arbeitslehre* and second, with the emphasis on promoting individuals' autonomy, to equip youngsters with the requisite skills to meet the challenge of a rapidly changing technocratic society. Despite the virtual abatement of attack, Ziefuss (1980) still views *Arbeitslehre* from a social reproduction perspective, as

It exhibits now as ever considerable deficits as regards preparing pupils in the perception and the making use of their rights to have a hand in forming their own environment. The historical separation of handicraft from brain-work, of general from vocational education has caused barriers till today. Furthermore, inequivalences arise and are legitimized because of these barriers.

(p. 70)

and he proceeds to stress the divisiveness of academic versus practical stratification which is seen by many to be a natural consequence of the tripartite system of secondary education. Despite the KMK's efforts to produce material which suggested that *Arbeitslehre* be an integral part of all Secondary I students' curriculum, reservations similar to those surrounding the 'education versus training' debate in Britain *are* articulated, and questions raised to which answers are not readily available. As Castles and Wustemberg (1979) observe:

> Technical processes, technological developments, economic organisa-tion and social change are all analysed in relation to the effect on the worker's job, and, since work has the purpose of satisfying material and mental needs, in relation to effects on family, recreation and public affairs. Understood in this way, *Arbeitslehre* becomes a combination of economics, technology and socio-ecology. . . . All this sounds very like the Marxist theory of polytechnic education, and curiously out of place in official publications of an Education Ministry in FRG. Why should the authorities of a capitalist state suddenly have an interest in politi-cally aware workers? Or could it be that this stated intention is ideo-logical window-dressing, and that the real contents of the projects in the schools have different aims?
>
> (p. 54)

Thus is offered a question which leads Castles and Wustemberg to con-sider the paradox of such a philosophy:

> . . . the end product is an illusion: namely that the worker possesses the autonomy to plan his or her life, as if it were not shaped by the decision-making of powerful economic groups, which decide on ration-alisation, redundancy, and transfer of production to other places.
>
> (p. 56)

Unlike in Britain, the 'paradox of training' issue is surprisingly one that has been rarely addressed. Should this criticism enter any debate sur-rounding *Arbeitslehre*, it would be countered by the retort that *Arbeits-lehre* is *not* training for jobs, but training and preparation for life, being much more about promoting an understanding of the relationship between theory and practice, i.e. *praxis*.

THE FUTURE OF *ARBEITSLEHRE*

Concern regarding the future of *Arbeitslehre* tends to focus on the actual logistics of implementation, e.g. knowledge overload and constraints of the timetable, rather than debate regarding its merit and/or content, as consensus in this area, albeit *Länder*-specific, has been achieved.

Timetabling

Woeppel (1980), at the Ministry of Education and Sport in Baden-Württemberg, identified two fundamental difficulties in the practical application of *Arbeitslehre*:

> – *Arbeitslehre* does not – like many school subjects – have only one

related area of learning as its foundation, but several, e.g. employment theory, engineering, economic affairs, industrial management, domestic science, social science. There is no teacher training able to create the super-teacher who is qualified to teach all aspects of *Arbeitslehre*. . . .

– For *Arbeitslehre* contacts with practice are much more important than in the case of all other school subjects (visits to firms, practical experience in factories, questioning experts) . . . this creates particular administrative problems.

(p. 11)

Thus *Arbeitslehre* faces the same problem as any 'new' subject in the British curriculum has faced in the past.

New technologies

Competing for time on the timetable, despite the headway *Arbeitslehre* has made in gaining acceptance and status, remains a concern as considerations such as ecology, leisure time and information technology gain advocates who, in their evangelism, see them warranting a space on the timetable. *Arbeitslehre* is now fighting the battle on this front, stressing that the time presently allocated to the study of *Arbeitslehre* should not be cut as the subject is under constant revision in light of current developments, and thus such concerns as ecology, leisure time and information technology are merely sub-themes of *Arbeitslehre*.

Infusion of separate subject?

There are differences in opinion as to whether *Arbeitslehre* should be a new subject or come through existing subjects, and whether or not it should be carried on into Secondary Phase II, or limited to Secondary Phase I and, if so, to age 15 or 16.

There is general agreement among college representatives, school administration, and planning administration groups that:

1 guidance about economics and the world of work;
2 understanding of the reciprocal dependence of technology, economy and politics;
3 guidance in planning, judgement about career work and household guidance;
4 contact with the employment agency to gain experience of the work process;
5 preparation for first career choice

are all the basic information of pre-vocational general education which should belong to the basic education of every student but are not presently there in general education. How to ensure that every student gains access to this basic information is a question left to individual *Länder* to address.

Cultural function

Kledzik (1983, 1988) stresses throughout his work the notion that 'man cannot in youth always learn what is required to become an effective citizen, worker, and family member. To be told is not enough – first-hand experience is required' (pp. 12–13). He thus perceives *Arbeitslehre* as having a cultural function, so to speak, in that it provides the scope to allow students to plan and organise their own lives by considering different courses of action, encouraging them to develop the confidence to enquire and negotiate, and allows them scope to develop skills of social co-operation – all in practice for their future roles in both work and society at large. Students need to be introduced to appropriate behaviours and provided with experiences in order to extend their own capabilities, talents and inclinations. This *Arbeitslehre* is capable of doing by examining the interdependence of man, society, the economy and technology. Here the 'experience' dimension cannot be overstressed. Teachers as *'Beamte'*, (civil servants) are not required to undergo further training once granted civil servant status. Thus ensuring that *all* teachers of *Arbeitslehre* are adequately equipped with the appropriate pedagogical skills, not solely the recently trained or those keen enough to volunteer for INSET, remains a problem.

CONCLUSIONS

The current state of *Arbeitslehre* in the FRG is very akin to developments and concerns expressed in each of the western industrialised countries:

> Each nation views itself in economic competition with other industrialized and trading nations, and believes that success in competition will depend importantly on the skills and adaptability of the labor force . . . [therefore] they want a more 'practical' curriculum, greater knowledge and appreciation of the world of work on the part of both teachers and students and more efficient management of the schools.
>
> (Noah and Eckstein 1988: 65–7)

Despite concerns regarding 'green' issues, 'utilitarianism' ultimately appears to be the guiding force of policy makers. However, regardless of the changes to the curriculum, the changes in teaching and learning styles in evidence in a growing number of classrooms are inevitably leading to an increasing population of students gaining first, a greater awareness of the society around them, be it a local or global understanding; second, a greater understanding of the factors and processes that led to the present social, political, economic and ecological situation; and finally, skills to empower them to take control of at least their own situation and to enable them to take an active role in influencing their future. These are all aims implicit in the rhetoric of *Arbeitslehre*: rhetoric that has been enthusiastically welcomed by many educationists striving for a broader interpretation and integration of the stratified tradition of classical education for the 'academically inclined' and vocational training for the 'less academically inclined', and aiming to counter the narrow utilitarian view of education that came to be endorsed by many in the 1980s. The tide of change has begun, and the spirit of co-operation as opposed to competition witnessed at present should indicate a positive reception to an enhanced notion of *Allgemeinbildung*.

REFERENCES

Bundesvereinigung der Deutschen Arbeitgeberverbände (1976), (1977), (1979), in: U. J. Kledzik (1988) *Lernfeld Arbeitslehre. Die Hinführung aller Schüler des Sekundarbereichs I auf die Arbeits-, Wirtschafts- und Berufswelt als vorberufliche Grundbildung* (Berlin, Pädagogisches Zentrum).

Castles, and Wustemberg, W. (1979) 'The new school subject', in: Further Education Staff College (1982) *Studies in Vocational Education and Training in the Federal Republic of Germany* (Bristol, Coombe Lodge).

Council of Europe (1983) *Empfehlung* (83) 13 (Strasbourg).

Council of Europe (1984) *Empfehlung* (84) 14–15.6 (Strasbourg).

Deutscher Gewerkschaftsbund (1977) Leitsätze des Deutschen Gewerkschaftsbundes zur Arbeitslehre, in: U. J. Kledzik (1988) *Lernfeld Arbeitslehre. Die Hinführung aller Schüler des Sekundarbereichs I auf die Arbeits-, Wirtschaftsund Berufswelt als vorberufliche Grundbildung* (Berlin, Pädagogisches Zentrum).

Groth, G. (1977) *Arbeitslehre: Fachdidaktik zwischen Bildungspolitik und Pädagogik* (Heusenstamm, Scriptor Verlag GmbH & Co.).

Groth, G. and Kledzik, U. J. (1983) *Arbeitslehre* (Basel, Beltz).

Hans, N. (1961) *Comparative Education. A Study of Educational Factors and Traditions* (London, RKP).

Hearnden, A. (ed.) (1978) *The British in Germany* (London, Hamish Hamilton).

Heimann, P. (1963) 'Zur theoretischen Grundlegung der Bildungsarbeit an Oberschulen Praktischen Zweiges', in: U. J. Kledzik (1963) *OPf in Berlin* (Berlin, Schneedel Verlag).

Kledzik, U. J. (1983) *Arbeitslehre 5–10* (Basel, Beltz Verlag).

Kledzik, U. J. (1988) *Lernfeld Arbeitslehre. Die Hinführung aller Schüler des Sekundarbereichs I auf die Arbeits-, Wirtschafts- und Berufswelt als vorberufliche Grundbildung* (Berlin, Pädagogisches Zentrum).

Kultusministerkonferenz (1968) *Empfehlung* 68 (Bonn, KMK).

Kultusministerkonferenz (1969) *Empfehlung* 7/69 'Empfehlungen zur Hauptschule, Beschluß der Kultusministerkonferenz vom 3. Juli 1969' (Bonn, KMK).

Kunze, A. (1982) 'The politics of utilitarianism: some notes on the history of working-class training in Germany', in *Paedagogica Historica*, Vol. 22, pp. 1–2.

Max Planck Institut (1983) *Between Elite and Mass Education* (Albany, State University of New York Press).

Noah, H. and Eckstein, M. (1988), 'Business and Industry Involvement with Education in Britain, France and Germany, in: J. Lauglo and K. Lillis (eds)

Vocationalizing Education: An International Perspective (Oxford, Pergamon Press).

Reisen, Barbara (1972) 'Wir brauchen eine neue Arbeitslehre. Ziel: Kritische Reflexion statt Anpassung', in: *Erziehung und Wissenschaft*, 24, 5, pp. 4–5 (Bonn).

Samuel, R. H. and Hinton Thomas, R. (1949) *Education and Society in Modern Germany* (London, RKP).

Schnitker, Paul (1986) *Die Welt*, 28 February 1986.

Technische Universität Berlin (1987) *Institut für Arbeitslehre am Fachbereich 2 der TU Berlin* (Berlin, TU).

Training Agency (1989) *What is TVEI?* (Sheffield).

Woeppel, J. (1980) *'Arbeitslehre* in the Federal Republic of Germany', in: Further Education Staff College (1982) *Studies in Vocational Education and Training in the Federal Republic of Germany* (Bristol, Coombe Lodge).

Ziefuss, H. (1980) *Technische Bildung als Teil allgemeiner Bildung in der Bundesrepublik Deutschland* (Kiel, Institut für die Pädagogik der Naturwissenschaften an der Universität Kiel).

Part IV

Education in the New Germany

13 Education in present-day Germany: some considerations as mirrored in comparative education (July 1991) [1992]

Wolfgang Mitter

EAST GERMANY AFTER REUNIFICATION

On 3 October 1990, Germany was legally reunified. The 'transitional' phase started by Erich Honecker's overthrow one year before had come to a formal end, insofar as the German Democratic Republic ceased to exist. Two months later, on 2 December 1990, the first all-German *Bundestag* was elected by the whole population (entitled to vote) of Germany. During the 'transitional' phase, represented by the 'farewell socialist' government under Hans Modrow and the first democratically elected government under Lothar de Maizière, East Germany resembled a boat on a river which had left its long-year harbour in rotten repair, as a consequence of the desolate condition the harbour itself had been in. However, the harbour at which the boat has arrived after being exposed to the power of rapids, looks more like a shelter or scaffolding than a solid house, all the more so as it is still loaded with heaps of scrap which has been taken over from the 'old' harbour.

To leave this metaphoric allusion, East Germans are certainly in a more favourable position than their neighbours in East Central Europe with whom they share the collapse of their socialist regimes. Their march to market economy and political pluralism does not only depend on their own efforts, as is in principle the case in Poland, Czechoslovakia and Hungary, but can get benefit from the unification with the (in socio-economic as well as in political terms) highly developed Western part of Germany. This bright picture is, however, far from free of shadows. First, the West German *Länder* have to cope with their own deficiencies which have recently been tremendously increased by the arrival of immigrants of German descent from the Soviet Union, Poland and Romania and of people from all over the world seeking 'political asylum'. Therefore they could not fulfil expectations which tend to be illusory, even if their readiness to 'share the challenge' had been less hesitant up to February 1991. There is some hope that the concerted measures which were announced on 28 February 1991 and consequently entailed a series of legal and administrative decisions, may set going a start for the better, but the prospects have raised some controversy (cf. P. Christ in *Die Zeit*, 28 June, p. 23). Secondly, the 'support' offered by the West German authorities, above all with regard to installing efficient administration units in East Germany, has been characterised by a good deal of 'dominance' or, at least 'interference' which, of course, has not proved to be helpful, insofar as it often neglects the concrete needs of the 'supported'. Education can be cited as a striking example, as will be demonstrated later. The fact that this unsatisfactory state of affairs has been provoked by the policies of the two aforementioned interim governments, may serve as a historical legitimation; yet it can hardly suffice as a remedy for the various social tensions and communicative disturbances which can be readily perceived as a widespread feature in present-day East Germany.

In legal terms, the German reunification has been based upon the 'accession' of the German Democratic Republic to the Federal Republic of Germany, according to article 23 of its Basic Law; the alternative provision as contained in article 146, namely to elaborate a new Constitution and to have it confirmed by general referendum (of all Germans) was also discussed, but finally rejected.

EDUCATION IN A PERIOD OF TRANSITION

According to article 30 of the Basic Law, responsibility for the education system in East Germany has essentially become the prerogative of the (re)constituted five *Länder* on the base of general elections held on 14 October 1990. Consequently, they have joined the Standing Conference of Ministers of Education and Culture and the Federal-*Länder* Commission of Educational Planning and the Promotion of Research. On the other hand, the Federal Ministry of Education and Science has taken over those responsibilities which have been assigned to it according to articles 75 and 91 of the Basic Law (namely in the areas of higher education and research). The *Land* of Berlin has undergone the change in a particular way, insofar as all the legal provisions hitherto in force in West Berlin only, have been extended to East Berlin as a consequence of the reunification of the previous and, though hitherto only formally, 're-established' German capital.

The regulations for implementing the 'accession' were fixed in the Unification Treaty (*Einigungsvertrag*) of 31 August 1990, concluded between the Federal Government and the (former) Government of the GDR. The procedures pertaining to the education system have been laid down in the following articles:

Article 13. This assigns all institutions and units of public administration to the *Länder* in which they are located. This decision includes 'establishments of culture, education, science and sport'. This assignment is of particular relevance to the central units of the former GDR which in principle have been allocated to the *Land* of Berlin.

Article 37

According to article 37 academic and vocational certifications which were acquired in the GDR are acknowledged in the whole of Germany provided they are 'equivalent' to those acquired in the 'old' Federal Republic. In each concrete case the equivalence must be confirmed by the 'responsible authority' which is in charge of the special matter. As regards secondary school-leaving certificates (*Abitur*) and teacher diplomas, assessment has been assigned to the Standing Conference of Ministers of Education and Culture which has to install special procedures for transition. Thus authorisation has already been exercised in the case of recognising the secondary school-leaving certificate after twelve years' school attendance (counted from the first grade of primary education) instead of the thirteen years' rule in West Germany.

Article 38

This deals with the future of the publicly financed institutions of science and research in the former GDR with explicit regard to the Academy of Sciences where the bulk of East Germany's research, in particular in the area of natural sciences, has been centred. This Academy has been subjected to assessment by the Science Council (*Wissenschaftsrat*), which must be completed by 31 December 1991. The outcome will lay the ground for the decision, whether and how the Institutes of the Academy of Science and other institutes will survive, 'provided they are not closed or transformed earlier'. Such 'earlier' closure (as from 31 December 1990) has already affected the three central (extra-university) institutions of educational research and planning, since neither the *Land* of Berlin nor the other new East German *Länder* had shown any interest in taking them over, namely the Academy of Pedagogical Sciences, the Central Institute of Vocational Education and the Central Institute of Higher Education.

The universities and teacher training institutions are also affected by article 38. At the end of 1990 a great number of the departments and faculties of education at the East German universities were dissolved in order to be replaced by newly organised units in the course of 1991, whereby the former professors and lecturers are given the chance of individually applying for reappointment. Similar decisions were made with regard to the Teacher Training Colleges (*Pädagogische Hochschulen*). The reorganisation of the whole system of higher education, though to a less radical degree than that of the extra-university research sector, has been subjected to preceding assessment of the previous institutions which the *Wissenschaftsrat* (Science Council) has been commissioned with by the Federal and *Länder* authorities.

NEW APPROACHES IN EAST GERMANY

Legal provisions

The 'interim year' of the post-Honecker GDR was marked by a series of debates whose participants were on the one hand members of the – then still existing – central research institutions, particularly the Academy of Pedagogical Sciences, while on the other hand the newly founded political parties as well as the teachers' associations came out with their programmes. The Ministry of Education in East Berlin issued several amendments to the Act Concerning the Uniform Socialist Education System (*Gesetz über das einheitliche sozialistische Bildungssystem*) of 25 February 1965 with special regard to invalidating its ideological foundations and democratising the hitherto rigid school administration which had rested upon the principle of 'democratic centralism' with its hierarchical ladder and the total control by the Social Unity Party (SED) at all levels – from the Ministry of Education down to the grass roots of the individual schools. One of the immediate consequences of the Unification Treaty was the constitution of the Joint Education Commission (*Gemeinsame Bildungskommission*) which convened representatives of the educational authorities from both Germanies. On 26 September 1990 it passed a document consisting of 'Principles and Recommendations' for the further development of general education in East Germany.

As regards the structural and curricular essentials, the education system remained untouched. The provisional 'Skeleton Syllabus' (*Rahmenlehrplan*) for the 10-year General Education Polytechnical Secondary School was slightly modified, insofar as the previous subject of 'civics' (*Staatsbürgerkunde*) – which had been cancelled already at the end of 1989 – was replaced by 'Social studies' (*Gesellschaftskunde*), whereas the up to then mandatory teaching of Russian made way for the choice of the first foreign language. A serious change was made in the transformation of the upper-secondary Institutes for Teacher Training (*Institute für Lehrerbildung*), serving as training places for primary school teachers, into post-secondary establishments.

After a short transitional period following reunification (under the direct control of the Federal Ministry of Education and Science) 'cultural sovereignty' has been taken over by the new East German *Länder* with their *Landtage* (parliaments), governments and administration agencies which, however, have been up to now far from functioning properly. The reason for this crucial deficiency results above all from the enormous shortage of experts who are not compromised by their former loyalty to or even activity in favour of the socialist regime. The gap has been filled, though to a very limited extent, by civil servants from West German education authorities. This policy certainly contributes to constructing efficient school administrations, but promotes, at the same time, the transfer of West German experiences into situations where they tend to end in failure, because the 'inherited' conditions are neglected. The widespread inclination of the East German organisations of the (all-)German political parties to copy or imitate 'examples' offered by their 'related' West German counterparts, reinforces this trend which has become manifest, first of all, by the way in which structural, curricular and participatory issues had been presented to the public so far.

The legislative procedures have passed their initial stages. They make clear that the East German *Länder* have been included in controversies which play an important part in the education policies in West Germany. This statement is particularly true of the debates on the structure of lower secondary education between the adherents of comprehensive schools and the defenders of the traditional tripartite system consisting of *Gymnasien* (grammar schools), *Realschulen* (intermediate schools) and *Hauptschulen* (secondary modern schools). This debate had dominated the education policies in West Germany at the end of the 1960s and the beginning of the 1970s. It has remained on the agenda up to now, although its dominant role in educational discussion has been reduced by initiatives in favour of curricular and pedagogical innovations.

Recent events have, however, awakened the impression that the transfer of 'Western experience' into the new *Länder* of East Germany has not operated in the way that some of the most committed advocates of both parties may have hoped for. Rather unexpectedly, policy makers have been confronted with utterances of opposition and protest among teachers and parents which have led to modifications of the original draft bills in some of the *Länder*. In this unstable state the enactment of laws as 'provisional' (with 2-year terms) certainly favours flexibility, although critical observers have plausibly pointed to the tendency towards a *fait accompli* inherent in such 'provisional' decisions. It is only Saxony which has announced its intention to pass a definitive Education Act.

It should be added that the interventions of the West German *Länder* and their political party organisations are reinforced by the efforts of the West German teacher association to expand their member structures to the new *Länder* in East Germany. Thus one can watch the conservative *Deutscher Philologenverband* (German 'Philologists'' Association) pleading for the establishment of *Gymnasien*, while the leftist *Gewerkschaft Erziehung und Wissenschaft* (Union of Education and Science) publicises *Gesamtschulen* (comprehensive schools), the *Verband Bildung und Erziehung* (Educational Association) taking a view in the middle propagating an open and mixed system (cf. *Forum E*, 1990, Vols 2 and 4). Finally, in the interim period private schools have already appeared on the scene as 'alternative competitors'. Above all, the Free Waldorf Schools have proved remarkably attractive. At this moment it has to remain open whether this recent trend is only a radical reaction to the former rigid state monopoly and therefore perhaps a 'fashion', or if it will continue, thus following the increased interest such schools have gained in West Germany. Irrespective of this trend one must, however, take into account the dominant role the state has played in Germany in the organisation, administration and control of schools since the beginning of modern school history to be traced back to the seventeenth and eighteenth centuries.

The education system

The texts of the Education Acts mirror the political scene as it has come out from the *Landtag* elections of 14 October 1990 (see: Documents, East German *Länder* 1991; cf. Avenarius 1991). Brandenburg, as the only *Land* with a Social Democrat dominated government, has presented the scheme of an education system providing, on the one hand, 6-year primary schools, which have existed only in West Berlin since the end of World War II. On the other hand it foresees the establishment of *Gesamtschulen* (comprehensive schools) with the status of 'ordinary' schools, alongside *Gymnasien* and *Realschulen*. The other four *Länder* dominated or (as is the case in Saxony) monopolised by the Christian Democrats have definitely given preference to 'conservative' models. While all of them provide 4-year primary schools, differences must not be overlooked nevertheless. They indicate options for the 'traditional' tripartite system with *Gymnasien, Realschulen* and *Hauptschulen* (secondary modern schools), as contained in the Education Act of Mecklenburg-Vorpommern, or a bipartite alternative. The latter is inherent in the Education Acts of Thuringia presenting *Gymnasien* and *Regelschulen* (regular schools) and Saxony where *Gymnasien* and *Mittelschulen* (middle schools) have been established; in Saxony-Anhalt the *Gymnasien* are paralleled by *Sekundarschulen* (secondary schools). In these three *Länder Hauptschulen* (secondary modern schools) are not foreseen, as in Brandenburg. However, *Realschulen* and *Hauptschulen* have remained as differentiated tracks within the non-*Gymnasien* types. Finally, the Mecklenburg-Vorpommern draft explicitly makes provision for *Gesamtschulen*, whereas the other three 'Christian Democrat' *Länder* have not included them in their Education Acts.

Summing up, the observer at first takes note of new approaches which, though originally modelled on West German examples (e.g. Saxony on Baden-Württemberg, Thuringia on Rhineland-Palatinate, Brandenburg on Northrhine-Westphalia) allow for modification in the course of the decision-making processes viewed from the present-day state of affairs (cf. Mitter 1990: 338–9; Rolff 1991). They resemble the current trends to be observed in the 'Northern' *Länder* of the 'old' Federal Republic (in contrast to the rigorous traditionalism dominating in the 'Southern' *Länder*). Second, particular attention should be paid to the apparently widespread aversion against *Hauptschulen* as independent types. In this respect the current debate in East Germany is likely to settle legally the trend set by real events and parental choices in West Germany, where in spite of various attempts made by *Länder* authorities, the *Hauptschule* has got into a critical position so far as its achievement levels and social status are concerned. Its official function can be fulfilled, more or less, only in rural areas. In towns it finds it increasingly difficult to compete with the expanding *Realschulen* and *Gymnasien*. The *Hauptschule* is in constant danger of declining into a school for 'left-overs', i.e. one which is attended by boys and girls of low achievement and, also, by the majority of children of migrant workers – a group which is (still) absent from the East German school scene.

Finally, all the new structural approaches bear witness to the definitive end of the 10-year general education polytechnic secondary school. Quite apart from its ideological base, its main deficiency is seen in its uniform structure built upon the equalisation of individual qualities and interests and thereby neglecting, in particular, both the talented pupils and the slow learners. Therefore the comprehensive schools (*Gesamtschulen*), like their West German counterparts, are to be provided with differential internal structures according to curricular criteria to be dealt with in the following section.

Curricular issues

These considerations will be restricted to curricular issues at the level of lower and upper secondary education. Let us start from the historically and philosophically supported idea of a broad core curriculum that curricular concepts and programmes in Germany have emphasised since the beginning of the nineteenth century. This idea is focused on the importance of a 'general education' which *all* children and youngsters must acquire. The standards, namely 'higher scientific education' in the *Gymnasien*, or 'popular education' in the elementary school (the forerunner of the secondary modern school) were indeed strictly distinct, one from the other, in the vertical system with the intermediate school occupying a position between the two 'wings'.

It is true that the radical distinction between the standards of 'general education' has been more or less blurred in West Germany for the past twenty years, since the principle of 'permeability' between the individual school types has been applied to secondary education. Nevertheless, the traditional distinction of standards is still an essential feature of (and, moreover, a legitimating argument for!) the tripartite system in West Germany which is likely to exercise its distinct influence on the curricula in East German secondary schools in the near future. On the other

Table 13.1 Learning areas in grade 9 as a percentage (including mandatory and optional sectors)

School type	German	Foreign languages	Math-ematics	Sciences	Total
Bavaria					
Grammar school					
languages oriented	9.38	34.38	9.38	9.38	62.52
sciences oriented	9.38	31.25	12.50	21.88	75.00
arts oriented	12.50	18.75	9.38	12.50	53.13
Intermediate school	12.50	9.38	15.63	15.63	53.14
Secondary modern school (with English as optional subject)	15.63	9.38	15.63	9.38	50.02
GDR					
General polytechnic Secondary school	11.43	17.14	14.29	20.00 (+ 14.29 polytechnic instruction)	62.86 (77.15)
Total		35	36	35	34

Source: Mitter, W.: 'Allgemeinbildendes Schulwesen, Grundfragen und Überlick', in: O. Anweiler *et al. Vergleich von Bildung und Erziehung* ... (see References), pp. 196–99 (according to the author's own calculations)

hand the aforementioned foundation of *Regelschulen* (regular schools) in Thuringia, *Mittelschulen* (middle schools), and *Sekundarschulen* (secondary schools) in Saxony-Anhalt is built upon the principle of integrating the curricula of the non-*Gymnasium* types at least in grades 5 and 6. From grade 7 on, however, *Realschule* and *Hauptschule* are retained in the form of separate 'courses', as regards organisation and curricula.

As regards the proportions of the main learning areas (in grade 9), the comparison with the tripartite system in Bavaria (where it is most traditionally oriented) exemplifies the position of the 10-year general education polytechnic secondary school (POS) 'somewhere between' intermediate school and *Gymnasium* – with the strong proportion of sciences marking its most significant trait. It must be added that Table 13.1 comprises the mandatory as well as the optional areas of learning.

Contrary to this rather rough comparison the curricular distance between the POS and comprehensive schools as they have developed in West Germany are introduced in more detail, whereby the case of Hessen is used as a significant example.

Tables 13.2 and 13.3 generally show that the POS, emphasising its appreciation of 'socialist general education' and allocating more than 90 per cent of the timetable to mandatory subject matter, can be placed nearer the traditional German philosophy than the West German compre-

Table 13.2 Ten-year general polytechnical secondary school (*Zehnklassige Allgemeinbildende Polytechnische Oberschule*) in the former German Democratic Republic (enacted in 1971)

Subjects/learning areas	Grade 7	Grade 8	Grade 9	Grade 10
German	5	5	4 + 1	3 + 1
Russian	3	3	3	3
History	2	2	2	2
Geography	2	2	1	2
Civics	1	1	1	2
Mathematics	6	4	5	4
Biology	1	2	2	2
Chemistry	2	4	2	2
Physics	2	2	3	3
Astronomy	—	—	—	1
Physical education	2	2	2	2
Polytechnic instruction	4	4	5	5
Art	1	1	1	—
Music	1	1	1	1
Optional sector				
Second foreign language	3	3	3	2
Total	35	36	35 + 1	34 + 1

Source: Sozialistisches Bildungsrecht. Volksbildung. Allgemeinbildende polytechnische Oberschulen. Ed. by Ministerium für Volksbildung 1982: 81

hensive schools (and, of course, the schools of the tripartite system). The Hessian case indicates, on the other hand, a trend towards reducing the mandatory section. To introduce the second distinctive criterion, the course setting in the Hessian comprehensive school based upon the arrangement of achievement levels, particularly in mathematics, the first foreign language and also German is presented by Table 13.4. In this respect the Hessian case clearly differs from the POS-concept based upon uniform classes for all youngsters, regardless of their achievement standards and their interests. (The alternative of 'internal differentiation' inside the classroom is here only mentioned, but not discussed. The same is true of the schools for the handicapped and of the 'specialised schools' for highly talented pupils which existed in the GDR though for a tiny minority.)

The aforementioned statement concerning the strong impact of the German 'inheritance' on the curricular development in the GDR included the extended secondary school (*Erweiterte Obserschule*) whose pupils had to take ten mandatory subjects throughout the 2-year course up to the final school-leaving examination. Contrary to this policy the West German *Gymnasien* have been strongly affected by the introduction of the re-formed upper stage (*Reformierte Oberstufe*) during the 1970s. Departing from the traditional system of instruction where subjects were taught in

Table 13.3 Integrated comprehensive school (*Integrierte Gesamtschule*) in Hessen (enacted in 1983, amended in 1989)

Subjects/learning areas	Grade 7	Grade 8	Grade 9	Grade 10
Mandatory sector				
German	4	4	4	4
First foreign language	4	4	3	3
Social studies[a]	4	4	6	4
Mathematics	4	4	4	4
Sciences[b]	4	5	4	5
Physical education	3	3	2	2
Polytechnic education[c]	1[c]	1[c]	—	—
Religion	2	2	2	2
Mandatory choice sector				
Group 1				
Art	2[d]	2[d]	2[d]	2[d]
Music				
Group 2[e]				
Foreign language				
Sciences courses				
Polytechnical courses	4	3	5[f]	6[f]
Courses in arts and music				
Courses in physical education				
Total	32	32	32	32
Social studies subjects				
Geography	—	2	2	—
History	2	2	2	2
Civics	2	—	2	2
'Science' subjects				
Biology	2	1	—	1
Chemistry	—	2	2	2
Physics	2	2	2	2

Source: Verordnung des Hessischen Kultusministers, 6 June 1989, in: *Schulrecht. Ausgabe für das Land Hessen*, pp. 262, 489

Notes:

[a] The learning area of 'social studies' is divided into the subjects of history, geography and civics

[b] The learning area of 'sciences' is divided into the subjects of biology, chemistry and physics

[c] Alternative: two lessons over a half-year

[d] Two weekly lessons devoted to art and music are allocated to half-year courses for each subject

[e] The choice must be made at the beginning of grades 7 and 9 for two years each. The foreign language courses can be used for the reinforcement of the first language or, as is more usual, for the second one

[f] The pupil can choose either two or three courses whereby one of them has to cover four weekly lessons

Table 13.4 Course setting in integrated comprehensive schools (*Integrierte Gesamtschulen*) in Hessen (enacted in 1989)

Subjects	Grade 7	Grade 8	Grade 9	Grade 10
German	2/3[a]	2/3	2/3	2/3
First foreign language	2/3	2/3	2/3	2/3
Second foreign language	—	2[b]	2[b]	2[b]
Mathematics	2/3	2/3	2/3	2/3
Biology	—	—	2[a]	2[a]
Chemistry	—	—	2	2
Physics	—	—	2	2

Source: Verordnung des Hessischen Kultusministers, 20 June 1988, in: *Schulrecht. Ausgabe für das Land Hessen*, p. 262
Notes:
2 = Courses at two achievement levels (A, B)
3 = Courses at three achievement levels (A, B, C)
[a] Course setting not mandatory
[b] Course setting dependent on minimum number of participants (were there is only one course possible, it must be allocated to the A-level)

self-contained classes according to the age-group criterion, it substituted a system of course instruction. Requirements for individual subjects or groups of subjects remained. But pupils were provided ample opportunities to choose the subjects they wanted to specialise in within an extended range of available subjects. It is to be expected that the policies in the new East German *Länder* will follow the West German example – probably including the intricate controversies concerning the status and proportion of the individual subjects and learning areas which have characterised the West German scene since the end of the 1970s.

Let us end this discussion by pointing to some special characteristics signalling the distinction between West and East German curricula up to 1989. Mostly, this was true of the field of social and political education where, of course, the divergencies came out most sharply. Whereas the West German variant has been based upon democratic principles, 'civics' (*Staatsbürgerkunde*) in the GDR was rigidly subjected to the Marxist–Leninist ideology.

Second, mention has to be made of the educational field covering the facts about, and conditions in, the working world. Here the introduction of polytechnical education and training as a school subject and as a cross-disciplinary learning area, can be made out as one of the most significant innovations in the education policies of the GDR since the end of the 1950s. It must be added – and emphasised – that polytechnic education and training was a curricular field which was mandatory for the uniform school system as a whole. On the other hand the subject 'polytechnical instruction' (or *Arbeitslehre*/teaching about work) which is taught in the West German *Länder*, has been, in principle, restricted to the non-selective secondary modern school and the comprehensive school. Third, up to now the diversified development for foreign language teaching has mirrored the supra- and international ties of the two Germanies. In particular this is true of the first foreign language which appears in the syllabuses mainly from the fifth grade upwards. While in the GDR Russian was mandatory in all schools, the curricula in the Western *Länder* include, as a rule, English as the first foreign language, with a minor group of schools left where Latin and French are offered as alternatives. While the future of polytechnical education and training in East Germany is still open, one can already observe a radical switch from Russian to English, although Russian is likely to remain in the syllabuses as an alternative offer.

Finally, the new syllabuses in East Germany will effect the (re-)introduction of religion as an ordinary subject differentially taught according to the demand of the Christian denominations. One must add the explanation that this had been the rule all over Germany until 1933 and has been reinstituted in West Germany since 1945. Here the 'socialist inheritance' seems to have left visible marks which have recently become manifest in utterances of opposition against the intended mandatory status of religion. In this situation the introduction of 'ethics' to be taught as an alternative to religion offers an expedient way out of the dilemma.

Pedagogical approaches

Pedagogical approaches in both Germanies have been significantly influenced by the socio-political framework of the education systems. Above all, one must take into account the ties of the curricula to the overarching philosophical and political norms in both Germanies, which mirror basic ideas about the education and socialisation of the young generation and, beyond that, about the relation between individual and society. Comparative indicators thus are offered, on the one hand, by the extent to which a teacher is allowed some choice of methods (linked with the range of freedom in curricular decision-making) and on the other hand by the teaching methods as such. Here the contrasting positions are represented by receptive learning and authoritarian teaching and by communicative teaching and learning to be traced back to the large-scale reform movement of the 1920s (*Reformpädagogik*). Generally speaking, the education systems of the two Germanies have embodied the contrast between these two fundamental method models.

This contrasting position can be investigated, in an exemplary way, by asking whether and how the heritage of the *Reformpädagogik* has been accepted and pursued after its suppression during the Nazi period. In West Germany this heritage, after experiencing a distinct revival in the post-World War II years, has never been excluded from both the experimental and the everyday practice. It is just the emphasis *Reformpädagogik* has laid on pedagogy at the micro-level of the classroom against the somewhat illusory confidence in the short-term effects of large-scale reforms of the 1970s that has stimulated its recent 'rediscovery'.

In the post-World War II period the *Reformpädagogik* exerted some influence in the Soviet zone too, because a few of its proponents were given the opportunity to re-activate their experiences from the Weimar period for the reconstruction of the education system.

However, this period of 'relative liberalism' came to a definitive end with the foundation of the GDR (1949) and the total subjection of education to the 'Soviet Model', and that just at the climax of its Stalinist variation. The radicalism of this imposition has determined pedagogy in the GDR throughout the four decades of its existence. Yet, during the 1980s one could observe some tentative steps signalling a certain tendency towards more individualisation and flexibility and even a communicative teaching and learning. Whether these modest steps to more openness might have led to genuine reforms, remains a question which recent historical events have made superfluous.

There can be no doubt about the significance of this problem area concerning the future of education in East Germany. Above all, schools must cope with those attitudes which have survived the collapse of the Marxist–Leninist ideology. In particular, pupils must learn how to overcome their internalised reluctance to make choices and decisions.

Teachers

In East Germany the chances of new pedagogic approaches towards communicative and interactive learning and, moreover, towards attitudinal changes among the pupils, is immediately connected with the self-awareness and search for identity among the teachers. The complexity of this challenge is reinforced by the reality that the problems must be solved with thousands of teachers who had predominantly been loyal executors of the hitherto official doctrines. During the second part of the 'transitional phase' under Lothar de Maizière headteachers and also teachers who had actively identified themselves with the socialist régime were dismissed or degraded. Moreover, in an attempt to 'democratise' appointments the schools were given the chance to elect their head-teachers. However, this initiative broke down halfway, all the more so as a good number of the grass-roots elections resulted in confirming the 'old' headteachers in their positions.

The new school authorities in the East German *Länder* have made efforts to solve the problem which, however, is very difficult in respect of the need for qualified teachers. It goes without saying that the situation is particularly aggravated in the area of political and social education. The press has repeatedly reported on parents complaining that this delicate subject is taught by former teachers of (Marxist–Leninist) civics.

Therefore in-service training has become an essential task in the 're-education' process.

The involvement of initial teacher education in the educational recon-struction in East Germany has already been intimated in connection with the planned reorganisation of universities and colleges of education. Here, of course, the question of appointing professors and lecturers who are both qualified and (in political terms) not incriminated appears at a higher and even more intricate level than in the classrooms.

Besides this actual problem teacher education in Germany has to tackle genuine changes in order to reach equivalence to the West German patterns. On the one hand this is true of the aforementioned transfer of primary teacher education to universities and colleges. On the other hand the change concerns the (re-)introduction of the 'two-phase' model consisting of organisation of a second-phase practical training under the direct responsibility of the regional school authorities. This question, in its turn, is immediately involved in the transformation of the teachers' status from 'employees' to 'civil servants'.

IMPACTS ON EDUCATION IN WEST GERMANY

East Germany is presenting itself as a huge 'laboratory' for educational change. It seems that the overall trend towards adjustment to the West German counterpart will dominate the near future. Yet, the contours to be recognised at this moment (March 1991) do not as yet allow any justified prediction. The current debates in the new East German *Länder* indicate uncertainties on the one hand, while 'deviations' from the 'West-bound' main line are not to be overlooked nevertheless. One should not be surprised that this trend might increase on a medium-term basis. Whether the 'assets' of the former GDR system will experience a certain revival (of course, related to the changed socio-economic and political framework) must remain an open question. In particular, such an 'asset' is given, above all, in the field of polytechnical education, although its theoretical concept as well as its implementation need to be reconsidered.

On the other hand education in West Germany will hardly be left unaffected by its co-operation with its Eastern counterpart. This predic-tion should be permitted for the reason alone that great numbers of school administrators and university lecturers have been delegated or invited to East Germany in order to help reconstruct education, teaching and research – which, in its turn, is an ambivalent enterprise, given the aforementioned 'closing-down' and 're-opening' activities. However, experiences won by 'Western people' under East German 'laboratory' conditions are likely to influence their minds and to have impacts on their further professional work 'at home' after their return.

Moreover, the overall debates in the public, pushed, among others, by the various teachers' associations and the media, can be regarded as catalysing stimuli in this process of mutual impacts, as has been already exemplified by the approaches to solving the controversial deliberations about 'comprehensive schools versus the tripartite system'. To give a second example, the current debates in the West German *Länder* about reducing the length of primary and secondary education from 13 to 12 years which have been motivated by 'European' concerns of equivalence (with regard to the march towards the Single Market), have been widened and reinforced by a look at the East German '12-year model'. The striking interest in private schools in East Germany appears as a third significant example. At present it can be interpreted as a substantial symptom of aversion to state control, and that as a corollary of people remembering the collapsed 'democratic centralism'. Further development will prove its ability to survive in a state of 'normalcy'.

Finally, reacting to the breakdown of the former 'command system', teachers, parents and also pupils have initiated pilot projects at their schools focused on 'quality in education' and 'school ethos' for the sake of humanising communication, interaction and learning. It seems that these initiatives have been small in number so far, but they have revealed remarkable commitment which might have its positive impacts on those efforts which have characterised the West German scene since the beginning of the 1980s.

CONCLUSIONS: COMPARATIVE CONSIDERATIONS

Has the reunification of Germany made 'German–German' comparisons obsolete? There is good reason not to answer this question in the affirmative. It is true that comparisons between the (old) Federal Republic and the GDR will become the domain of historians of education. Yet they will benefit from the conceptual and methodological assets having been collected by those comparativists who had dealt with 'West–East' issues in the context of their socio-economic, political, cultural and ideological background conditions.

Furthermore, comparative education will not lose this field as a task of investigating contemporary events and developments either, including their predictable conclusions. Here comparison is likely to maintain its place beyond the 'intra-national' range dealing with similarities and differences among the *Länder*. In the curricular sphere the subject of history offers an exemplary case, insofar as pupils in both 'Germanies' will go on facing the post-World War II history of Germany and Europe with 'different eyes'. Finally, the prediction is self-evident that the attitudinal problem area concerning pupils, teachers and parents (and, of course, citizens on the whole) in 'West' and 'East' will continue to be an important field of enquiry in comparative education in the foreseeable future. In this respect the 'intra-national' comparisons related to the two previous separate States, is involved in a transformation process aimed at its inclusion in research on multicultural education – due to the historically determined fact that Germany has long since developed into a multicultural society.

REFERENCES

Documents

GDR (until 1989)

Gesetz über das einheitliche sozialistische Bildungssystem (Act Concerning the Uniform Socialist Education System), in Siegfried Baske (ed.) *Bildungspolitik in der DDR 1963–1976* (Berlin: Ost-europa-Institut an der Freien Universität Berlin) 1979, pp. 97–130.
Sozialistisches Bildungsrecht. Volksbildung. Allgemeinbildende Polytechnische Oberschulen (*Socialist Educational Law of Public Education. General Education Polytechnical Secondary Schools*). Ed. by Ministerium für Volksbildung, Berlin (GDR) 1982.

GDR (October 1989–October 1990)

Thesen zur Bildungsreform (Theses Concerning Educational Reform). Ed. by Akademie der Pädagogischen Wissenschaften der DDR, Berlin; Bildungswesen aktuell, 10/1990 (cit. Thesen).

Unification Treaty

Vertrag zwischen der Bundesrepublik Deutschland und der Deutschen Demokratischen Republik über die Herstellung der Einheit Deutschlands/Einigungsvertrag (Treaty between the Federal Republic of Germany and the German Democratic Republic Concerning the Completion of the Unity of Germany/Unification Treaty). Bonn, Presse- und Informationsdienst der Bundesregierung, Bulletin, Nr 104/S. 177, 6 September 1990 (cit. Einigungsvertrag).

East German Länder (1991)

Erstes Schulreformgesetz für das Land Brandenburg: Vorschaltgesetz-1, SRG-vom 28. Mai 1991 (First School Reform Act for the Land Brandenburg: Provisional Act – 1st SRA – of 28 May 1991). (Potsdam, Ministerium für Bildung, Jugend und Sport des Landes Brandenburg) 1991.
Erstes Schulreformgesetz des Landes Mecklenburg-Vorpommern (SRG) in der vom Landtag am 25. April 1991 verabschiedeten Fassung (First School Reform Act of the Land Mecklenburg-Vorpommern/SRA, in the Version passed by the Landtag on 25 April 1991). (Schwerin, Kultusministerium des Landes Mecklenburg-Vorpommern) 1991.
Schulgesetz für den Freistaat Sachsen (SchulG): Entwurf der Landesregierung vom 9. April 1991 (Schools Act for the Free State of Saxony/School Act: Draft of the Land Government of 9 April 1991). (Dresden Sächsisches Staatsministerium für Kultus) 1991.

Schulreformgesetz für das Land Sachsen-Anhalt (Vorschaltgesetz) vom 24. Mai 1991 (School Reform Act for the Land Saxony-Anhalt/Provisional Act of 24 May 1991). (Magdeburg Ministerium für Bildung, Wissenschaft und Kunst) 1991.

Vorläufiges Bildungsgesetz (VBiG) vom 25. Mai 1991 (Provisional Education Act/PEA of 25 March 1991). (Erfurt, Gesetz- und Verordnungsblatt für das Land Thüringen) Nr 5/1991.

Basic literature

Anweiler, Oskar (1988) *Schulpolitik und Schulsystem in der DDR (School Policy and School System in the GDR)*. (Opladen, Leske & Budrich).

Anweiler, Oskar; Mitter, Wolfgang; Peisert, Hansgert; Schäfer, Hans-Peter and Stratenwerth, Wolfgang (eds) (1990) *Vergleich von Bildung und Erziehung in der Bundesrepublik Deutschland und in der Deutschen Demokratischen Republik (Comparison of Education in the Federal Republic of Germany and the German Democratic Republic)*. (Köln, Verlag Wissenschaft und Politik).

Avenarius, Hermann (1991) *Die Schulgesetzgebung in den neuen Bundesländern* (School Legislation in the New Länder). *Deutsche Lehrerzeitung* 38, 21, p. 3; 22, pp. 6–9; 24, p. 6.

Hörner, Wolfgang (1990) *Bildung und Wissenschaft in der DDR. Ausgangslage und Reform bis Mitte 1990 (Education in the GDR. Departure and Reform until the Middle of 1990)*. (Bonn, Bundesminister für Bildung und Wissenschaft).

Mitter, Wolfgang (1986) 'Continuity and change – a basic question for German education', *Education* (Tübingen), 33. pp. 7–23.

Mitter, Wolfgang (1990) 'Educational reform in West and East Germany in European perspective', *Oxford Review of Education*, 16, 3. pp. 333–41.

Rolff, Hans Günter (1991) 'Zwischen Westimport und eigenem Weg: Ein Überlick über die Schulgesetzentwürfe in den fünf neuen Ländern' ('Between western import and individual direction: an overview of the school Bills in the five new Länder'), *Frankfurter Rundschau* 68, p. 27.

Schaumann, Fritz and Hofmann, Hans-Georg (1990) *Bildungspolitischer Reformbedarf in der Bundesrepublik und in der DDR (Needs for Reform of Educational Policies in the Federal Republic and in the GDR)* (Köln, Deutscher Institutsverlag).

Schmidt, Hans-Dieter *et al.* (1991) *Dem Kinde zugewandt. Überlegungen und Vorschläge zur Erneuerung des Bildungswesens (Devoted to the Child. Considerations and Proposals Concerning the Innovation of the Education System)* (Hohengehren, Schneider Verlag).

Journals: special volumes

Bildung und Erziehung, 43 (1990) 1; theme: 'Bildungsprobleme in beiden deutschen Staaten (Educational Issues in both Germanies)'.

Forum E: Zeitschrift des Verbandes Bildung und Erziehung, 23 (1990) 2; theme: 'Bildungsreform in der DDR: Grundlegende Erneuerung der Schule?' (Education Reform in the GDR: Fundamental Innovation of the School?) 43 (1990) 4: theme: 'Schule im Deutschland der Zukunft (School in Future Germany).

Pädagogik, 45 (1990) 3; theme: 'Thema DDR (Theme GDR)'.

Pädagogik und Schule in Ost und West (1990) 2; theme: 'Ein Bildungswesen im Umbruch – DDR (An Education System in Transformation – GDR).

(Furthermore, the present chapter has been prepared on the base of numerous information derived from the daily press, information brochures and pamphlets of different kinds.)

14 Transitions and traditions: educational developments in the New Germany in their historical context [1992]

David Phillips

In this chapter I shall attempt to place current concerns about the future of education in the New Germany against a historical background of those traditions and transitions that have shaped the system since the early years of the last century. In so doing I shall draw particularly on recent personal experience as a member of a commission appointed by the German Science Council, the *Wissenschaftsrat*, to report on the future of teacher education in the territory of the former German Democratic Republic, that part of the New Germany whose description now causes such difficulty both in English and in German.

Generally the Germans have been using terms like *die fünf neuen Länder* (the five new states), or *die neuen Bundesländer* (the new federal states), but such nomenclature by its very nature has to be temporary. Other terms like *die ehemalige DDR* (the former GDR) or even *die Ex-DDR* are similarly problematic. *Ostdeutschland* will not do, since it has been used as a synonym for the GDR itself, or can be taken, as a geographical rather than a political term, to include eastern territories now no longer part of Germany. At least we can now use 'Germany' and *Deutschland* to describe the merged territory of the old Federal Republic (*die alte Bundesrepublik, die Altbundesländer*) and the former GDR. In English 'West Germany' is now a redundant term, since it was a synonym for the (old) Federal Republic. The adjectives 'western' and 'eastern', however, are more helpful that 'west' and 'east', and so I shall use 'eastern Germany' to describe the New Federal Republic's five new states, with their evocative names: Mecklenburg-Vorpommern, Brandenburg, Sachsen, Sachsen-Anhalt and Thüringen.

As the countries of Eastern Europe began the process of reforming their education systems in the light of the events of 1989, the GDR faced a rather different set of problems from those of its eastern neighbours. Hungary, for example, could draw on a Central European tradition in education which had lain under the surface throughout the post-war period. Anyone who has visited a Hungarian *gimnázium* – the famous *Sagvári gimnázium* in Budapest would be a good example – will have recognised in the institution the 'feel' of a grammar school in the Austrian tradition. Writing in 1937, a Hungarian commentator demonstrated – if in somewhat simplistic terms – the ease of the assumption about the common tradition of the schools of Central Europe:

> Every Central European [Gymnasium] has eight classes. Their curriculum, text-books and the method of teaching is absolutely uniform all over the country. They all begin to teach Latin from the first year, German from the third, Geometry from the fourth, Physics from the seventh, and teach Philosophy in the last. [...] If one says 'So-and-so's son is in the fifth class of the Gymnasium, a Hungarian at once knows that the boy in question is about fourteen to fifteen years of age [...] and that at present he is encouraged to appreciate the beauties of Ovid and the lighter verse of Heine and Goethe.[1]

The same association with an earlier tradition could be claimed for Czechoslovakia and Poland; even Romania has been able to call upon its original leanings towards the French model. For the countries of Eastern Europe the notion of a return of sorts to older traditions has helped to guide plans for reform, though the precise model might be the unique creation of the newly independent states.

The GDR, however, was the only country of Eastern Europe not to have had a separate historical identity reaching back for more than forty-odd years, and is the only country now to have been absorbed into another. What remains of its education system has languished in a state of great uncertainty following the events of November 1989 and unification less than a year later. The problems for the system are immense, and their inevitably slow solution is causing considerable pain and bitterness to many of those whose lives are affected by the compelling need to adapt to western norms.

Parallels with the immediate post-war period in education are in some respects unfair but in others inevitable, and I shall devote more space to them below. Suffice it for the moment to state that now too, if not in quite the same sense, Germany stands at Year Zero (*Stunde Null*); now too, solutions are sought in previous experience, usually of the conservative kind; now too, there are recriminations about the past and anxieties about the future. But the main difference lies in the integration of 'East Germany' into the Federal Republic, in the absorption of an alien system into one that is well established and by most standards highly successful and competitive, and in the inevitable contrasts which such a dramatic bringing-together of two very different cultures (albeit of common origin) has created.

The five new *Länder* have not only that common Central European tradition to draw upon that has informed the development of education in the old Federal Republic as well as in the other countries of Eastern Europe, but also the ready-made model of modern educational provision as it exists in the eleven western *Länder*, and the decision has been whether they should simply copy that provision or go their own way. The decision was quickly taken to 'mesh' or 'dovetail' the systems – *Verzahnung* is the German expression – and the governments of the new *Länder* have opted for structures which draw very closely on existing western German models. The then Federal Minister of Education Jürgen Möllemann argued in May 1990 that all institutional reform in the GDR should be discussed in terms of how it would fit with West German equivalents: 'Das Schlüsselwort für die deutsch-deutsche Bildungspolitik heißt "Verzahnung" ', he said ('the key to educational policy in the two Germanies is dovetailing').[2]

Verzahnung could, however, be taken to suggest that two separate parts can stay basically intact while coming together in an inter-relationship which would not preclude transition from one part to the other. It is a different concept from, say, *Verschmelzung* or *Zusammenführung* or even *Verbindung*, each of which terms suggests bringing together, integrating, in a way that Möllemann's advice did not necessarily imply.

And so we find that by the end of March 1991 a pattern was emerging in the reform plans of the *Länder* of eastern Germany that relied heavily on the traditional tripartite model of secondary education as it exists for the most part in the rest of the Federal Republic. Thus Sachsen, Sachsen-Anhalt and Thüringen were not envisaging introducing the *Gesamtschule*, the comprehensive school. Brandenburg and Mecklenburg-Vorpommern saw such schools as existing alongside the *Gymnasien*. Brandenburg (the only non-CDU-governed *Land*) was not planning to introduce the so-called 'main' secondary school, the *Hauptschule*; and Sachsen, Sachsen-Anhalt and Thüringen were proposing the introduction of a type of school (called respectively *Mittelschule, Sekundarschule* and *Regelschule* which would embrace in a single institution with different streams the kind of education available in both the *Hauptschulen* and the *Realschulen* of the western systems. These three *Länder* would also be introducing the *Gymnasium*. In addition Thüringen was considering introducing an entrance examination for the *Gymnasium*; Brandenburg intended to introduce the thirteenth school year (as in the *Gymnasien* of the western *Länder*), while Thüringen felt constrained for economic reasons to keep the *Abitur* at the end of the twelfth year.

This pattern is roughly what had emerged by 30 June 1991, the time by which, according to the *Einigungsvertragsgesetz*, the unification treaty law, the parliaments of the new *Länder* had to have promulgated new school laws. Brandenburg decided upon the *Gesamtschule*, the *Gymnasium* and the *Realschule*; Mecklenburg-Vorpommern chose all four types of secondary school, Sachsen a dual system of *Gymnasium* and a differentiated *Mittelschule*, and Sachsen-Anhalt and Thüringen opted for the West German pattern of *Hauptschule, Realschule* and *Gymnasium*.

What is remarkable about these structures for the school system is not so much the introduction of the grammar school – though there is an important problem in that decision to which I shall return – as the accompanying dislike for one of the other two prongs of the tripartite system, the *Hauptschule*. It is true that the *Hauptschule* has become a great worry in the western *Länder*. Often described as the *Restschule* ('school for left-overs') it has gradually lost its way in comparison to the other types of secondary school. A team from the Max Planck Institute for Human Development and Education in Berlin concluded as long ago as 1983 that 'on the whole ... there is no reason to believe that the *Hauptschule* will be able to overcome its disadvantages *vis-à-vis* the other types of secondary school'.[3] An English commentator has confirmed this view:

> A strong body of opinion in the five new states holds that nothing short of the full *Gymnasium* structure will achieve *Abitur* standards acceptable throughout Germany.
>   But the corollary of introducing the tripartite system would be creating schools like the *Hauptschule* for pupils who fail to make the grade. Nobody, though, wants the *Hauptschule*, and for good reason: in the Federal Republic, it is now universally regarded as the 'left-overs' school' and studies constantly confirm the growing difficulties of [its] school-leavers in securing adequate training or employment.[4]

It could surely be argued that *if* the *Hauptschule* has proved to be so unsuccessful in the western *Länder* that its introduction in eastern Germany is undesirable, then the whole notion of a *tripartite* structure is thrown into question. By disguising the problems of the *Hauptschule* through the introduction of a new type of differentiated secondary school, the new *Länder* are simply creating the situation that existed for the most part in England and Wales prior to comprehensivisation. It could indeed be said that the grammar school, and certainly the *Realschule*, can only have a proper identity by virtue of their relationship to the other types of school.

The English commentator quoted above develops the question of the acceptability of the present structure of the western German school system:

> Part of the difficult legacy left by the communist regime is the lasting effect of East Germany's isolation from the West: the degree to which West Germany is out of step with most western countries in its adherence to early selection is often not understood in eastern Germany.

It is feared that wholesale copying of western German models will serve to reinforce a tripartite system that is already somewhat isolated. An OECD report of 1972[5] had been very critical of the conservative nature of education in the Federal Republic, and the system remains the most 'traditional' in western Europe, though perhaps for that very reason it has attracted considerable attention from the United Kingdom in recent years.[6] Keen on preserving the status quo in the western *Länder*, the Chairman of the prestigious grammar school teachers' association (*Deutscher Philologenverband*), Bernhard Fluck, is quoted as arguing in September 1990 that selection must be introduced in the schools of the old GDR to ensure that they would become 'ability and performance oriented'; Germany, once united, could not have a disunited education system.[7]

There is considerable enthusiasm for the introduction of the grammar school. Teacher training institutions have been keen to start training for *Sekundarstufe II*, the upper classes of the secondary school – training that distinguishes the *Gymnasiallehrer*, the grammar school teacher. Yet it is clear that many of those who speak so positively about the *Gymnasium* can have little idea what such a school actually entails; no teacher in the school service of the old GDR had experienced a grammar school of the West German kind; indeed, only those who had been at school before 1933 would have known anything approaching a 'normal' German education system. The enthusiasm for the *Gymnasium* is of course attributable to the urgency of achieving parity with the western *Länder*, but it probably has as much to do with a yearning for the past, a faith in the inherited tradition of the common origin of the two systems, now so suddenly thrown together.

The GDR was the only country of Eastern Europe, apart from Bulgaria, to have an all-through ten-year school system. In Hungary, by contrast, the *gimnázium* proved an academic curriculum for pupils aged 14–18 upon completion of the eight-year general school, the *általános iskola*. Alongside the *gimnázium* were two other types of secondary school, one having the same kind of higher level vocational aims as the West German *Realschule*. The system of the GDR, however, allowed no differentiation between children until the so-called 'extended upper school' (*erweiterte Oberschule*), which followed on from the ten-class general polytechnical school.

The polytechnical schools represented, if we leave aside the ideological framework which guided all they did, comprehensive provision of a 'pure' kind, and it is perhaps appropriate to reflect on the extent to which they might have provided a starting-point for a new approach to the structuring of a school system in each of the new *Länder*. There were no rival institutions in the system as it existed in the GDR, and there was no ability grouping within the schools. The teaching staff were used only to a common system of schooling, and to teaching mixed-ability classes. Once embraced within the democratic federal structure of a united Germany, they might have formed the basis for the first genuine comprehensive schools on German soil; comprehensive schools, that is, in the UK interpretation, but without the problem of competing schools for a parallel age range. But such an option seems not to have been seriously considered, and the decision to devise systems closely allied to West

German models must be seen as consistent not only with a particular interpretation of *Verzahnung* and with CDU policy (in the case of four of the new *Länder*), but also with a general tendency, at times of significant historical change, to react with an antithesis to what has gone before and often with an antithesis rooted in a familiar previous tradition.

This brings us to the parallels that can be drawn with the situation in education in Germany at the end of World War II. After the unconditional surrender the Allies had complete control over education, as they did over all other areas. Policy in the four zones of occupation varied considerably, with the Soviet Zone quickly developing strategies at variance with those of the three western Allies. The Potsdam Agreement had simply stated that 'German education shall be so controlled as completely to eliminate Nazi and militarist doctrines and to make possible the successful development of democratic ideas'.[8] And it was concern with democratic processes that informed the approach to education in the western zones.

The western Allies, however, could not quite come to terms with the fundamental paradox of their position: as victors they were in full control, but to *direct* people to be 'democratic' would in itself have made use of the very processes they were trying to eradicate. The solution lay in allowing the Germans as far as possible to sort out their problems for themselves, a solution for which the western Allies have received many a reproach.[9] By January 1947 – far too early in the view of many Allied officers working in Germany at the time – power over educational matters had been restored to the German authorities. And those authorities, unimpressed by the model of the American high school or by French or British approaches to education, took refuge in the catchphrase 'On from Weimar!' and reinstated in effect the pre-1933 system.

A famous article by Robinsohn and Kuhlmann characterised the first 20 years of education in the Federal Republic as 'two decades of non-reform'.[10] And it was of course understandable that after a period of thirteen years of Nazi rule, and faced with the immense material destruction that was its legacy, the Germans were primarily concerned to put the new Republic on a stable footing. Experiments with new models were not on the agenda. The same consideration – the need to ensure stabilisation and stability and not to take risks – has applied in policy making in eastern Germany since the turn of events (*seit der Wende*, as the Germans put it) of November 1989.

Let us turn to the tasks which confronted education in Germany immediately after the war. A checklist of problems would include:

- purging the teaching force at all levels;
- dealing with admissions to schools and universities;
- democratising decision-making processes in all institutions;
- providing new textbooks and other teaching materials;

- coping with the reconstruction of buildings and plant generally and providing modern equipment;
- restocking libraries in every type of institution;
- redesigning syllabuses in schools and universities;
- instituting emergency training programmes;
- establishing contact with the world outside Germany.

Each of these tasks is paralleled in the problems facing the new *Länder*. One of the most serious concerns the teaching force. After the war denazification processes, planned for by the Allies before hostilities ceased, enabled the occupiers (and later the Germans themselves) to rid the teaching force of those whose past record rendered them unfit to continue teaching. It would be unjust, indeed quite wrong, to postulate direct parallels with what has been happening in eastern German institutions – the association would be offensive to large numbers of teachers who have now lost their jobs – but the processes and resulting recriminations are similar enough to make comparison and contrast inevitable.

If we consider higher education, it is clear that the closing of whole departments has created enormous problems. The German term for the process involved, *Abwicklung*, means literally 'unwinding'; in its business sense it usually signifies 'liquidation', but the notion of 'unwinding' is closer to what has been happening. Those teaching in a department that has been *abgewickelt* have been suspended, placed in what has become known as the *Warteschleife*, a term which normally describes the 'stacking' of aeroplanes before they are given permission to land. The closing of departments – and even of a huge institution like the Berlin Academy of Pedagogical Sciences – has been predicated on the assumption that they were suspect *en bloc*. Decisions about the reinstatement of individuals have had to await the outcome of evaluation processes to determine to what degree they are *belastet* ('burdened [by the past]') to use a term from the post-war period.

But it is difficult to decide to what extent a matter like membership of the SED makes somebody unfit to teach. It appears that co-operation with the Stasi, or participation in the higher levels of the Party, have been used as the main criteria, rather than normal Party membership, which was required of so many with posts of any responsibility. What has been happening in higher education is a kind of self-evaluation, through internal processes. Deans of faculties have been elected, and institutions have set up procedures to vet their existing staff. In the schools of Thüringen the 27,000 teachers have had to fill in a questionnaire in which they are asked about work for the Stasi and functions in the Party – a reminder again of the post-war period, when the notorious *Fragebogen* (questionnaire) had to be completed by all citizens seeking employment, even in the lowliest jobs.

Following the evaluation process, the question of retraining the teaching force acquires considerable urgency. Those confirmed in their posts are as unused to freedom of thought and action as their students. After the war the policy of re-education was by no means straightforward. There is indeed something offensive in the very notion of trying to 'turn' the thinking of a nation, and it is a brave re-educator who thinks he can provide the key to the problems facing both teachers and learners as they emerge from several decades of suppression. The Allies were often accused of coming to war-torn Germany with the patronising attitudes of 'knowing what was good for the Germans'. Federal Minister Möllemann warned before unification against precisely that kind of approach in the speech referred to above:

> We must beware of coming forward with the 'I know best' attitudes of a rich uncle. What is important is to encourage the forces of reform, to strengthen self-confidence, and to support the capacity to introduce into the process of reform a high degree of intellectual self-achievement. [Present author's translation]

There is, however, some evidence that West German visiting academics (*Gastprofessoren*), not always those of the highest calibre, have seen involvement in eastern Germany as a chance to further their own careers, and they have not always behaved with appropriate sensitivity and circumspection. One West German professor encountered in a famous university in an eastern *Land* replied, when asked what he was doing there: *Ich wollte hier was retten* ('I wanted to rescue something here'). That is the kind of arrogance that the hard-pressed academics of the eastern German universities can do without.

After the war there were many who wanted to 'do something for Germany', and most, certainly in the early part of the occupation, were fired with admirable motives, among them some highly respected members of Education Branch in the British zone. But there were temptations of various kinds, one being the opportunity the *tabula rasa* a devastated country afforded for the trying-out of pet ideas. Some of the ideas proposed for the reform of the universities of the British zone, for example, would have been given short shrift in the England of 1945. Stefanie Rehm, education minister of Sachsen, has criticised visiting West German 'missionaries' who have wished to introduce their own favoured type of school into the systems of the new *Länder*. The *Hauptschule* had no chance in Sachsen, she added, however hard the *Philologenverband* might fight for it.[11]

It was clearly important for the new *Länder* to look to their western neighbours for assistance, and they have drawn on the expertise not only of visiting academics – often dashing for an intensive day's work to an eastern university – but also of civil servants seconded from the ministries of western *Länder*. Many departments have recruited West Germany *Gründungsdekane* (founding deans) to oversee their re-establishment under new conditions. But the fear that West Germans will step in to fill a large proportion of vacant positions is a very real one. The apprehension in this connection is such that positive steps have been taken to encourage foreign applicants for those chairs that have been advertised since unification – as in the case of ten professorships in Education at the Humboldt University in Berlin, for example. Applications from eastern Germany are also encouraged, many advertisements stating specifically that, all things (i.e. qualifications) being equal, they will be given preference. Chair-holders at present in post are having to face the unenviable prospect of applying for their own jobs once they are advertised anew.

Unemployment threatens large numbers of people in all types of institution. Thousands of lecturers have been affected – at the Humboldt University in Berlin, for example, the teaching staff was cut by more than 6,000. In Sachsen only 10,000 out of a total of 24,000 lecturers in institutions of higher education were due, in July 1992, to keep their jobs.[12] But unemployment has resulted not only from ideological vetting: the favourable staff : student ratios common in the old GDR can simply no longer be afforded in the tight budgets of the new *Länder*.

Academics in the eastern universities and colleges have of course been cut off from contact with the west for a couple of generations, and their own education and training cannot compare in most subjects with that of their western counterparts, even of those subjects, such as medicine, least susceptible to ideological interference. The *Rektor* of one teacher training college told me that he had waited several months for permission to read Henry Ford's autobiography; an English lecturer nearing retirement had never been given permission, during 37 years of specialist teaching, to visit the UK or America; a 48–year-old academic, despairing of the task of catching up with her western counterparts, said *Man kann nicht in einem Jahr nachlesen, was man in 30 Jahren nicht lesen konnte* ('You can't catch up in one year on the reading you haven't been able to do for 30 years'); laboratory facilities in many institutions resemble those of western schools and colleges of the 1950s; doctoral theses and academic publications are forever tainted by references to what Margot Honecker had said at such-and-such a Party congress, in the way that some otherwise respectable scholarly writings in the Nazi period were topped and tailed with similar ritualistic sops to the prevailing ideology.

That democratic processes should be introduced at all levels of the education system has been a priority since the dramatic changes of 1989. But what is to be understood by 'democratic' is problematic, and reminds us again of the post-war years. At one four-power meeting in Berlin after the war it was suggested that each delegate should define 'democracy'; the British representative concluded that democracy was what four powers could agree to inflict on a fifth.[13] Now those planning the future of education in the eastern *Länder* have the model of West Germany before them, but they have gone beyond that model in electing people to posts of responsibility within institutions: in Potsdam, for example, about 90 per cent of the leadership of the college has been chosen by democratic voting processes.

Democratic freedom has also of course resulted in the expression of views, usually of an extreme right-wing kind, which are considered unacceptable in other democracies. I recall being struck by a conversation in Leipzig in the spring of 1989 with a class of *Abiturienten* (18-year-old school-leavers) who questioned me closely about neo-Nazi groups then hitting the headlines in West Berlin. When we consider that the GDR had consistently sought to justify its obsessions with secure boundaries in terms of keeping 'fascist' forces at bay – the Berlin Wall was after all known as *der antifaschistische Schützwall* – it is frightening that such forces should now be emerging from within its own former territory. The very same arguments about democracies allowing freedom of expression (so that the views of extremists can be defeated) that were regarded in the GDR as a typical Western fudge, can now be utilised to defend the kind of behaviour we have seen reported from eastern Germany in recent months.

In the post-war years an urgent problem was the need for quick production of new teaching materials. In the schools of the new *Länder* there has been a great shortage of suitable teaching materials. The immediate availability of appropriate textbooks from West German publishers has provided an advantage that did not exist after the war, but the process of change is slow, and is hampered by the non-existence of that accumulated material on which teachers depend to construct teaching programmes. The problems have been caricatured by an English observer:

> Hello everyone in East Germany! My name is James Sherman and I am an unemployed Welsh miner . . . I've been helping all you good socialist schoolchildren to learn what life in Britain is really like. Today I am going to teach you important English words such as 'strike committee', 'solidarity' and 'picket-line'. [. . .]
>
> The adventures of the mythical James Sherman during the 1974 miners' strike (and other similarly gruelling episodes from East Germany's standard secondary school texts) will soon be consigned to the dustbin.
>
> East German language students are looking forward to bright new West German textbooks, in which ideologically inscrutable British children race happily around on their bicycles and play games with Dick the dog.
>
> It is all part of a classroom revolution that will, at least in theory, free East Germany's schools from the shackles of communist theory and transform a generation of pupils from docile doctrinaire dullards into inquisitive, intelligent dynamos.[14]

Caricatures, to be recognisable, must at least have a grain of truth in them, and that is no exception. But the main import of the description lies in the aim to produce a new generation used to making their own decisions and attuned to the imperatives of Western capitalist democracy. Günter Grass reminds us that in the common perception 'what triumphed in Leipzig and Dresden, in Rostock and East Berlin, was not the people of the GDR but Western capitalism',[15] and it is adjustment to the alien norms implicit in that interpretation that is proving so difficult, despite their expectations, for the average citizens of the eastern *Länder*.

That adjustment will take time. The people are still in a state of shock; indeed there is a kind of national trauma as a result of the effective disappearance of their country and the widely held view, constantly reinforced, that nothing of worth had been achieved during the four decades and more of its existence.

Visitors to eastern German universities and colleges have been struck by the extent to which people at all levels have been waiting for directives, expecting something to happen that would solve their immediate problems. Simply making them aware that decisions now rest with the democratically elected parliaments of the *Länder* and not with an all-powerful central administration has not been as easy as might be imagined. And in addition the functions of federal bodies like the standing conference of education ministers of the *Länder* (the *Kultusministerkonferenz*), or the *Wissenschaftsrat*, or the West German Rectors' Conference, have had to be explained and their potential to help has needed to be made explicit. Those bodies, and others like the German Academic Exchange Service (DAAD), have been overburdened with work on a host of initiatives to encourage development in the eastern *Länder* that will help to achieve some kind of parity with provision in the old Federal Republic. The *Wissenschaftsrat* in particular has been reporting with astounding regularity on a very wide range of issues facing higher education. Its activity during 1991 was frenetic. The general view seems to be that it will take some ten years before the new *Länder*, despite the many initiatives, reach the standard of their western German counterparts.

But let us return to the question of tradition upheld in times of transition. I have intimated that a future verdict on what is happening in the new *Länder* might well be that opportunities were missed to experiment, to capitalise on what might be seen as strengths of the old GDR provision. Were there any such strengths? The answer is: 'Yes, but . . .'. Proponents of comprehensive education will argue that the polytechnical schools provided a model non-selective education that could have been developed under Western-type conditions; vocational training experts might see positive aspects in the compulsory work experience that was an essential part of polytechnical education, and in the East German bringing-together of general and vocational education; nursery school provision was highly developed, though no doubt out of necessity, since so many women were needed in the workforce; lecturer : student ratios in higher education were much smaller – as were institutions – than in the 'mass universities' of the old Federal Republic, and advantages might be seen in the selection which governed access to higher education; teacher education, organised in one phase rather than the two phases of the western *Länder*, involved lecturers in a much closer association with the world of practice than their western counterparts enjoyed.

But it was clear from an early stage after the agreement to move towards unification that the dovetailing of the two systems was to be given high priority, and that few tears would be shed over the passing of a system which lacked those roots in the country's culture and history that the models of the western *Länder* offered.

Those models have been remarkably resilient. I have referred to the criticism levelled against the Federal Republic in terms of its having the most conservative or 'traditional' education system in Europe. After the war Adenauer's dictum 'No experiments!' (*keine Experimente!*), was instrumental in preventing reform, and even with his departure the country was in no hurry to emulate the changes which were taking place in the education systems of her Western neighbours. A policy of 'wait and see' required that comprehensive schools (*Gesamtschulen*) could have only experimental status and be allowed for the most part to exist only alongside the schools which make up the tripartite system. In taking such a cautious line, the Germans may well feel they have been justified in view of the criticisms now levelled against systems which were ready to embark on radical reform.

The Humboldtian tradition has survived for nearly two centuries, and provides quite remarkable continuity in the academic education offered in the *Gymnasien*. If we look at the curricula of these schools since Humboldt's brief tenure as Prussian Minister of Education (he held office in 1809–10), it is striking how consistent the provision has been.

But this continuity has not been restricted to the grammar schools. A parallel tradition of serious attention to high-quality non-academic education and training, exemplified in the prestigious *Realschulen*, can be taken to have contributed significantly to Germany's growth as an industrial nation in the second half of the last century. The *Realschule*, described as a 'semi-academic intermediate school'[16] has provided a strong backbone to the tripartite nature of the German secondary school system; it has been praised as 'a model . . . for a type of school that should be made universal'.[17]

By the turn of the century the Germans had evolved an education system which was in many respects the envy of Europe. The two main periods of nationalistic fervour during the nineteenth century had provided considerable impetus to the system's development, but it was recognised that Germany's powerful industrial growth depended on soundly based educational provision, and the highly developed system of vocational training in force in the Federal Republic today owes much to the forward outlook of the late nineteenth- and early twentieth-century planners. Michael Sadler, writing of what he called the 'ferment' in education at the time, summarised the merits of German education in enthusiastic terms:

> The German system excels in the grade of academic and of higher technological instruction. It also excels in the provision of cheap, standardised, well-staffed and easily accessible secondary day-schools for boys, where much is taught (perhaps a little too much taught) that equips a man to take a well-informed and intelligent part in modern trade and professional life, and prepares him to submit to the further discipline of special technical training. A third, but not least important, excellence of German education is to be found in the combination of well-informed municipal initiative with expert supervision on the part of the State. At the present time this is perhaps the most remarkable characteristic of the whole system, and evidence of its success may be seen in the widespread appreciation, among parents of all classes, of the importance of well-chosen curricula, of sound rather than showy teaching, and of prolonged courses of intellectual discipline.[18]

There is here, as in much of Sadler's writing, an uncannily accurate reflection of today's educational issues.

Sadler touches on several issues which provide an explanation for the durability of the German approach. First, there is a strong and much-prized academic tradition, but alongside it is a similarly prized tradition of technological education and training that is not regarded as inferior. The *Realschule* does not compete with the *Gymnasium*, rather it complements it; likewise the *Technische Hochschulen* (now for the most part called *Technische Universitäten*) have existed alongside the universities at least as equal partners; many would claim to be superior, at least to some of the younger western German universities. (The qualification of Dipl. Ing., incidentally, has always been highly regarded in Germany.) Now the German near-equivalents of polytechnics, the *Fachhochschulen*, enjoy a reputation based on their being able to offer high-status training seen to lead to specific types of responsible employment.

Second, the state, despite all the complications of a political system predicated on federalism, has provided that oversight of education which ensures that all involved in the education system – whether pupils, parents, teachers, or administrators – know unequivocally what to expect from it.[19] Where the British have a wary attitude to the state and would wish to keep its influence – or to use the term most commonly used, 'interference' – at bay for the sake of academic freedom, the Germans have seen state control, in terms of a kind of benevolent paternalism, as a guarantee of such freedom.

But while there has been an acceptance of *die Aufsicht des Staates* ('the supervision of the state') as Article 7 of the German *Grundgesetz*, the

Basic Law of the Federal Republic, puts it, there has also been great faith in the federal principle (with autonomy in educational matters devolved to the *Länder*), and a distrust of national decision-making bodies. The only time there has been an all-powerful national Minister of Education was under the Nazis, and the experience of the GDR has served simply to reinforce the undesirability of centralisation. On the other hand, the task of the *Kultusministerkonferenz* to co-ordinate policy – difficult enough with the views of eleven *Länder* to accommodate – is now made much worse with the accretion of another five.

Third, what Sadler called 'intellectual discipline' is furthered by a national reverence for the concept of *Leistung*, 'performance', as understood in the so-called 'achievement principle', the *Leistungsprinzip*, that informs the content and processes and the assessment of outcomes of education at all levels. That is why Bernhard Fluck was so quick to talk about the need in the last months of the GDR for its schools to become 'ability and performance oriented'. So fundamental is the concept of *Leistung* in German education that it is virtually impossible to contemplate alternative approaches in which its importance would be diminished.

As to 'sound rather than showy teaching', the echoes will reverberate in all directions. Suffice it to say that the German teacher, for good or ill, has stuck to the old-fashioned teacher-dominated approach to the classroom, *Frontalunterricht*, as it is known, and this has been perceived to have advantages over other more pupil-centred approaches.

There is no doubt that the future of education at all levels in the new *Länder* will be problematic. Adjusting to western norms will be a slow and painful process; competition with parallel institutions in the western *Länder* will be difficult until a more confident teaching force, retrained where necessary, and up-to-date teaching materials and equipment are in place; the influx of people from the western *Länder*, many of whom will be filling posts made vacant by the dismissal of East Germans, will create tensions locally that will not be easily resolved; many will feel that much that was good in their institutions has been changed without proper reason; students will suspect, despite reassurances, than an 'eastern' education will not be so highly regarded for many years to come as an education in the West. The German language has already divided people into *Ossis* and *Wessis*, and there must be fears about the social tensions and conflicts that will result if that division is perpetuated in some way through the education system.

But the imperatives of history are so strong in the German context that there can be little doubt that a school and higher education system will emerge that will have drawn on the perceived strengths and security of the West German model. There is indeed something very exciting about the great universities in Leipzig and Halle and Jena, despite their present sorry state, being brought back into the fold of the western democratic tradition – and indeed in the prospect of the renewal of education in Dresden and Potsdam and in such jewels of towns as Erfurt and Mühlhausen.

The eastern *Länder*, however, will have to face up to some of the problems confronting the German system as a whole as we approach a new Europe with redefined notions of boundaries within systems. Among those problems are the reduction of the length of the full academic secondary course from 13 to 12 years, tighter regulation of access of higher education, and a shortening of the time taken to complete higher education courses. It might be hoped that wider developments in Europe will provide an impetus for reform in German education which the forces of tradition have resisted for so long and which unification has failed to bring about.

That the future verdict might well be one of missed opportunity to experiment, or to allow a distinctively eastern German style of educational provision to develop, pales into insignificance compared to the hopes for an education system at last released from the ideological stranglehold that denied those freedoms which the West has taken for granted for so long, and which the West Germans in particular have had such good reason to cherish.[20]

NOTES

1 Adam de Hegedus (1937) *Hungarian Background*. London: Hamish Hamilton.
2 Jürgen W. Möllemann (1990) Deutschland nach dem 9. November 1989 – Chancen, Perspektiven und Probleme, speech delivered in Nordkirchen, 3.5.90; Presse Info BMBW, 61/1990.
3 Max Planck Institute for Human Development and Education (1983) *Between Elite and Mass Education: Education in the Federal Republic of Germany*, Albany: State University of New York Press, p. 181.
4 Paul Bendelow (1990) 'Eastern pendulum swings back to western selection', *The Times Educational Supplement*, 2 November.
5 OECD (1972) *Reviews of National Policies for Education: Germany*. Paris.
6 See, for example, DES (1986) *Education in the Federal Republic of Germany: Aspects of Curriculum and Assessment*, London: HMSO; (1991) *Aspects of Vocational Education and Training in the Federal Republic of Germany*. London: HMSO; S. J. Prais and Karin Wagner (1985) 'Schooling standards in England and Germany: some summary comparisons bearing on economic performance', *National Institute Economic Review*, May 1985, No. 112 and *Compare*, 16, 1986.
7 See Paul Bendelow (1990) 'Youth training campaign opens amid job fears', *The Times Educational Supplement*, 21 November.
8 *Protocol of the Proceedings of the Berlin Conference, Berlin, 2 August 1945*, London (HMSO) 1947, paragraph II A 7.
9 See, for example, Hellmut Becker (1978) 'Retrospective view from the German side', in Arthur Hearnden (ed.) *The British in Germany: Educational Reconstruction after 1945*, pp. 268–82. London: Hamish Hamilton.
10 Saul B. Robinsohn and J. Caspar Kuhlmann (1967) 'Two decades of non-reform in West German education', *Comparative Education Review*, 11 (3).

11 'Saxony and Thuringia striving for new paths', is In Press (Bildung und Wissenschaft), BW 1991 1/2, p. 10.

12 Mike Gardner (1991) 'Germans join the dole' and 'New law devastating for Humboldt', *The Times Higher Education Supplement*, 5 July.

13 Russell Hill (1947) *Struggle for Germany*, p. 12. London: Gollancz.

14 Tony Allen-Mills (1990) 'East Germans axe dogma in the classroom', *The Sunday Times*, 2 November.

15 Günter Grass (1990) *Two States – One Nation? The Case against German Reunification*, p. 2. London: Secker & Warburg.

16 Arthur Hearnden (1976) *Education, Culture and Politics in West Germany*, p. 82. Oxford: Pergamon.

17 Max Planck Institut, *Between Elite and Mass Education*, p. 194.

18 Michael Sadler (1903) *The Ferment in Education on the Continent and in America*, Proceedings of the British Academy, pp. 4–5.

19 This point is developed in David Phillips (1987) 'Lessons from Germany? The case of German secondary schools', *British Journal of Educational Studies*, 35, pp. 211–32.

20 I am grateful to Britta Baron for her helpful comments on an earlier draft of this paper, which was delivered as the keynote lecture at the British History of Education Society's annual conference in Liverpool in December 1991 on the subject 'Education: the European context'. It has appeared simultaneously in Maurice Whitehead (ed.) (1992) *Education and Europe: Historical and Contemporary Perspectives*, in the series 'Aspects of Education' (University of Hull, No. 46).

15 On the education system in the five new *Länder* of the Federal Republic of Germany

Brandenburg, Mecklenburg-Western Pomerania, Saxony, Saxony-Anhalt, Thuringia [1992]

Christoph Führ

INTRODUCTION

Far-reaching reforms at all levels of the education system are at present taking place in the five new *Länder*. They affect structures as well as educational objectives and curricula. The same applies to universities and colleges which should once again become centres of free research and teaching rather than 'forges of socialist cadres'. One could speak of the greatest 'school and university experiment' in modern German educational history. This by no means merely involves adopting well-tried West German regulations. Autonomous models have been, and still are being, developed in the new *Länder*. In some cases they go beyond the 1964 Hamburg Agreement on unifying general schooling and beyond the University Outline Law.

These new developments require greater legal 'latitude' for a transitional period. As the cultural and educational autonomy of the *Länder* is at the heart of their sovereignty, people in the West should show understanding for the fact that the new *Länder* make use of this opportunity for once again implementing their own educational policy and thereby gaining an identity of their own. (Appendix 15.1 provides information about the area, population, and political structure in these *Länder*.)

When 'Schools and Institutions of Higher Education in the Federal Republic of Germany' was published in 1988, no one could foresee that the revolutionary events of autumn 1989 in the GDR would put an end, on 3 October 1990, to 45 years of the division of Germany. At the end of that book, attention was devoted to 'All-German Aspects' and reference made to the Conference of Ministers of Education's trail-blazing 1978 resolution on 'The German Question at School'. In the meantime reunification has taken place. Redevelopment of the education system is well under way. So what follows can only be an interim report reflecting the situation in December 1991.

THE STARTING-POINT: THE GDR EDUCATION SYSTEM

The treaty of unification laid down that the new *Länder* established in 1990 had to have reorganised their education systems by 30 June 1991. That deadline created unusual pressure. Replacing the socialist unified school by a flexibly structured school system and restructuring higher education created great problems. It is therefore necessary to outline the starting-point – i.e. the GDR education system – especially as the new *Länder* also have a right to expect that innovations should be viewed and evaluated in terms of their individual historical preconditions. Unlike the federal structure of the education system and the *Länder* autonomy in the (former) Federal Republic, education in the GDR was centrally administered and strictly directed in accordance with Socialist Unity Party ideology, steered by party functionaries. The extent to which schools and universities were infiltrated by the State Security Service has only recently become completely apparent.

Schoolchildren and students had to be members of youth organisations (Young Pioneers, Free German Youth) and participate in the 'Jugendweihe' (a socialist ceremony replacing confirmation class and confirmation itself) if they wanted to get ahead in their education or job. As in most totalitarian states, pre-military training also formed part of the programme at schools and universities. Nevertheless, it must be recognised that many teachers and professors endeavoured – particularly during the first ten years of the GDR – to provide a proper education.

As early as July 1945, the Soviet military authorities in Berlin established the 'German Central Administration for National Education'. From the very start the intention was that postwar redevelopment of the school and university system should follow the central directives of the communist leadership, which at that time presented itself as being more anti-fascist than socialist. The ministries of education and culture in the *Länder* created in the postwar era and maintained until 1952 – Thuringia, Saxony, Saxony-Anhalt, Brandenburg, and Mecklenburg – played a subordinate role. In 1946 the Berlin central administration promulgated the 'Law on Democratisation of the German School', which constituted the foundation for joint *Länder* legal provisions. The *Länder* were more or less forced to step into line. When the GDR was established in 1949, the Ministry of National Education was set up, responsible for schools and institutions of higher education. From 1951 vocational training and the higher education system were assigned to other ministries. The Ministry of National Education retained responsibility for the school system. The higher education and technical school system was initially entrusted to a secretary of state and then to a separate ministry. Vocational training was assigned to its own state secretariat.

The traditional structured school system was replaced in 1946 by the 'democratic unified school':

- pre-schooling (*Kindergarten*);
- primary level (*Grundschule*, classes 1 to 8);
- upper level: vocational school (3 years), technical school; upper school (classes 9 to 12), evening schools, special courses at colleges of adult education (the university admission qualification could also be gained here and in technical schools);
- institutions of higher education (university).

New laws relating to education came into force in 1959 and 1965. After 1959 the eight-year *Grundschule* was transformed into the ten-class general polytechnical upper school (*allgemeinbildende polytechnische Oberschule – POS*). The expanded upper school (*Erweiterte Oberschule – EOS*) with classes 11 and 12 led to the *Abitur*, the qualification for entering university. The diagram in Appendix 15.2 provides information about school structure.

Up to 1969 the upper school was organised in three branches (mathematics and natural sciences, modern languages, and classics which were only available at very few schools). Since that time a unified curriculum has existed for class-levels 11 and 12 with an emphasis on mathematics and the natural sciences. Until 1982 there still existed special classes in preparation for the expanded upper school (class-levels 9 and 10 of the polytechnical upper school).

Russian was a compulsory subject for all pupils from class 5. The polytechnical sphere of education prepared the way for choice of a career, providing an introduction to industrial and commercial practices. There were several attempts at making the alternative forms of access to universities (by way of vocational training) into the norm. Compulsory general education extended over ten years in the GDR – a year longer than in the majority of *Länder* in the former Federal Republic. However, about 14 per cent of the pupils left the ten years of compulsory schooling after the eighth class so as to start vocational training.

Vocational training and the vocational schools were structurally similar to their western counterparts. Practical training on-the-job was accompanied by general education in part-time vocational schools (*Betriebsberufsschulen* or *Zentralberufsschulen*) within a dual system. Intermediate-level specialists were trained at full-time technical schools (*Fachschulen*). Some of those followed on directly from the polytechnical upper school (such as 63 medical schools and 47 schools of education for training nursery-school and primary level teachers); and some required prior completion of vocational training.

Both educational attainment and political/ideological attitudes were decisive for gaining access to the expanded upper school and university studies. For instance, an objection by the school Free German Youth leadership was enough to prevent pupils with very good grades from gaining admission to university studies. In actual fact a *Numerus clausus* existed: Only as many pupils were admitted to the expanded upper school as university places were available. That is why only about 12 per cent of an age-group gained the *Abitur* – in the 2-year expanded upper school, in 3-year vocational training, or in special schools and classes. The latter, based on a Soviet model, existed after 1965 for pupils especially gifted in the arts, sport, languages, mathematics, or the natural sciences.

In the Federal Republic of Germany the choice of form of education or training was left to pupils and their parents, but in the GDR a strictly controlled 'planned educational economy' prevailed. All school, study-, and training-places beyond the period of compulsory schooling were assigned by the state in the GDR. Planned targets within state employment policy were the crucial factor. Teachers played a decisive part in this 'distribution of social opportunities'. One of the most esteemed experts, Oskar Anweiler, said that this process involved 'the most rigid of all selection systems as compared with other socialist states including the Soviet Union'.

After 1945 some 20,000 out of around 28,000 teachers were dismissed because of their Nazi activities. About 28,000 'new teachers' – of whom 54 per cent had only received an elementary school education – were trained in crash-courses. The German Socialist Unity Party (SED) simultaneously gained a large potential reservoir of members and functionaries. Parallel efforts were made to transfer teacher training to the universities, and educational faculties were established. Colleges of education were also set up. In 1953 teacher training was fundamentally reorganised in accordance with the Soviet model, aligned thenceforth with levels within schools rather than with types of school. From 1953 to 1969 three types of teachers existed:

- *Teachers for classes 1 to 4.* They were trained at institutes of teacher training akin to technical schools.
- *Specialised teachers for classes 5 to 10.* They were trained in 4-year study-courses at colleges of education and universities.
- *Specialised teachers for classes 9 to 12 and part-time vocational schools.* They were trained in 5-year study-courses at universities and technical universities.

In 1969 differentiation of specialised teacher training into two categories was replaced by a unified 4-year course of studies (two subjects), which concluded with a diploma and qualified for teaching classes 5 to 12. The precondition for access to such studies was the *Abitur*, and this teaching diploma could only be gained at universities and colleges of education. In 1982 the period of training was extended to 5 years. All courses of teacher training included study of the foundations of Marxism-Leninism. The training of primary-level teachers, following completion of the tenth class at the polytechnical upper school, continued to take place at institutes of teacher training (with the status of technical schools).

Teachers were obliged to support the 'building of socialism', the 'leading role of the SED', and the educational objective of 'the all-round and harmoniously developed socialist personality'. All those active in teacher training were expected to demonstrate outstanding political loyalty and vigilance.

While in the West the number of students rose rapidly, there was a decline in the GDR from the beginning of the 1970s (1972: 161,000; 1985: 130,000). In 1985 there were 195 students for every 10,000 inhabitants in the Federal Republic, and only 78 in the GDR. In 1989 the percentage of students among their 18 to 24 age group was 22.3 per cent in the Federal Republic, and only 11.2 per cent in the GDR. That also explains the current 'need to catch up' and the present increase in the number of students in the new *Länder*. The higher education system in the GDR was characterised by the co-existence of universities and special colleges. In 1989 there was a total of 54 institutions of higher education:

- 6 universities;
- 3 technical universities;
- 12 technical colleges;
- 3 colleges of engineering;
- 3 medical academies;
- 2 colleges of agriculture and forestry;
- 3 colleges of economics and law;
- 10 colleges of education;
- 12 colleges of art and music.

After 1946 the entire realm of higher education was reorganised step by step in accordance with Marxism-Leninism, a move that was partly accompanied by considerable resistance from so-called bourgeois professors and students. Faculties of social science were established at universities as centres for this ideology. The Socialist Unity Party in 1946 set up the 'Karl Marx Parteihochschule', a college for training SED leaders. Within about five years Marxism-Leninism became a compulsory subject in all curricula. From 1951 courses were strictly organised in study-years rather than semesters. Teachers and students in higher education were increasingly subjected to rigid ideological controls. In 1987 Jürgen Kuczinski, a prominent communist social scientist, complained that 'the universities have become factories for training mediocrities'.

INITIAL REFORMS IN THE GDR: FROM THE CHANGEOVER IN AUTUMN 1989 TO REUNIFICATION ON 3 OCTOBER 1990

Many changes occurred in the school and higher education system after the Honecker regime was replaced by the Modrow government (SED/PDS) in November 1989 – and to an increasing extent under the de Maizière government (CDU) from April to October 1990. Schools and universities started reforms on their own initiative. These primarily involved the political climate in education. The previously crucial ideological links between teaching and university training were relaxed and gradually abandoned. On their own initiative teachers and parents sought new ways in reshaping the school system. From the start of the 1990/1 school year, schools were run by headteachers elected by school conferences. The involvement of pupils, teachers, and parents in school life was intensified. The ideological guidelines for GDR curricula were revoked. Commissions began to develop new curricula. The subject '*Staatsbürgerkunde*' (citizenship), involving the ideological education of socialist citizens, was replaced by 'Social Studies' in classes 7 to 12. The contents of lessons now concerned the establishment of a democratic constitutional order and a liberal economic and social system. The history curriculum was also reformed, taking into account Western textbooks and concepts of history teaching. The predominance of teaching Russian was also called into question. Lessons in other modern languages, such as English and French, were introduced to the extent that trained teachers were available. The subject 'Introduction to Socialist Production' was also revised to correspond to 'Work Studies' (*Arbeitslehre*) as taught in the West where basic information is provided to prepare the way for the world of work. As there had been almost no private schools in the GDR, there was an initial wave of new foundations (e.g. Rudolf Steiner schools and ecclesiastically maintained institutions). After the former rigidly centralised control fell away, a hitherto unfamiliar degree of autonomy developed in schools and universities from autumn 1989. Many teachers and professors were not prepared for a situation allowing 'freedom of choice', and experienced an identity crisis as a result of their often close ideological ties with Marxism-Leninism.

At the universities, the problematic nature and limitations of 'ideological self-purification' quickly became apparent when the question of dissolving ('winding up') or restructuring particularly contaminated spheres of study had to be tackled. Leipzig historian Karl Czok's 'History of Saxony', published just before the 1989 changeover, stated with regard to educational policy in the postwar period: 'Every revolutionary upheaval exerts a profound impact on intellectual and cultural life.' This declaration, which served to justify Marxism-Leninism's 'seizure of power' in higher education, also applies, however, to its surmounting. And thus, as is well known, every revolution is followed by a change of personnel.

RESTRUCTURING OF THE *LÄNDER* AND THEIR EDUCATION SYSTEMS FROM AUTUMN 1990

A new phase of educational policy got under way with the restructuring of the *Länder* by way of the GDR law dated 22 June 1990, regulating their introduction. The first *Länder* elections on 14 October 1990, decided the relative strengths of political forces. The territorial re-ordering took up the *Länder* structures prevailing in 1952 – apart from a few regional changes. This fundamental restructuring was and is a great political and organisational challenge. Like all other branches of administration, the educational administration also had to be completely reshaped. Many experts from the West helped with that. The new *Länder* were also integrated in all the institutions (developed in the old Federal Republic during recent decades) whereby the federal and regional authorities co-ordinate educational policy. In December 1990 their ministers of education became members of the Conference of Ministers of Education. The same applies to participation of the new *Länder* in the Federal-*Länder* Commission for Educational Planning and Advancement of Research, and the Science Council.

The Science Council had been asked by the last GDR government, and also by the federal and *Länder* governments, to evaluate non-university research institutions and plans for the development of institutions of higher education, especially with regard to the restructuring of teacher training. Recommendations were immediately discussed in many Science Council working groups and committees with participation by experts from the new *Länder*, and prepared after detailed consultation on the spot with those involved. Agreement was reached in the course of 1991, and these recommendations now serve the *Länder* governments as a basis for appropriate further developments.

The new education laws

The new *Länder* school laws were discussed and approved by parliaments between March and July 1991 with great efforts made to attain consensus.

- *Brandenburg*: First School Reform Law, dated 28 May 1991.
- *Mecklenburg-Western Pomerania*: First School Reform Law, dated 26 April 1991.
- *Saxony*: School Law, dated 3 July 1991.
- *Saxony-Anhalt*: School Reforms Law, dated 11 July 1991.
- *Thuringia*: Provisional Education Law, dated 25 March 1991.

The diagrams in Appendix 15.3 provide information on school structure.

A flexibly structured school system was introduced in Brandenburg, Mecklenburg-Western Pomerania, Saxony-Anhalt, and Thuringia at the start of the 1991/2 school year. Saxony, on the other hand, continued with a modified form of the existing school system (general and expanded upper schools) during a transitional year, and will only initiate the new structure in the 1992/3 school year. The legislation in Brandenburg, Mecklenburg-Western Pomerania, Saxony-Anhalt, and Thuringia was expressly termed 'provisional' or 'first' education laws. Comprehensive *Länder* school laws will be enacted later. Saxony has already approved a long-term school law, but – as already mentioned – will only start implementing these reforms after a year's delay. Saxony-Anhalt and Thuringia have made express provision for the revision or replacement of their laws by 31 December 1992 and 31 July 1993 respectively. The legal regulations applying to education in West Berlin were implemented in the Eastern part of the city, so Berlin has been omitted in what follows.

Length of compulsory schooling

The new *Länder* have regulated the start of compulsory schooling on the basis of the Hamburg Agreement (paragraph 2, section 1). As in West Germany, schooling is compulsory for all children who are 6 years old by 30 June in the current year. Regulations regarding the length of compulsory schooling differ. Mecklenburg-Western Pomerania, Saxony-Anhalt, Saxony, and Thuringia have legislated for 9 years of full-time schooling, and Brandenburg for 10. That is followed by what is usually 3 years of obligatory attendance at part-time vocational school, which extends until vocational training is concluded or attainment of the age of 18.

Special schools

The existing system of special schools for handicapped children and young people is being continued. However, the policy objective is extensive integration of the handicapped in normal schools. In Brandenburg and Saxony the special school is called a 'mixed-ability school'. The different types of special or mixed-ability schools are listed in school laws in Mecklenburg-Western Pomerania, Saxony-Anhalt, and Saxony. Thuringia intends to regulate specific issues in a law concerning special schools.

Private schools

Private schools (dependent on private backing) can be established in all the *Länder* with official permission. Brandenburg, for instance, has adopted the corresponding regulations in the *Land* of Berlin. Thuringia plans a special private school law. The guidelines for state subsidies differ. In Mecklenburg-Western Pomerania, for example, between 60 and 90 per cent of the grants available to state schools are available to private institutions on application.

Religious instruction

Religious instruction, which according to article 7 section 3 of the Basic Law is a regular subject at public schools, was the object of fierce discussions in the five new *Länder*. Religious instruction was banned from schools after 1945 in the Soviet occupied zone and later in the GDR. The churches organised denominational instruction on a voluntary basis. Now lessons in religion are to be compulsory again at public schools, even though, compared with the West, the role of the church is much reduced in the area that was formerly the GDR – also as an outcome of decades of totalitarian rule and atheistic state education of the young. The preconditions are thus completely different from those in the West.

There has been much discussion about whether the 'Bremen clause' (in article 141 of the Basic Law) is applicable in the new *Länder*. This runs: 'Article 7, paragraph 3, clause 1 is not applicable in a *Land* where another legal regulation applied on January 1, 1949.' This only refers to Bremen and Berlin where the churches and other religious communities are themselves responsible for the provision of religious instruction. The Bremen clause does not apply to the new *Länder*. Different regulations prevailed on 1 January 1949 in Brandenburg, Mecklenburg, Saxony, Saxony-Anhalt, and Thuringia – but the new *Länder* established on the basis of the GDR law of summer 1990 are not, however, identical with the territories existing at that time. Nevertheless, account must be taken of the fact that parents have the right (in accordance with article 7, paragraph 2 of the Basic Law) to withdraw their child from religious instruction. The pupils themselves have this right from the age of 14 – on the basis of the 1921 Reich Law on the religious upbringing of children.

The reintroduction of religious instruction at public schools is not easy even in terms of the lack of teachers. School laws lay down that religious instruction or ethics (for pupils who do not take part in religious instruction) is an obligatory subject. Brandenburg leaves ultimate regulation to the *Land* school law. Some time will pass before religious instruction can be offered to a sufficient extent by trained teachers at every school. Anyone who wants to educate young Germans as Europeans must also impart basic knowledge about religion and its history – without which German history and our European present day cannot be understood.

Concepts of structural reform in general education

Let us now consider ideas about reforming the organisation of schools in the new *Länder*.

Attendance at the *Grundschule* extends over four years – except in Brandenburg, which follows the Berlin model of six years.

• *Secondary levels I* and *II* are structured as follows: *Mecklenburg-*

Western Pomerania comes closest to West German models of a flexibly structured school system with the *Hauptschule* (non-academic secondary school – classes 5 to 9), *Realschule* (intermediate school – classes 5 to 10), and *Gymnasium* (grammar school – classes 5 to 12). Special regulations apply to the establishment of comprehensive schools (classes 5 to 10) – e.g. comprehensives must satisfy the precondition of triple streaming.

- In *Saxony-Anhalt* the primary school (*Grundschule*) is followed by the 'secondary school', which is structured in a differentiating mixed-ability level (classes 5 and 6) succeeded by either a *Hauptschule* course (classes 7 to 9/10) or a *Realschule* course (classes 7 to 10). The *Gymnasium* comprises classes 5 to 12 with a 2-year upper level termed a 'course level'.

- *Saxony* plans to follow the *Grundschule* with the 'middle school'. Class levels 5 and 6 serve an orientational function. From class 7 a 'qualification-related differentiation' applies. The middle school can be differentiated into several emphases. Two separate courses – for *Hauptschule* and *Realschule* – are possible. The *Hauptschule* leaving qualification is gained after conclusion of the 9th class, and the *Realschule* leaving qualification after taking an examination at the end of the 10th class. In addition the middle school can also accentuate certain subjects such as languages, mathematics and the natural sciences, the arts, technology, and sport. The *Gymnasium* involves classes 5 to 12 (with a 2-year course-based upper level).

- School reforms in *Thuringia* are going in a similar direction. What in Saxony is called the middle school is known in Thuringia as the '*Regelschule*' (regular school – classes 5 to 9/10). Differentiation gets under way in class 7, leading pupils to either the *Hauptschule* leaving qualification or the *Realschule* leaving qualification (in both cases after a final examination). The *Gymnasium* comprises classes 5 to 12 (with a 3-year upper level for entrants from *Realschule*).

- As already mentioned, *Brandenburg* diverges from that structure. Six years at *Grundschule* are followed by either a comprehensive school (classes 7 to 10, and as a *Gymnasium*-equivalent upper level classes 11 to 13), the *Gymnasium* (classes 7 to 13), or the *Realschule* (classes 7 to 10). The comprehensive offers – by way of inner and outer differentiation (differential subject demands) – a general education leading to all secondary level I qualifications. The *Realschule* concludes with a qualification allowing admission to a technical secondary school. The law may not say anything about the length of the *Gymnasium*-equivalent upper level, but in the preceding negotiations reference was always made to 13 graduated school years.

Vocational training (secondary level II)

The structure of vocational schools completely corresponds with the Western model. In all of the new *Länder* there are part-time vocational schools, full-time vocational schools, technical schools, and technical secondary schools. Saxony-Anhalt and Thuringia also have institutions for supplementary vocational training (*Berufsaufbauschulen*). Vocational or technical *Gymnasien* (classes 11 to 13) are envisaged in Mecklenburg-Western Pomerania, Saxony-Anhalt, Saxony, and Thuringia.

Alternative forms of access to university

Admission to university is possible in all the new *Länder* by way of evening schools for the employed or sixth-form colleges.

Overview of school statistics

At present only provisional statistics indicate how these regulations work out in practice, i.e. the availability of individual kinds of school (see Table 15.1).

Summary of innovations in school organisation

Brandenburg is the only *Land* that has introduced a 6-year *Grundschule* and envisages a total of 13 years leading up to the *Abitur*. The other four *Länder* conclude – as in the former GDR – with the 12th class. Brandenburg also acts differently with regard to comprehensives. Only Mecklenburg-Western Pomerania has a tripartite organisation of secondary level I as in West Germany. Saxony-Anhalt, Saxony, and Thuringia are experimenting with new dual models of differentiation. Alongside the *Gymnasium* there exists a type of school (*'Regelschule'*, *'Mittelschule'*, or *'Sekundarschule'*) where *Hauptschule* and *Realschule* courses are combined. The qualifications attained are the same as in the West. Flexible ways are being sought with regard to inner differentiation of courses. Permeability is an important objective. So there will probably be a dual rather than a tripartite structure for secondary level I in the majority of the new *Länder*.

The *Hauptschule* constitutes a special problem. This exists as an autonomous form of school only in Mecklenburg-Western Pomerania and Berlin. In the other *Länder* provision has been made for a '*Hauptschule* leaving qualification', but not for the *Hauptschule* as an independent type of school. People avoid that designation. There are probably two reasons for this. On the one hand, critical discussions in the West during the past couple of decades have had an impact. After all, the Education and Science Trade Union (GEW) has long propagated 'Farewell to the

Table 15.1 School statistics

Pupils, teachers, and schools at the start of the 1991/2 school year				
	M-W. Pom.	*Brandenb.*	*Sa.-Anh.*	*Thur.*
No. of pupils	280,000	370,000	415,000	376,000
No. of teachers	21,300	35,000[a]	32,000	27,250
Total no. of schools	953	1,135	1,715	1,436
Of these:				
Primary schools	302	563[b]	870	770
Secondary modern	37[c]	—	—	—
Intermediate schools	403[d]	68	—	—
Secondary schools	—	—	618	—
Regular schools	—	—	—	458
Gymnasien	92[e]	79	140	105
Comprehensive schools	18[f]	300	—	—
Special/mixed ability	101	125	87	103

Data on schools in Saxony	
No. of pupils	660,000
No. of teachers	52,000
No. of schools	2,000

Numbers of schools in West and East Berlin		
	West Berlin	*East Berlin*
Primary schools	232	230
Secondary modern	40	12
Intermediate schools	38	30
Gymnasium (I and II)	60	41
Comprehensives	28	54
Gymnasium-level at comprehensives	16	18

Source: Hans Döbert, Renate Martini: *Schule zwischen Wende und Wandel – Wie weiter mit den Schulreformen in Deutschland-Ost?*
Notes:
[a] This high quota results from a special regulation stipulating 80% employment for every teacher
[b] 92 in conjunction with comprehensive
[c] With a primary section
[d] Of these 340 have a primary/secondary modern section
[e] Of these two have an intermediate section
[f] Of these fifteen are integrated and three co-operative comprehensives

Hauptschule', which it declared to be a 'discontinued model'. Conference of Ministers of Education documentation no. 114, issued in February 1991, showed that in 1989 at class-level 8 in the West: 35 per cent of pupils attended *Hauptschulen*, 28.8 per cent *Realschulen*, 29.9 per cent *Gymnasien*, 5.7 per cent integrated comprehensives, and 0.6 per cent Rudolf Steiner schools. The *Hauptschule* was therefore still the most attended form of school at secondary level I – and yet people act as if this were close to its end everywhere. Another factor may be responsible for the reservations shown in the East with regard to the *Hauptschule*.

In the GDR there were only 'upper schools'. Deceptive labelling led parents and pupils to believe that all schools were virtually the equivalent of a *Gymnasium* since the term 'upper school' accorded with the earlier designation of grammar school. That was also reflected in the curricula. For instance, the mathematics curriculum at polytechnical upper schools was largely the same as at the *Gymnasium* in the West. But what was the reality at these GDR 'upper schools'? About 14 per cent of pupils went on to vocational training after the 8th class. Only 12 per cent of pupils in the 10th concluding class at a polytechnical upper school had a chance of gaining the *Abitur*. If some pupils from the former polytechnical upper school should in future 'only' go to a *Hauptschule*, that will – unjustly but understandably – be experienced as a social come-down.

The most important fact to be noted is that in all five new *Länder* the unified school is being replaced by different forms of a flexibly structured system. This generates an abundance of problems. For instance, what teachers should teach in the new kinds of school? On what basis should teachers be assigned to the different kinds of schools? What criteria are decisive there? Secondary moderns are now being developed without *Hauptschule* teachers, intermediate schools without *Realschule* teachers, grammar schools without *Gymnasium* teachers. Teachers who can offer English, Latin, or French are particularly sought.

In conclusion it can be said that secondary level I in the new *Länder* is diversely organised. The structuring of secondary level II is largely identical with regulations in the Western *Länder*. This comprises, on the one hand, the upper level at *Gymnasien* and, on the other, the types of vocational school (part-time and full-time vocational school, technical secondary school, technical school, and *Berufsaufbauschulen* – the vocational extension school). As already mentioned, usually only two years are spent in the upper level at *Gymnasium* as compared with three in the West (followed only by Brandenburg). So the overall time spent at *Gymnasium* is at present disputed between the *Länder*. In four of them the general qualification for university admission is gained after twelve years at school, in Brandenburg after thirteen. This shortened form of upper level runs counter to the Hamburg Agreement (paragraph 11, section 2) and recommendations (dated 10 May 1990) by the Conference of Ministers of Education.

Innovations in school organisation viewed from the perspective of the Hamburg Agreement

How do the ideas of the new *Länder* about school reforms appear in the light of the 1964 Hamburg Agreement? That Agreement does not, for instance, cover what terminology should be applied to designate the various types of schools such as '*Regelschule*', '*Mittelschule*', and '*Sekundarschule*', or the decision by four of the *Länder* to reduce the length of the *Gymnasium* course by a year. Strictly speaking, a formal application should have been made to the Conference of Ministers of Education which regulates the implementation of school experiments in accordance with paragraph 16 of the Hamburg Agreement. Article 37, paragraph 4 of the Treaty of Unification says that the Hamburg Agreement and other relevant accords reached by the Conference of Ministers of Education constitute the 'basis' for reshaping the school system in the new *Länder*. This formulation is very cautious. Perhaps it would be useful in this context to recall how the Hamburg Agreement came into being.

In the West at the beginning of the 1950s there was extensive discussion of supposed 'school chaos'. After 1945 the cultural autonomy of the *Länder* resulted in the development of diverse school structures. Public opinion urged greater unification. The Conference of Ministers of Education took account of that, and prepared for the Conference of Minister-Presidents a state agreement on unification of the school system, which was adapted in 1955 and named the 'Düsseldorf Agreement' after the place where it was signed. Since 1964 the new version of that agreement has been known as the 'Hamburg Agreement' because that is where it was signed. This agreement contains regulations about when the school year starts, compulsory schooling, and holiday dates. At its heart are accords on unified terminology and forms of organisation for schools providing general education. Types of school such as the *Grundschule, Hauptschule, Realschule,* and *Gymnasium* were redefined (with the term *Realschule* replacing the '*Mittelschule*' which still appeared in the Düsseldorf Agreement). Recognition of examinations, designation of grading levels, and the organisation of experiments in schooling are also regulated here. During the 1980s the experimental nationwide introduction of comprehensive schooling was accepted by the Conference of Ministers of Education on this basis so that comprehensive schools were accepted de facto as regular schools despite their not being mentioned in the Hamburg Agreement itself (as they did not even exist in 1964!). If the qualifications attained at integrated comprehensive schools were recognised by the Conference of Ministers of Education, then such recognition should be all the more forthcoming in the case of school forms (such as the *Regelschule, Mittelschule,* and *Sekundarschule*) entailing lesser problems with regard to differentiation.

The Hamburg Agreement thus maintained the necessary freedom of action for the *Länder*. They were able to continue developing their school systems within the framework of a federal order. In addition, the Agreement ensured far-reaching structural correspondence. If the Agreement had not proved its worth, it would long since have been revoked in the course of the past twenty-seven years.

In the West one would therefore be well advised to allow the new *Länder* to gather their own experience during the next few years, even putting up with some measure of 'school chaos' in the process. Any attempt at precipitately adapting these developments in the sphere of school terminology and structures to the Hamburg Agreement would only slow down impulses towards reform in the new *Länder*, which would be regrettable. We should not forget how difficult it is for the new *Länder* to replace the unified school by flexibly structured forms. There is no single 'ideal way'. Cultural autonomy has been the heart of *Länder* sovereignty in the West since post-1945 reconstruction, so it should go without saying that the new *Länder* are given an opportunity of seeking their own solutions.

Teacher training

The Science Council adopted detailed recommendations about teacher training on 5 July 1991. Just shortly before reunification, the de Maizière government revoked single-phase teacher training (18 September 1990). In imitation of the West German model, the first teacher-examination is followed by a period of in-service training which is concluded with the second state examination. Transitional arrangements apply to students still involved in the 'old' training. For instance, lower-level teachers, who took their examination in 1990, will have to undergo additional training, concluding with the first state examination. The *Länder* education laws, which only refer to the principles involved in teacher training (special regulations will cover the details), also take the two phases of teacher training as their starting-point.

In its resolution dated 5 October 1990, the Conference of Ministers of Education established the basic equivalence of teaching diploma examinations in two or three subjects at GDR universities and the first state examination for teaching in *Hauptschule* and *Realschule* – or in secondary level I – and, with additional qualifications, also the examination for teaching at *Gymnasien* or in secondary level II. In the meantime the training of primary school teachers has been removed from institutes of teacher training and integrated in colleges and universities.

Basic Marxist-Leninist studies, and obligatory lessons in Russian and sport, have been abolished. The sections for Marxism-Leninism, and for citizenship and history, have been closed ('wound up') at colleges of education – and so, in general, have the sections for pedagogics and psychology. The courses for teacher training are at present being devised anew with the assistance of visiting professors and newly appointed university teachers.

The Science Council recommendations with regard to teacher training are highly detailed, containing differentiated proposals for individual universities and colleges of education. At present the integration of or co-operation between these colleges and universities has been established or is still being prepared in a variety of ways. The Academy of Educational

Sciences, which had a staff of over 600 and was responsible for drawing up curricula, was closed at the end of 1990.

Surplus of teachers

In 1987 167,230 teachers were employed at schools providing a general education in the GDR. There were 81.4 teachers for every 1,000 pupils at such schools in the GDR, compared with 66.6 in the Federal Republic. The teacher–pupil ratio in the GDR was about 1 : 9, and in the Western *Länder* the average figure was 1 : 15. As a consequence the size of school classes was considerably less than in the Federal Republic. The number of student-teachers in the GDR in 1988 was approximately 39,000. In 1987 they constituted 22 per cent of the students at GDR universities and colleges of education – but only 8 per cent in the Federal Republic. As the number of established teaching posts in the individual *Länder* is being revised, taking into account average figures drawn from past experience in the former Federal Republic, this leads to the dismissal of teachers. Those affected are primarily politically compromised teachers (e.g. pioneer leaders, teachers of citizenship, and informal associates of the State Security Service), inadequately qualified teachers, and teachers who were active as state functionaries (e.g. in the State Security Service) or in business but were reassigned to schools by the Modrow government after the 'changeover'.

Pioneer leaders at schools are also affected because they are generally not trained to teach a second subject (and instead acted as extramural teachers). Teachers regard these dismissals as primarily a 'political purge'. It is expected that a total of around 30,000 teachers will be dismissed in the five *Länder*. Saxony, for instance, planned to fire about 10,000 out of 52,000 teachers by the end of 1991. Brandenburg chose another course so as to continue to employ as many teachers as possible. The *Land* government, the Education and Science Trade Union, and the other teacher associations reached agreement on reducing the number of obligatory lessons and wages by 20 per cent for all teachers. Up to now Brandenburg has only dismissed 700 out of 34,500 teachers, and a further 3,800 went of their own accord.

The new university laws

The new university laws serve the purpose of renewing the entire university system with the objective of comprehensively guaranteeing freedom of research and teaching.

- *Brandenburg*: University Law dated 24 June 1991.
- *Mecklenburg-Western Pomerania*: Law for the Restoration of Universities, dated 19 February 1991.

- *Saxony*: Law for the Restoration of Universities, dated 25 July 1991.
- *Saxony-Anhalt*: Law for the Restoration of Universities, dated 31 July 1991.
- *Thuringia*: Provisional University Law, dated 14 May 1991.

The 1976 Federal University Outline Law and its amendments constitute the crucial model for the new *Länder* university laws. East Berlin was incorporated in the area of application of the existing Berlin University Law. Special regulations applied until 31 March 1994. Brandenburg has largely followed the West German University Outline Law, while Saxony and Saxony-Anhalt diverge in some respects. Mecklenburg-Western Pomerania and Thuringia have enacted interim laws. The Provisional Thuringia University Law no longer applies after 29 February 1992, and is to be replaced by legislation founded on the University Outline Law. The most important regulations concern changes in staff. The treaty of unification stipulates that the situation of the existing scholarly staff must be clarified within three years. They can be given notice because of absence of demand, inadequate qualifications, or lack of personal integrity. Commissions concerned with staffing and subject-matter are at present evaluating university personnel and making recommendations about the dismissal of professors or other scholars. Special appointment committees are working on proposals for refilling professorial posts. All such activities create considerable unrest and uncertainty at universities. That must be put up with. Only in that way can qualitative restoration be initiated, guaranteeing comparable scholarly standards at all German universities.

Degree-granting colleges of higher education, roughly equivalent to a polytechnic, did not exist in the GDR. Such institutions are now being established in all the *Länder* – for the most part in continuation of existing colleges. Hitherto Brandenburg had neither a university nor a technical university, but has now set up universities at Potsdam and Frankfurt an der Oder as well as a technical university at Cottbus. Table 15.2 lists the number of students according to *Länder* and different forms of higher education during the 1990/1 winter semester.

Reform programme for universities and research

On 11 July 1991 the federal and *Länder* authorities reached agreement on a comprehensive 'Renewal Programme for University and Research' to run for a term of five years. The 1.76 milliard DM available – 75 per cent from the federal authorities and 25 per cent from the New *Länder* – is to go towards the following:

1 *New professorships*. Funds for 200 new professorships in university and college faculties in need of renewal and 100 inaugural professorships at degree-granting colleges of higher education are being employed in accordance with the Science Council's recommendations. Assistance is,

Table 15.2 German, foreign and first-year students in the 1990/1 winter semester, according to type of higher education and *Länder*

Land	Total		Universities		Comprehensive universities		Of these at art colleges		Degree-granting college of higher education		Degree-granting colleges of administration	
	Total	Women	Total	Women	Total	Women	Total	Women	Total	Women	Total	Women
Brandenburg	5,415	2,605	5,246	2,563	—	—	151	42	—	—	—	—
Mecklenburg-Western Pom.	13,160	6,230	13,160	6,230	—	—	—	—	—	—	—	—
Saxony	53,813	21,666	52,145	20,891	—	—	1,668	775	—	—	—	—
Saxony-Anh.	20,861	10,437	20,184	10,111	—	—	677	326	—	—	—	—
Thuringia	13,711	6,055	13,012	5,682	—	—	699	373	—	—	—	—
East Berlin	26,642	13,557	25,439	12,982	—	—	1,203	575	—	—	—	—
Total	133,602	60,550	129,186	58,459	—	—	4,398	2,091	—	—	—	—

Source: Conference of Ministers of Education

for instance, being given to 35 professorships in legal studies, 43 in economics and business studies, 48 in education, and 53 in the humanities.

2 *Visiting scholars.* Visiting scholars are also to contribute towards the redevelopment of faculties. Under consideration here are professors on sabbaticals, delegated professors, professors in retirement, as well as qualified lecturers.

3 *Assistance for up-and-coming scholars.* Assistance will be granted towards obtaining doctorates and qualifications as lecturers (habilitations) as well as establishment of graduate colleges, since a large number of university teachers will reach retiring age in the 1990s.

Since 1 January 1991 the 54 institutions of higher education in the new *Länder* have been included within the measures of the law regulating assistance for the construction of institutes of higher education. The treaty of unification lays down that the federal legislation regulating educational assistance also applies to students since 1 January 1991, making available grants and loans (at present still less munificent than in the West).

CONCLUDING REMARKS

German reunification came as a surprise. During the initial phase of political euphoria in autumn 1990, there was much talk of an 'all-German educational union'. This was intended to stand alongside the economic and social union within the immediate future. For some experts this meant a rapidly effective and far-reaching transference of West German school and university structures to the new federal *Länder*. However, such transfers came up against limiting factors because the completely different preconditions existing in those *Länder* were not always sufficiently taken into account. In short, these short-term expectations of an educational union have vanished. As time passes, the difficulties involved in redevelopment of the education system become much more apparent. Education administrations, teachers and professors, pupils and students, teachers' associations, and parents all need time for orientating themselves within changed structural conditions. In this reconstruction they also justifiably want to make the most of the experience gained in completely different circumstances. All this demands that the West show understanding for the East's great problems. Effort will still be required before 'inner unity' is achieved in the all-German education system.

NOTE

The author would like to thank Gerhard Fengler (Federal Ministry of Education and Science), Peter Fränz and Klaus Stöppler (Secretariat of the Conference of Ministers of Education), and Hans Döbert and Renate Martini (DIPF) for their reliable and rapid assistance; Hermann Avenarius, Rudolf Raasch, and Gerlind Schmidt (DIPF) for their critical reading of the manuscript and many suggestions; and Barbara Launer for the trouble and care she took during the final stage of editing.

APPENDIX 15.1   STATISTICS

Statistics on the area population, and political structure of the new *Länder*. Information as of 30 June 1991. *Source*: Informationen zur politischen Bildung Nr. 230 (1st quarter, 1991).

Mecklenburg-Western Pomerania

* *Area*: 23,838 sq. km.
* *Population*: 1.96 million.
* *Land parliament*: CDU 38.8%, SPD 27%, FDP 5.5%, PDS 15.7% (Elections on 14 October 1990). Governed by a CDU/FDP coalition.

Brandenburg

* *Area*: 29,059 sq. km.
* *Population*: 2.64 million
* *Land parliament*: SPD 38.3%, CDU 29.4%, FDP 6.6%, PDS 13.4%, Bündnis '90, 6.4% (Elections on 14 October 1990). Governed by a SPD, FDP, and Bündnis '90 coalition.

Saxony-Anhalt

* *Area*: 20,445 sq. km.
* *Population*: 2.96 million.
* *Land parliament*: CDU 39%, SPD 26%, FDP 13.5%. Governed by a CDU/FDP coalition.

Thuringia

* *Area*: 16,251 sq. km.
* *Population*: 2.7 million.
* *Land parliament*: CDU 45.4%, SPD 22.8%, PDS 9.7%, FDP 9.3%, Grüne/Bündnis '90 6.5%. Governed by a CDU/FDP coalition.

Saxony

* *Area*: 18,337 sq. km.
* *Population*: 4.9 million.

- *Land parliament*: CDU 53.8%, SPD 19.1%, PDS 16.2%, Grüne/Bündnis '90 6.5%, FDP 5.3%. Governed by the CDU.

APPENDIX 15.2   School Structure in the German Democratic Republic

Class

Class				
13			Vocational training with *Abitur*	
12	Extended secondary school	Vocational training		
11				
10	10-class general upper school			Special schools
9				
8				
7	(upper level)			
6	(middle level)			
5				
4				
3	(lower level)			
2				
1				

Source: Hans Döbert, Renate Martini: *Schule zwischen Wende und Wandel*

APPENDIX 15.3   School Structure in the New Länder

Brandenburg

School year

School year				
13	*Gynasium* upper level at Comprehensive	*Gymnasium* upper level at *Gymnasium*		Upper level centre
12				
11				
10	Comprehensive	*Gymnasium*	*Realschule*	Educational facilities for handicapped children and young people and special schools
9				
8				
7				
6	*Grundschule*			
5				
4				
3				
2				
1				

Mecklenburg-Western Pomerania

School year

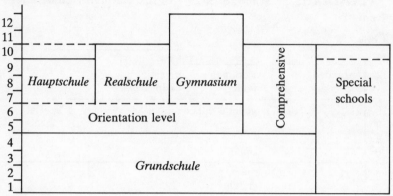

Saxony[1]

School year

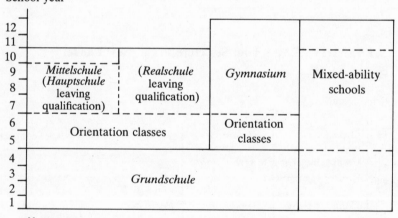

Note:
[1] This structure only applies from the 1992/3 school year

Saxony-Anhalt

School year

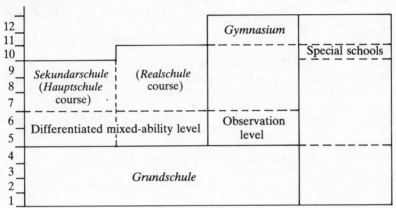

Thuringia

School year

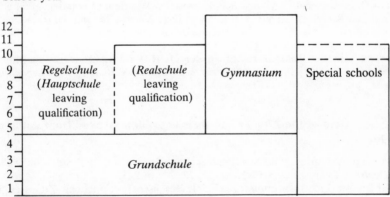

Source: Appendix 15.3 source: Hans Döbert, Renate Martini: *Schule zwischen Wende und Wandel*

APPENDIX 15.4   SOURCES

The starting-point: the GDR education system

Oskar Anweiler: *Schulpolitik und Schulsystem in der DDR*. Opladen 1988.
Oskar Anweiler (ed.): *Vergleich von Bildung und Erziehung in der Bundesrepublik Deutschland und in der Deutschen Demokratischen Republik (Materialien zur Lage der Nation. Herausgegeben vom Bundesministerium für innerdeutsche Beziehungen)*. Cologne 1990.
Karl Czok (ed.): *Geschichte Sachsens*. Weimar 1989.
Christoph Führ: 'Bildungssysteme im Wandel'. In: *Deutschland, Deutschland. 40 Jahre. Eine Geschichte der Bundesrepublik Deutschland und der DDR. Mit einem Vorwort von Peter Scholl-Latour*. Gütersloh 1989. pp. 224–30.
Wolfgang Hörner: *Bildung und Wissenschaft in der DDR. Ausgangslage und Reform bis Mitte 1990. Herausgegeben vom Bundesminister für Bildung und Wissenschaft*. Bonn 1990.
Freya Klier: *Lüg Vaterland. Erziehung in der DDR*. Munich 1990.
Gerhard Neuner: 'Pädagogische Wissenschaft in der DDR. Ein Rückblick auf Positionen und Restriktionen'. In: *Die Deutsche Schule. Jg.* 83 (1991) 3, pp. 281–95.
Helmut Stoltz: 'Thesen zur Entwicklung und Überwindung der DDR-Pädagogik vom 15.11.1991' (unpublished manuscript).

Initial reforms in the GDR: from the changeover in autumn 1989 to reunification on 3 October 1990

Hans Döbert, Renate Martini: 'Schule zwischen Wende und Wandel – Wie weiter mit den Schulreformen in Deutschland-Ost? Vortrag bei der Jahrestagung der Gesellschaft zur Förderung Pädagogischer Forschung am 22./23.11.1991 in Frankfurt a.M.' (Conference documentation).
Gerlind Schmidt: 'Bildungsreform in der DDR. Grundlegende Erneuerung der Schule?' In: *FORUM E. Zeitschrift des Verbandes Bildung und Erziehung* 2 (1990), pp. 9–12.

Restructuring of the *Länder* and their education systems from autumn 1990

Hermann Avenarius: 'Die Schulgesetzgebung in den neuen Bundesländern'. In: *Deutsche Lehrerzeitung* 1991, Nr. 21, 22, 24, and 25.
Karl Dienst: 'Eine Institution für Schüler, Gesellschaft und Kirche. Zum Religionsunterricht in den neuen Bundesländern'. In: *Evangelische Verantwortung*. Heft 9/1991, pp. 6–8.
Dokumentation der Schulgesetze der Länder: Brandenburg, Mecklenburg-Vorpommern, Sachsen, Sachsen-Anhalt und Thüringen. Herausgegeben vom Sekretariat der Ständigen Konferenz der Kultusminister der Länder in der Bundesrepublik Deutschland 1991.
Förderung von Bildung und Wissenschaft in den neuen Ländern. Informationen für die Länder Brandenburg, Mecklenburg-Vorpommern, Sachsen, Sachsen-Anhalt, Thüringen und Berlin (Ost). Herausgegeben vom Bundesminister für Bildung und Wissenschaft. Bonn 1991.
Hochschulgesetzgebung in den neuen Ländern. Interne Dokumentation des Bundesministeriums für Bildung und Wissenschaft.

Christoph Führ: 'Kultur ist Reichtum an Problemen. Überlegungen zu den Schulreformgesetzen in den neuen Ländern'. In: *Realschule* 99 (1991) 7, pp. 261 ff.

Harald Kästner: 'Zur Einheitlichkeit des Schulwesens in Deutschland nach der Beschlußlage der Kultusministerkonferenz unter Berücksichtigung des Einigungsvertrages und der Schulgesetze der neuen Länder'. In: *Die Höhere Schule*, Heft 8/91, pp. 242–8.

Mecklenburg-Vorpommern, Brandenburg, Sachsen-Anhalt, Thüringen, Sachsen: Informationen zur politischen Bildung. Heft 230. Herausgegeben von der Bundeszentrale für politische Bildung. Bonn 1991.

Studienentscheidung und Studienaufnahme im Wintersemester 1990/91 in Deutschland. Analyse der Studienanfängerzahlen im Wintersemester 1990/1. Hochschulinformationssystem Hanover June 1990.

Empfehlungen des Wissenschaftsrates zur Lehrerbildung in den neuen Ländern vom 5.7.1991.

Dieter E. Zimmer: 'Rausschmiß nach Bedarf. Politisch belastet, fachlich ungeeignet, einfach zu viel: Wie in Sachsen die Lehrer auf die Straße gesetzt werden'. In: *ZEIT* Nr. 49 vom 29.11.1991, pp. 12–13.

Index